The Psychology of Abilities, Competencies, and Expertise

The goal of this book is to characterize the nature of abilities, competencies, and expertise and to understand the relations among them. The book therefore seeks to integrate into a coherent discipline what formerly have been, to a large extent, three separate disciplines. Such integration makes both theoretical and practical sense because abilities represent potentials to achieve competencies and, ultimately, expertise. Chapter authors (a) present their views on the nature of abilities, competencies, and expertise; (b) present their views on the interrelationships among these three constructs; (c) state their views on how these three constructs can be assessed and developed; (d) present empirical data supporting their positions; (e) compare and contrast their positions to alternative positions, showing why they believe their positions to be preferred; and (f) speculate on the implications of their viewpoints for science, education, and society.

Robert J. Sternberg is IBM Professor of Psychology and Education and Director of the Center for the Psychology of Abilities, Competencies, and Expertise (PACE Center), Department of Psychology, Yale University. He is currently President of the American Psychological Association and Editor of *The APA Review of Books: Contemporary Psychology*. The author of more than 900 published works, including multiple books and articles, Sternberg has won numerous awards for his work.

Elena L. Grigorenko holds a Ph.D. in general psychology from Moscow State University and a Ph.D. in developmental psychology and genetics from Yale University. Dr. Grigorenko has published more than 100 books and articles and has won a dissertation award and three early career awards. She has worked with American, Russian, Indian, and African children in multiple countries around the world. Her main interests are individual differences, child development, and exceptional children. Currently, Dr. Grigorenko is Associate Professor of Child Studies and Psychology at Yale and at Moscow State University.

The Psychology of Abilities, Competencies, and Expertise

Edited by

ROBERT J. STERNBERG
Yale University

ELENA L. GRIGORENKO
Yale University and
Moscow State University

CAMBRIDGE
UNIVERSITY PRESS

PUBLISHED BY THE PRESS SYNDICATE OF THE UNIVERSITY OF CAMBRIDGE
The Pitt Building, Trumpington Street, Cambridge, United Kingdom

CAMBRIDGE UNIVERSITY PRESS
The Edinburgh Building, Cambridge CB2 2RU, UK
40 West 20th Street, New York, NY 10011-4211, USA
477 Williamstown Road, Port Melbourne, VIC 3207, Australia
Ruiz de Alarcón 13, 28014 Madrid, Spain
Dock House, The Waterfront, Cape Town 8001, South Africa

http://www.cambridge.org

First published 2003

Printed in the United States of America

Typeface Palatino 10/13 pt.   *System* LATEX 2$_\varepsilon$ [TB]

A catalog record for this book is available from the British Library.

Library of Congress Cataloging in Publication data

The psychology of abilities, competencies, and expertise /
Robert J. Sternberg, Elena L. Grigorenko, editors.
    p.   cm.
Includes bibliographical references and index.
ISBN 0-521-80988-6 – ISBN 0-521-00776-3 (pb.)
1. Ability.   2. Performance – Psychological aspects.   3. Expertise.
I. Sternberg, Robert J.   II. Grigorenko, Elena.

BF431 .P375   2003
153.9–dc21   2002034809

ISBN 0 521 80988 6 hardback
ISBN 0 521 00776 3 paperback

Contents

Preface

Some people study abilities, some study expertise, but few study both. Traditionally, the study of abilities has been seen as relatively distinct from the study of expertise, and the literatures that have developed in these two areas are largely distinct as well.

Ability theorists have argued about alternative factorial, process, biological, contextual, or other models of expertise, but, with few exceptions (such as Howard Gardner), have drawn only sparse links between their studies and studies of expert performance. Individuals with high levels of expertise are simply assumed to have developed these high levels of expertise as a function of their high levels of abilities.

Expertise theorists have argued about what it is that makes someone an expert, such as outstanding information processing or a highly organized knowledge base, or they have argued about how expertise is acquired, for example, through deliberate practice or skilled apprenticeship. They have failed to consider fully the role of expertise in the development and maintenance of expertise, and indeed, few expertise theorists have used any tests of abilities in their research.

Competencies often have been viewed as an endpoint in the study of abilities (for example, as providing criteria against which measures of abilities are validated) or as a beginning point in the study of expertise (for example, as providing a baseline for novices, or at least, nonexperts, against which expertise performance can be compared). Competency theorists have sometimes linked their work to abilities, and sometimes to expertise, but rarely to both.

The result of this separation among the studies of abilities, competencies, and expertise is that the field of psychology lacks relatively comprehensive accounts of how abilities, competencies, and expertise relate, for example, through the development of abilities into competencies and later into varying levels of expertise.

The mission of this book is to present alternative viewpoints of the relationships among abilities, competencies, and expertise. The book therefore seeks to integrate into a coherent discipline what formerly have been, to a large extent, separate disciplines. Such an integration makes both theoretical and practical sense, because abilities are of interest because they represent potentials to achieve competencies and, ultimately, expertise.

Psychology students often wonder how there can exist within the field of psychology widely discrepant theories of the same phenomenon. They also wonder how theories can be so well able to account for certain kinds of facts pertaining to a given phenomenon, but not for other kinds of facts. One of the reasons that such puzzles arise is that investigators tend to limit their research to particular paradigms, to particular aspects of phenomena, or both.

For example, one might argue that g (general intelligence) theorists tend to rely on studies showing the internal and external validities of measures of the so-called general factor of intelligence, but largely discount many studies that show discriminant validity for other, non-g-based measures. At the same time, multiple-intelligence theorists largely discount the voluminous evidence that seems to favor a general factor. More generally, abilities theorists largely ignore the literature on expertise that shows the importance of deliberate practice in the development of expertise, whereas expertise theorists largely ignore the literature on abilities showing how much difference abilities can make to the attainment of expert levels of performances of diverse kinds. This book integrates both paradigms and multiple facets of what we believe to be three highly interrelated phenomena that force psychological researchers as well as consumers of such research to confront other paradigms and aspects of phenomena that they may not have fully confronted in their past thinking.

The book may be of interest to differential, cognitive, educational, school, industrial/organizational, counseling, and biological psychologists who wish to learn about the relations among abilities, competencies, and expertise. It may also be of interest to educators, cognitive scientists, and cognitive neuroscientists interested in questions related to these constructs. The book has been written at a level comprehensible to advanced undergraduate students.

Authors of chapters have been asked to do six things in their individual chapters:

1. To present their views on the nature of abilities, competencies, and expertise (including its nature and development)
2. To present their views on the interrelationships among these three constructs
3. To state their views on how these three constructs can be assessed and developed
4. To present empirical data supporting their position
5. To compare and contrast their position to alternative positions, showing why they believe their position to be preferred
6. To speculate on the implications of their viewpoint for science, education, and society

This book is dedicated to the memory of our contributor, colleague, and friend, Michael Howe.

Preparation of this book was supported by Contract DAS W01-00-K-0014 from the U.S. Army Research Institute; by Grant REC-9979843 from the National Science Foundation; by a government grant under the Javits Act Program (Grant No. R206R000001) as administered by the Office of Educational Research and Improvement, U.S. Department of Education; by a grant from the W. T. Grant Foundation; and by a grant from the College Board. Grantees undertaking such projects are encouraged to express freely their professional judgment. This book, therefore, does not necessarily represent the positions or the policies of any of the funding agencies.

Contributors

Philip Ackerman, *Georgia Institute of Technology*

Paul B. Baltes, *Max Planck Institute for Human Development and Education, Berlin, Germany*

Susan M. Barnett, *Cornell University*

Margaret E. Beier, *Georgia Institute of Technology*

Stephen J. Ceci, *Cornell University*

Michael W. Connell, *Harvard University*

Jane W. Davidson, *Sheffield University, United Kingdom*

K. Anders Ericsson, *Florida State University*

Howard Gardner, *Harvard University*

Elena L. Grigorenko, *Yale University and Moscow State University*

Michael J. A. Howe (deceased), *University of Exeter*

Tomoe Kanaya, *Cornell University*

Ralf T. Krampe, *Max Planck Institute for Human Development and Education, Berlin, Germany*

Richard E. Mayer, *University of California, Santa Barbara*

Kimberly Sheridan, *Harvard University*

Dean Keith Simonton, *University of California, Davis*

Robert J. Sternberg, *Yale University*

The Psychology of Abilities, Competencies, and Expertise

1

Trait Complexes, Cognitive Investment, and Domain Knowledge

Philip Ackerman and Margaret E. Beier

The study of expertise has a long and varied history across over one hundred years of modern psychology. Along the way, various approaches and perspectives have been applied to examination of two central questions: "Who becomes an expert?" and "How does one become an expert?" Traditional experimental psychology researchers have focused on describing the processes involved in acquisition of expert performance (for example, Bryan and Harter, 1899), or on specifying the methods one should adopt for successfully acquiring expert performance (for example, James, 1890/1950). In contrast, traditional differential psychology researchers have focused on differentiating individuals from some specified group (for example, novices) who will acquire expertise during the course of training or job tenure from those who will fail to acquire expertise, given the same exposure. Researchers from a third perspective, which is best characterized as an "interactionist" approach, have attempted to build representations that consider both trait differences and childhood and adulthood experiences as spurs to the development of expertise (for example, Snow, 1996).

The focus of our discussion in this chapter is mainly on the differential and interactionist approaches. That is, we seek to understand the development of expertise as an interaction between individual characteristics (abilities, personality, interests, self-concept, and so forth) and the environment, as jointly influencing which persons develop expertise and which persons do not. In addition, we concern ourselves with the *direction* of investment of cognitive resources, which in turn determines the domains of expertise that are developed. The "environment" in this context can be highly constrained, as in elementary school and secondary school, or much less constrained, as post-secondary education and the world of work.

This chapter will first review some central issues of our perspective, such as the distinction between typical and maximal performance and the concept of aptitude complexes or trait complexes. Next, we describe a theoretical approach that encompasses the interactions between trait complexes and knowledge acquisition, followed by a brief review of empirical evidence associated with the theory. The current theoretical perspective will be placed in the context of other theories of abilities and expertise. We close with a discussion of some implications of this approach for science, for education, and for society.

TYPICAL BEHAVIOR VERSUS MAXIMAL PERFORMANCE

By the mid-1900s, researchers concerned with individual-differences theories and assessment procedures had split into essentially non-overlapping groups. Cronbach (1957) identified the field of correlational (differential) psychology as "sort of a Holy Roman Empire whose citizens identify mainly with their own principalities" (p. 671). For example, ability theorists and practitioners had little contact or communication with personality theorists and practitioners. As Cronbach (1949) earlier pointed out, abilities (in terms of both theory and assessment practices) were associated with "maximal performance." That is, when individuals were administered intelligence, aptitude, or achievement tests, they were exhorted to "do your best." The goal of the assessments was explicitly to measure the performance of an individual at his/her level of maximum cognitive effort. Individuals who did not try hard on such assessments effectively invalidated the inferences that could be made on the basis of the resulting test scores. In contrast, according to Cronbach (1949), personality theory and assessments were not concerned with maximal performance. Instead, they focused exclusively on how the individual "typically" behaved or focused on what were the individual's typical likes and dislikes. Operationally, personality assessment measures asked, for example, "Do you like to attend parties?" to obtain an estimate of the individual's underlying level of introversion-extroversion. Although Cronbach (1957) initially argued for the integration of experimental and differential approaches to behavior, subsequent investigators have attempted to better integrate the disparate streams *within* differential psychologies of cognition (abilities), conation (motives and volition), and affect (personality). Such approaches were advocated by Snow (1963), Cronbach (1975), and others (see Ackerman, 1997, for a review).

When it comes to expertise, the traditional concept of ability-as-maximal-performance leaves a lot to be desired. The contrasting contexts for ability assessment and achievement assessment make this point in a salient fashion. On the one hand, ability tests (such as standard omnibus intelligence tests) generally attempt to *remove* the benefits of specific expertise on overall performance, by (a) sampling very broadly (maximizing the heterogeneity of test content), and (b) specifically selecting content that is not associated with expertise (for example, neither the Stanford-Binet nor the Weschler Adult Intelligence Scales require that the examinee know how to read). Thus, the expert chef and the expert chemist are confronted with little test content that could benefit from their respective fields of expert knowledge. On the other hand, achievement tests (especially specialized domain-knowledge tests, such as professional certification tests) attempt to focus only on the specialized knowledge domain in question. For example, the Graduate Records Examination (GRE) Subject test in Chemistry can be expected to effectively discriminate between the chemist and the cook in a way that demonstrates the differences between their respective cumulative knowledge about chemistry. (It should be noted, though, that such tests have their limitations, such as the potential confound of individual differences in reading comprehension abilities that might influence performance on a time-limited domain-knowledge test. For a discussion of this issue, see Carroll, 1982.)

Looking at so-called intelligence and achievement tests through the perspective of maximal effort and typical behavior, it becomes clear in theory (though not entirely certain in practice) that without the application of directed cognitive effort toward domain-knowledge acquisition over extended time, performance on specific achievement tests will suffer. In contrast, tests of maximal effort, especially when presented in decontextualized formats (such as working-memory tests with letters and numbers as stimuli), are likely to be less influenced by cognitive investment toward developing expertise *in any specific domain*, though the cumulative effects of investment across domains can be expected to influence performance somewhat. Such considerations suggest that tests of general intelligence (as measures of maximal effort) are likely to have diminished associations with individual differences in the development of expert knowledge when compared with measures that are more appropriate to the assessment of typical levels of cognitive investment over extended periods of time.

APTITUDE COMPLEXES AND TRAIT COMPLEXES

In a seminal study of learning in post-secondary physics that considered interactions among abilities, attitudes, personality variables, and prior knowledge, Snow (1963) asked whether there are "combinations of levels of some variables which are particularly appropriate or inappropriate for efficient learning?" (p. 120). The concept of these kinds of combinations of traits was ultimately described by Snow as "aptitude complexes," in the same kind of framework as Cronbach's (1957) generic usage of "aptitude" as any individual-differences construct. Over the course of the subsequent three decades, Snow and his students (for example, Peterson, 1976; Porteus, 1976; for reviews see Snow, 1976, 1989) revealed the existence of several interesting personality-ability aptitude complexes that were related to the relative effectiveness of different instructional treatments (such as high structure/low structure class environments).

Although not directly resulting from an analysis of learning outcomes, Ackerman and Heggestad (1997) performed a large-scale meta-analysis and review of the literature associated with relations among ability, personality, and interest variables. They identified four broad sets of traits that shared significant and meaningful levels of common variance, which they called "trait complexes" after Snow's aptitude complex conceptualization (the term "traits" replaced "aptitude" in order to address the larger context of the overlapping characteristics across learning and other contexts). The four trait complexes were identified as (1) Social, (2) Clerical/Conventional, (3) Science/Math, and (4) Intellectual/Cultural, and the component traits are shown in Figure 1.1. These complexes have elements in common with Snow's aptitude complexes, but are, in fact, derived outside of the educational context. These trait complexes are posited to coalesce during child and adolescent development. Moreover, they represent combinations of traits that will, in turn, affect both academic and vocational orientations. Trait complexes affect the direction and intensity of the investment of cognitive effort and ultimately lead to differentiation between individuals in the breadth and depth of knowledge/expertise acquired during adulthood. Initial indications suggested that many sources of domain knowledge were

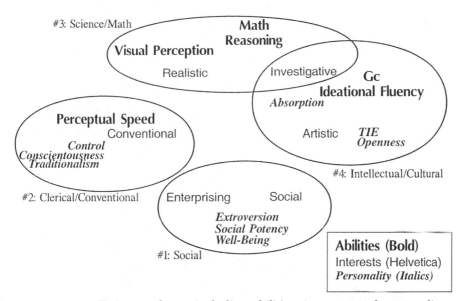

FIGURE 1.1. Trait complexes, including abilities, interests, and personality traits showing positive commonalities. Shown are (1) Social, (2) Clerical/Conventional, (3) Science/Math, and (4) Intellectual/Cultural trait complexes. Ability traits = bold; Interests = Roman font; Personality traits = Italic font. (Figure 7 on p. 239 of Ackerman and Heggestad, 1997, "Intelligence, personality, and interests: Evidence for overlapping traits." *Psychological Bulletin, 121,* 219–45. Copyright American Psychological Association. Reprinted by permission.)

positively associated with high levels of Science/Math and Intellectual/ Cultural trait complexes, and were associated with lower levels of Social and Clerical/Conventional trait complexes. Some of the subsequent empirical research on this topic will be discussed in a later section, but first we review a theoretical perspective that puts many of these constructs into a single theoretical framework, called PPIK.

PPIK

By integrating the concepts of typical versus maximal performance together with considerations of commonality among cognitive, affective, and conative traits, Ackerman (1996) has proposed a representation of the development of intellect across much of the adult lifespan. The approach is called PPIK for the four major components of the framework: intelligence-as-Process, Personality, Interests, and intelligence-as-Knowledge. Figure 1.2 provides a general description of these components, within a developmental framework. The PPIK approach draws

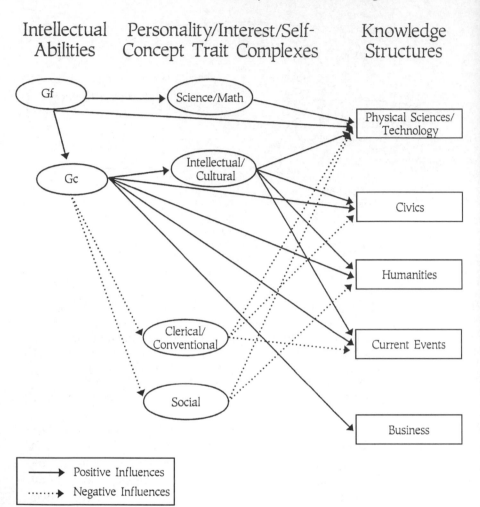

FIGURE 1.2. Illustration of constructs and influences in the PPIK theory (Ackerman, 1996). Gf (fluid intelligence) represents "intelligence-as-process"; Gc = crystallized intelligence. "Negative influences" mean that lower levels of one construct (for example, Gc) lead to higher levels of the other construct (for example, Clerical/Conventional trait complex). (Phillip L. Ackerman, Kristy R. Bowen, Margaret E. Beier, and Ruth Kanfer (2001). Determinants of Individual Differences and Gender Differences in Knowledge. *Journal of Educational Psychology*, 93, Number 4. Copyright American Psychological Association. Reprinted by permission.)

on the conceptualizations of Cattell and Horn (Cattell, 1943, 1971/1987; Horn and Cattell, 1966), the concepts of trait complexes (Ackerman and Heggestad, 1997), and Cattell's Investment Hypothesis (Cattell, 1957). Individuals start with differing levels of intelligence-as-process, which is similar to Cattell's fluid intelligence (Gf), but is limited to abilities that are based on substantially decontextualized processes (for example, working memory, abstract reasoning). Through interactions between intelligence-as-process and the development of key personality and interest variables (such as the trait complexes discussed earlier), individuals devote greater or lesser amounts of cognitive effort to the acquisition of domain-specific knowledge. These variables have mutually supporting or mutually impeding influences. For example, initial success in performing math problems may lead to an increment in math interests and supportive personality traits, which in turn may lead to increments in cognitive investment toward acquiring new knowledge in the mathematics domain (see Holland, 1959, 1973). In contrast, initial failures in performing math problems may lead to a decrement in associated interests and personality traits and in turn may lead to a decrement in cognitive investment toward acquiring new knowledge in the mathematics domain.

Across child and adolescent development, as the individual invests greater or lesser amounts of cognitive effort across different knowledge domains, coherent patterns of supportive and impeding traits are expected to coalesce into trait complexes. As individuals move from experiencing a common curriculum (for example, in elementary school) to increasingly differentiated experiences (both in secondary and post-secondary educational situations and in occupational and avocational activities), knowledge and expertise develop in increasingly differentiated repertoires. From the PPIK perspective, intelligence-as-knowledge is similar to Cattell's (1957) conceptualization of crystallized intelligence (Gc), but is much broader in operationalization than traditional measures of Gc (see, for example, Ackerman, 1996, for a discussion). In contrast to intelligence-as-process, intelligence-as-knowledge has an accumulative pattern across much of the adult lifespan (except for knowledge that is not regularly accessed and used, e.g., foreign language knowledge that is acquired in secondary school, but rarely used in subsequent years). Figure 1.3 illustrates the broad developmental patterns of intelligence-as-process, Gc (as traditionally assessed), and both occupational and avocational intelligence-as-knowledge. The figure indicates that, despite declines in intelligence-as-process during adulthood,

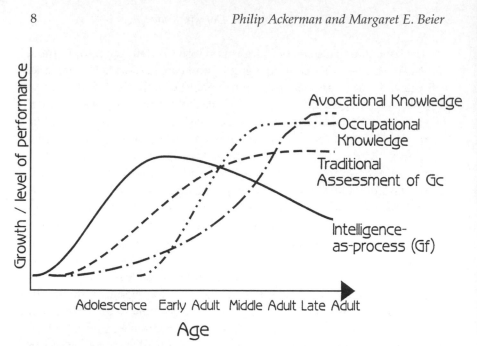

FIGURE 1.3. Hypothetical growth/level of performance curves across the adult lifespan, for intelligence-as-process, traditional measures of Gc (crystallized intelligence), occupational knowledge, and avocational knowledge. (Intelligence-as-process [Gf] and Gc modeled after Horn [1965].) (From Ackerman [1996].)

domain-specific knowledge and expertise tend to increase during the same period. Such increases, though, represent average standings – individual differences in trajectories are expected to be found, resulting from differential investment of cognitive effort toward or away from particular domains.[1]

EMPIRICAL FINDINGS RELATED TO THE PPIK THEORY

In a continuing series of studies over the past decade, we have investigated the relations among demographic variables of age and gender, intelligence-as-process, Gc, and several trait complexes in predicting individual differences in domain-specific knowledge. These studies are

---

[1] Note that the discussion of intelligence-as-process and intelligence-as-knowledge does not deny the potential influences of other abilities, either those traditionally defined empirically (for example, Carroll, 1993) or rationally (for example Gardner, 1999). The current approach focuses on what we consider the major sources of influence on intellectual performances, while remaining agnostic about the utility of other relevant cognitive traits.

described in detail elsewhere (Ackerman, 2000; Ackerman and Rolfhus, 1999; Beier and Ackerman, 2001; and Rolfhus and Ackerman, 1996, 1999), but we provide a brief review of this work below.

Study 1

In our first major study, we administered twenty academic and technology-oriented tests to a sample of 135 adults between the ages of thirty and fifty-nine (Ackerman and Rolfhus, 1999), and compared their performance with a group of 141 younger college students between ages eighteen and twenty-seven (Rolfhus and Ackerman, 1999). The middle-aged adults were found, on average, to know a great deal more about nearly all the various knowledge domains. In addition, this investigation showed that individual differences in knowledge are partly predicted by general intelligence, but especially well predicted by verbal/crystallized abilities, independent of general intelligence. The results were generally supportive of the Ackerman (1996) PPIK theory. A factor analysis of personality, interest, and self-concept traits, illustrated in Table 1.1, provided support for three of the trait complexes proposed by Ackerman and Heggestad (1997). The patterns of correlations between these three

TABLE 1.1. *Factor Analysis (Varimax Rotation) Showing Trait Complexes*

	Intellectual/Cultural	Science/Math	Social
Openness to experience	**.803**	−.005	−.046
Typical intellectual engagement (TIE)	**.838**	.135	.109
Investigative interests	**.638**	.250	−.033
Artistic interests	**.670**	−.085	.040
Verbal self-concept	**.630**	−.070	.066
Verbal ability	**.608**	.152	−.373
Realistic interests	.320	**.390**	.112
Math self-concept	−.339	**.628**	.014
Mechanical self-concept	.216	**.653**	.066
Spatial self-concept	.211	**.688**	.141
Math ability	−.190	**.502**	−.263
Spatial ability	.034	**.616**	−.274
Extroversion	−.092	−.075	**.662**
Social interests	.234	.047	**.688**
Enterprising interests	−.067	.004	**.586**

Note: N = 135, from study reported in Ackerman & Rolfhus (1999).
Salient factor loadings shown in boldface.

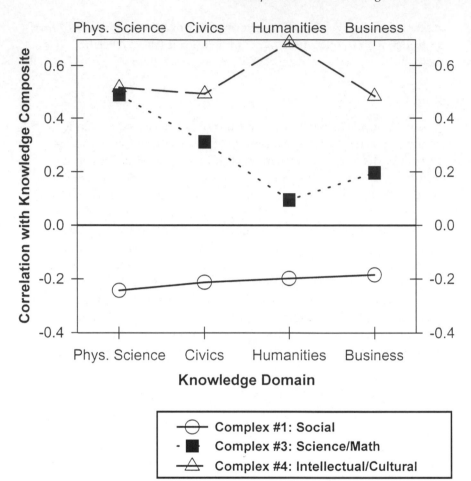

FIGURE 1.4. Correlations between trait complex scores and knowledge composites. $N = 276$ (Ages 18–59).

trait complexes (Social, Science/Math, and Intellectual/Cultural) and domain knowledge were consistent with the PPIK theory. Specifically, as shown in Figure 1.4, individuals with higher Intellectual/Cultural trait complex scores were more knowledgeable about all assessed knowledge domains than those with lower scores on the trait complex. The highest correlations between Intellectual/Cultural trait complex scores were found for knowledge in the humanities domain (for example, literature, music, art). Individuals with high Science/Math trait complex scores were broadly more knowledgeable than those with low scores, but especially more knowledgeable in physical sciences knowledge (for example, chemistry, physics, technology). Conversely, individuals with high scores on the Social trait complex showed lower levels of knowledge in all domains – even in domain knowledge about business.

Study 2

A second study centered on a cross-sectional investigation of 228 adults between the ages of twenty-one and sixty-two (Ackerman, 2000). The subjects were administered a large battery of ability tests to specifically assess Gf and Gc, a battery of personality and interest measures, and a set of eighteen knowledge tests. The study was designed to address three questions derived from Ackerman's PPIK theory: (1) Are middle-aged adults more knowledgeable than younger adults (or at least equally knowledgeable)? Or more generally, what is the relationship between age and individual differences in knowledge? (2) Are individual differences in knowledge well accounted for by traditional measures of Gf and/or Gc? and (3) What are the non-ability correlates of individual differences in knowledge? The study generated the following conclusions:

1. Supporting evidence was found for a coherent view of adult intelligence-as-knowledge, that is, in turn, quite different from the extant data and discussion of adult intelligence as representing only abstract reasoning or working memory abilities. First, there were significant *positive* correlations between age and knowledge scores in ten of the eighteen domains we investigated. Five of the remaining correlations between age and knowledge showed no significant relationship with age, and only the remaining three knowledge scales showed significantly negative correlations with age – all three were science tests (chemistry, physics, and biology) that were also the most highly correlated with Gf (in contrast to Gc). Overall, a single composite score computed across all the knowledge scales yielded a correlation of .19 ($p < .01$) between age and knowledge, indicating that at least across the domains and participants we sampled, older adults were on average more knowledgeable than younger adults. For comparison purposes: Gf yielded a correlation of $-.39$, ($p < .01$) with age; and Gc yielded a correlation of $+.14$, ($p < .05$).

2. The results of the analyses to determine the respective contributions of Gf and Gc to predicting individual differences in knowledge were differentiated by knowledge domain. Gf had a quite

considerable explanatory power in predicting knowledge in the science domain, accounting for 38.5 percent of the variance in the Science composite scores. It had a much diminished role in accounting for individual differences in any of the other areas we tested, accounting for less than 15 percent of the variance. In contrast, Gc accounted for an additional 34 percent of the variance in Civics knowledge and 42.8 percent of the variance in the Humanities, with a lesser role in Science and in Business/Law. A reasonable conclusion from these results is that Gf is mostly related to Science knowledge, Gc is mostly related to Civics and Humanities knowledge, but there is much variance in knowledge that is unaccounted for by these traditional intelligence assessments.

3. Selected personality traits of Social Closeness, Traditionalism, and Typical Intellectual Engagement accounted for significant variance in knowledge in every domain except for Business/Law. Individual differences in Realistic, Investigative, and Artistic interests accounted for significant amounts of variance in knowledge for all the broad domains we assessed. After trait measures were considered, individual differences in educational attainment and age provided relatively *little* additional explanatory power to predicting knowledge, suggesting that age may only be a useful predictor of knowledge in the *absence* of measures of relevant traits. As such, the influence of chronological age, in and of itself, on individual differences in knowledge may be substantially overemphasized. Personality/interest/self-concept trait complexes measures accounted for a substantially greater amount of variance in domain knowledge than did age.

4. The coherence between trait complexes and cognitive investment over time are illustrated by the pattern of trait complex scores across college majors. Figure 1.5 provides a breakdown of mean trait complex scores by college major, for domains of physical sciences, social sciences, arts/humanities, and business. Participants who had majored in one of the physical sciences showed higher levels of Science/Math-oriented personality/interest/self-concept traits, but lower levels on Social and Intellectual/Cultural trait complexes. In contrast, participants who majored in arts and humanities fields had higher scores on the Intellectual/Cultural trait complex and lower scores on the Science/Math trait complex. Social science majors were much more differentiated, in that they did not show a coherent pattern of different trait

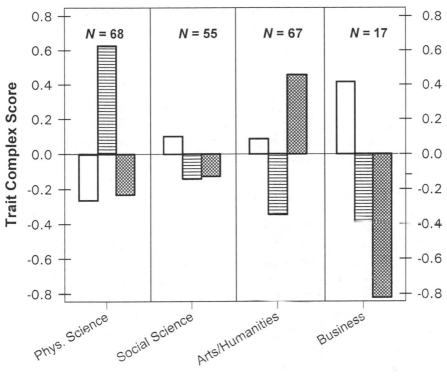

FIGURE 1.5. Mean trait complex scores, broken out by participants' college major. $N = 207$ (Ages 21–62); Phys. = Physical.

complexes (perhaps partly attributable to the diversity of areas within this classification – such as the difference in orientations between social work and econometrics). Business majors had the most coherent pattern, with high Social trait complex scores and low Intellectual/Cultural and Science/Math trait complex scores. When considered in the context of the negative correlations between Social trait complex scores and domain knowledge across all the areas, such a pattern suggests that these individuals would have high interest in interpersonal relations, but poor knowledge about the physical, political, and aesthetic world around them.

Study 3

The next study in the sequence was a cross-sectional study of 154 adults between the ages of twenty-one and sixty-nine (Beier and Ackerman, 2001). In this study, the scope of knowledge was expanded to include domains of current events from the 1930s to the 1990s, across areas of art, politics and economics, popular culture, and science/nature and technology. Results indicated that age of participants was significantly and positively related to knowledge about current events. Moreover, fluid intelligence was a substantially less effective predictor of knowledge levels than was crystallized intelligence. Selected personality measures, such as Traditionalism, were negatively related to current events knowledge, whereas Openness to Experience was positively related to current events knowledge. This study provided compelling evidence regarding the relative contributions of Gf, Gc, level of education, and age on current events knowledge. A most interesting pattern appeared for age and current events knowledge, with the largest correlation ($r = .55$) for the 1950s knowledge, and declining correlations for both earlier and later decades. A steep decline was seen for more recent knowledge than the 1950s, with a zero correlation between age and current events knowledge for the 1990s, even though Gc correlated with 1990s knowledge at a level of .73! Those individuals with high levels of Gc were much more knowledgeable about current events, regardless of the decade in which the events occurred. Interestingly, though, the trait complexes discussed earlier failed to substantially correlate with current events knowledge – suggesting that this is a domain where "expertise" is less likely to be influenced by intensive cognitive effort investments over time, and more likely to be influenced by a general orientation toward "intellectual engagement."

Study 4

In a recently completed study (Ackerman, Bowen, Beier, and Kanfer, 2001), we investigated the influences of individual differences in trait complexes in the prediction of individual differences in knowledge across several broad domains. In this study of 320 college students, we replicated and extended our previous work that showed the relative importance of Gc over Gf in predicting individual differences in knowledge. Moreover, we demonstrated that individual differences in two trait clusters (Science/Math/Technology and Verbal/Intellectual) had positive associations with acquired knowledge, and that three trait clusters (Social Potency/Enterprising, Social Closeness/Femininity, and Traditionalism/Worry/Emotionality) had broadly negative associations with acquired knowledge.

Summary

The studies conducted to date provide broad support to the PPIK approach, in several important respects: (1) Middle-aged adults were shown to be more knowledgeable on several broad and specific domains of knowledge when compared with younger adults – supportive of the notion that focused cognitive investment over extended periods of time yields clear differences between individuals in the depth and breadth of expertise; (2) Measures of Gf, which show declines as adults enter middle age, fail to fully account for either individual differences in knowledge structures (except for knowledge in the physical sciences) or the fact that middle-aged adults know more than their younger adult comparison groups in many areas. Gc measures, which represent intelligence-as-knowledge at the most broad conceptualization, are more predictive of individual differences in knowledge, but do not capture the rich sources of the breadth and depth of domain-specific knowledge; (3) The Science/Math Trait Complex and the Intellectual/Cultural trait complex represent constellations of characteristics that are supportive of domain-knowledge acquisition, whereas Social and Clerical/Conventional trait complexes are largely impeding of domain-knowledge acquisition.

GENDER DIFFERENCES

One major finding from the investigations described above was that the "ubiquity" of intellectual decline during adulthood heralded by many researchers is clearly a myth (for example, see Horn and Donaldson, 1976, 1977; however, see also Baltes and Schaie, 1976), when the repertoire of domain-specific knowledge is included in the conceptualization of adult intellect. However, a serendipitous finding from these investigations was that, rather than balanced differences in performance of men and women on domain-specific knowledge tests, women performed more poorly, on average, on most of the tests. Within the context of science, humanities, business, and civics knowledge domains, women either had substantially lower mean scores, or mean scores that were essentially equal to those of the men. Across all tested knowledge domains, the mean performance of women was nearly .36 lower than that of men, in *standard deviation units*. Women, on average, were not significantly better performers than men on any of the domain-knowledge tests. Although our tests of domain knowledge were predominantly objective multiple-choice tests, similar results are frequently found in both objective and essay test assessments (such as with the Advanced Placement [AP] tests taken by highly selected high school students). On AP tests, women only perform better than men, on average, on foreign language tests, despite ostensibly similar curricular backgrounds (see Cole, 1997; Willingham and Cole, 1997).

There are many potential explanations for these differences between men and women on accumulated domain-specific knowledge tests. One salient possibility from the PPIK and trait complex perspectives, is that gender differences in supportive and impeding trait complexes may explain differences in cognitive investment over time, that, in turn, lead to divergent patterns of knowledge and expertise. Our recent research (Ackerman et al., 2001) and ongoing studies (Beier and Ackerman, in press) suggest that gender differences in the key trait complexes can account for significant and substantial portions of the variance in gender differences. In an ongoing study of health and nutrition domain knowledge, we have found substantial mean gender differences in knowledge favoring women. Such findings support the notion that there is not an inherent method factor (that is, using multiple-choice tests of domain knowledge), but rather there are strikingly different patterns of accumulated knowledge between adult men and women. The interacting influences of intelligence-as-process, personality, and interest traits appear to be at least partially responsible for these differential patterns of developed expertise among identifiable demographic groups, such as men and women, groups that differ in socioeconomic status, and whether or not the individual has devoted time and effort toward child-rearing (see Beier and Ackerman, in press).

CONTRAST WITH OTHER THEORIES

Two major alternative theories that purport to address the determinants of individual differences in expertise, are "*g*- theory" and the "deliberate practice theory." In some ways, these two theories are actually straw-person arguments. Few researchers really believe, as perhaps Spearman (1927) did, that individual differences in *g* univocally determine individual differences in expertise, in the absence of deliberate practice. Similarly, few researchers seriously believe Watson's (1926) claim that with "a dozen healthy young infants, well-formed, and my own specified world to bring them up in and I'll guarantee to take any one at random and train him to become any type of specialist I might select" (p. 10). (At least Watson specified only "healthy" infants, and then also noted "I am going beyond my facts and I admit it" [1926, p. 10].) However, it is important to note that the set of researchers who make such claims is not a "null set" (for example, see Jensen, 1998, for a *g*-theory perspective, and Ericsson, 1996, for a deliberate-practice perspective). It is useful to review how these approaches consider the development of individual differences in expertise, while also recognizing that they are essentially extreme views.

g-theory

Spearman's (1914) early theorizing identified *g* as a *"general fund of mental energy"* (p. 103, italics in original) that could be applied to any tasks that required cognition. Later work by Spearman and his followers have variously identified *g* (or general intelligence) with a variety of different kinds of measures (for example, Sensory Discrimination, Common Sense [Spearman, 1904], eduction of relations and correlates [Spearman, 1927], performance on the Penrose & Raven Matrices Test [Spearman, 1938], and tests of working memory [Kyllonen and Christal, 1990]). Regardless of the operationalization of *g* assessment, mainstream *g-theory* (for example, Jensen, 1998) generally fails to take account of either aging effects or, more broadly, development in general across the lifespan (for a more detailed discussion, see Ackerman and Lohman, in press). In fact, Spearman stated: "For, as we have seen, the very essence of what is measured by [*g*] consists in its originativeness: that is to say, in its *not* being experiential" (Spearman, 1939, p. 250, italics in original).

   Clearly, *g-theory* has difficulties in explaining performance differences between individuals who are educated in Western European school systems from those individuals raised in impoverished developing countries without formal schooling or a high level of literacy. More specifically, the question is as follows: If *g* is not experiential, then how can one take account of individual differences in developed knowledge and expertise? One approach (see Jensen, 1998, p. 113) is to assert that a child's exposure to a traditional Western educational environment is needed to yield meaningful performance on g measures. Even if one were to limit the discussion of g to those individuals sharing a common curricular background, though, it is clear that measures of g that are closely related to Spearman's notions of eduction of relations and correlates (for example, Raven's Progressive Matrices Test, and other non-verbal reasoning tests) fail to account for a large portion of the individual differences variance in developed knowledge and expertise.

Moreover, in situations where g measures are substantially correlated with real-world performance measures (for example, scholastic and occupational performance), the general pattern of results is that such measures attenuate in their predictive validity, as the individuals progress from novice to skilled performers (for example, see Hulin, Henry, and Noon, 1990; Lin and Humphreys, 1977). Although such attenuation of the influence of g on performance is not universal (see Ackerman, 1994; Barrett, Alexander, and Doverspike, 1992, for examples and discussion), the general findings of reduced correlations between g and performance in real-world endeavors is consistent with the notion that g lacks the universal importance for all cognitively related activities, especially once initial stages of education or training are completed.

As illustrated from our own empirical studies (see Ackerman, 2000; Ackerman and Rolfhus, 1999; Beier and Ackerman, 2001; Rolfhus and Ackerman, 1999), individual differences in intelligence-as-process measures (which are based on such reasoning tests) show diminished predictive validity, especially in comparison to measures of broad verbal knowledge (for example Gc measures, such as vocabulary, reading comprehension, fluency, and general information). The important exception to the diminished correlations of g with knowledge and expertise lies in the math and physical sciences domains (see Ackerman, 2000). Interestingly, these are also knowledge domains most highly associated with creative works by younger investigators (see Simonton, 1988, for an extensive discussion), in contrast to creative works in the domains of the humanities and social sciences. Such a conjunction is consistent with a perspective on g that highlights peak ages for expressions of intelligence-as-process (see Figure 1.3), and the intense demands on abstract reasoning abilities in the math and physical sciences fields.

In the final analysis, either *g-theory* fails to provide a satisfactory account of development of individual differences in knowledge across the lifespan, or *g-theorists* must assert that knowledge and expertise are not "intellectual." Our perspective is that g is an especially important construct early in life (where it operates as intelligence-as-process), but g becomes diminished in influence (but certainly *not* eliminated in influence) in determining differences in knowledge acquisition, as individuals progress from common educational experiences (for example, core curricula in the elementary school systems) to differentiated experiences (such as in post-secondary schooling and occupational experiences).

Deliberate practice theory

According to Ericsson and his colleagues (1996; Ericsson and Charness, 1994; Ericsson, Krampe, and Tesch-Römer, 1993; Ericsson and Lehmann, 1996) attaining expert, even elite performance in any domain is not related to innate talent or ability. Rather, expert performance can be acquired by anyone through focused effort and hard work – what Ericsson calls deliberate practice (Ericsson, 1996; Ericsson and Charness, 1994; Ericsson et al., 1993; Ericsson and Lehmann, 1996). Deliberate practice is defined as an effortful enterprise focused on feedback and corrective action, which can only be sustained for a limited period of time each day (Ericsson et al., 1993). Deliberate practice is distinguished from work or play in that it is "specifically designed to improve the current level of performance" (p. 368, Ericsson et al., 1993). Another important characteristic of deliberate practice is that it is not inherently rewarding (Ericsson, 1996). Those who engage in deliberate practice are motivated or even obsessed by improvement in their performance. In Ericsson's theory, it is this difference in motivation, not innate talent or ability, that determines whether expert performance is reached in any domain. Based on retrospective studies of those who have attained expertise in various domains including music and chess, at least ten years of deliberate practice in a specific domain is required to achieve expert level performance. According to this view, expertise leads to an acquired memory skill – domain-specific long-term working memory (Ericsson and Kintsch, 1995)

Similar to the theory of deliberate practice, Ackerman's (1996) PPIK theory examines the role of experience and motivation in knowledge acquisition. However, the PPIK theory also incorporates a component of talent or ability (intelligence-as-process). As discussed above, research from the PPIK framework has shown that Gf (or intelligence-as-process) is an important determinant of knowledge across all domains – though the strength of the importance of Gf depends on the domain in question

(Ackerman, 2000; Ackerman and Rolfhus, 1999; Ackerman et al., in press; Beier and Ackerman, 2001; in press). In contrast, Ericsson's view ignores the role of ability entirely and posits that anyone, regardless of cognitive raw material or even disability, can become an expert at anything – provided he or she is motivated enough (Ericsson, 1996; Ericsson et al., 1993).

The omission of talent or ability in Ericsson's theory may be a function of the design of much of the research conducted to support it. For example, to understand the determinants of expertise, Ericsson et al. (1993) asked those who have achieved expert performance to report on the effort expended to achieve it. In this type of retrospective design, there is likely a restriction of range in ability of those studied. Consequently, individual differences in expert performance may well *not* be accounted for by talent or ability *for these groups of already highly talented individuals*. However, it would be erroneous to believe that the same conclusion (that is, that talent is not related to achieving expertise) would be reached if, for example, this research were conducted prospectively (that is, a longitudinal design) with a random sample of initially untrained individuals. It is useful also to point out that, despite a belief that pre-existing individual differences in intelligence or other abilities are irrelevant to the development of expertise, Ericsson and his colleagues have not attempted to develop world-class expertise in math or physics domains with a set of mentally retarded individuals. More broadly, in the absence of a random sample or a control group (Sternberg, 1996) it is difficult truly to understand the role of individual differences in intellectual and other abilities in the development of expertise.

We do not argue that the role of effortful practice is not important in attaining expert level performance in a domain – certainly, Nobel Laureates such as Richard Feynman and Murray Gel-Mann (for example, see Gleick, 1992) spent many years developing their expertise. However, if talent or ability were not important, we would question why individual differences in expert performance persist when it appears that many individuals work hard and participate in deliberate practice in their domains of choice. Ericsson (1996) would attribute these differences in expert performance to differences in deliberate practice, or to differences in motivation. As pointed out by Sternberg (1996), retrospectively attributing different levels of performance to different levels of deliberate practice is problematic, essentially rendering Ericsson's theory non-disconfirmable. In essence, the view that deliberate practice is "necessary and arguably sufficient for expertise – becomes unfalsifiable by virtue of any expertise that contradicts such a claim as being labeled as nondeliberate" (p. 349).

In summary, the theory of deliberate practice (Ericsson and Charness, 1994; Ericsson et al., 1993; Ericsson and Lehmann, 1996) is important in that it highlights the role of experience and effort expended in attaining expert performance and acquiring knowledge. Unfortunately, the "straw-person" argument proposed by these researchers (ignoring the contribution of individual differences in pre-existing abilities) places the theory at odds with decades of research on the role of ability in skill acquisition and ability-performance relations (for reviews, see Ackerman, 1988; Hunter and Hunter, 1984). Sending the message that only hard work is important in achieving one's goals, although appealing in a meritocracy, is undoubtedly the wrong message for those who are low in ability or new to a task. Such individuals would be much more likely to benefit from setting more realistic goals (Kanfer and Ackerman, 1989).

IMPLICATIONS FOR SCIENCE

The PPIK and trait complex perspectives discussed in this chapter are broadly developmental in scope. The early development aspects of these approaches pertain to discovering how abilities, personality, and interests develop together – whether they are more influenced by signal experiences, or by accumulated exposures and feedback/feedforward processes. One context for such issues is in how children learn to engage or avoid the pursuit of knowledge and expertise in particular domains, such as in extracurricular activities (for example, see discussion by Holland, 1959, 1973). Another context has to do with choices that are made by children within otherwise highly constrained learning environments (for example, choosing a particular topic for a book report within a general elementary school curriculum). For adolescents and adults, similar questions need to be addressed – though within the context of less structured learning, occupational, and avocational situations. Moreover, the mechanisms that give rise to the trait complexes and their impact on developed intelligence-as-knowledge have yet to be determined.

Although cross-sectional studies have provided important information on these issues, it is necessary to conduct extensive longitudinal studies to adequately evaluate various competing hypotheses regarding trait interactions during development over the lifespan. With the exception of some older literature (for example, Bayley, 1949; Honzik,

MacFarlane, and Allen, 1948) and studies that address more narrow aspects of these issues (for example, Moffitt, Caspi, Harkness, and Silva, 1993), there are almost no existing longitudinal studies that provide essential information on the developmental interactions between key ability, personality, and interest traits. There are, of course, logistical problems in conducting large-scale longitudinal studies that would involve assessment of intelligence-as-process, personality, interests, and intelligence-as-knowledge over extended periods of time. In addition, when considering the development of knowledge during the adult lifespan, Cattell's (1971/1987) assessment reflects the enormity of the problem. That is, for assessment of adult intelligence-as-knowledge, it may be necessary to create as many tests as there are different occupations and/or avocational activities.

Historically, there have been two "solutions" to such questions (for example, assessing Gc in adults – see Cattell, 1971/1987). The first solution is to assess only what has been learned within a relatively common school curriculum (for example, high school math and geometry) – which is what Cattell (1971/1987) called "historical Gc." The second solution is to focus only on a single knowledge domain (such as the architecture knowledge of architects, or the physics knowledge of physicists). The problem with assessments of intelligence-as-knowledge based on the first solution is that it does not give adults much credit (if any) for anything they have learned outside of the standard secondary school curriculum. Such assessments preclude any study of the knowledge that adults acquire within occupational or avocational contexts. The repertoire of a physicist might include knowledge of classical mechanics, electricity and magnetism, relativity theory, quantum mechanics, and so on, but none of this material would be considered to be part of the individual's intellectual capabilities. The second solution – to focus on a single knowledge domain – is similarly limited, because it ignores both knowledge outside of a narrow domain (which might frequently be used to solve problems in the domain of interest) and it fails to allow for comparisons between individuals with different occupations. A knowledge test developed for bank managers, for example, would be generally useless for assessing the knowledge of physicists. The interactions among ability/personality/interest traits could only be examined in groups of individuals who have either been self-selected or otherwise placed into a particular occupation. Such an approach would most certainly result in a restriction of range-of-talent on at least some of these variables, yielding obscured correlational information, and would be of little value to general questions of adult intellectual development.

Conducting large-scale longitudinal studies that sample individuals with both a wide range of talent and a wide range of occupations is clearly necessary to address the broader issues of trait interactions in the context of adult intellectual development. Such studies will need to include a broad sampling of the cognitive, affective, and conative trait domains as predictors, and a very broad sampling of domain-specific knowledge. These kinds of studies are obviously not easy or inexpensive to conduct – but the potential payoff seems to be proportional to the investment of scientific effort.

IMPLICATIONS FOR EDUCATION

The *interactionist* perspective inherent in the PPIK theory has several implications for educational and instructional systems. Across the entire educational lifespan from childhood to adult and non-traditional student there are two central issues related to education: (1) An increased focus on domain-specific knowledge, in contrast to general problem solving or intelligence; and (2) An orientation that trait-trait interactions may be more important than traditional aptitude-treatment interactions.

Domain-Specific Knowledge

Many recent attempts at innovation in educational policy have tried to reduce the time spent in the classroom on the development of domain knowledge in favor of an array of other topics (for example, development of ability, critical thinking skills, learning styles, or more simply "nurturing" students [Alexander & Murphy, 1999, p. 434]). Although some of these instructional innovations may indeed impact personality and interest traits that orient the students toward future acquisition of domain knowledge, little available evidence supports such a view. There are certainly cogent arguments against tracking individuals at an early age into particular vocational pursuits. However, there is generally a finite number of hours in the instructional day, and time taken to train such general strategies must be taken away from developing principled domains of knowledge.

In contrast, some secondary education and certainly most post-secondary education programs have become more focused on domain knowledge as a criterion of educational success (for example, Advanced

Placement tests and similar examinations figure prominently in selection of applicants for higher educational placements; see Watzman, 2000). The Chancellor of the University of California (UC) System, Richard Atkinson (Brainard, 2001), has recently proposed eliminating the traditional aptitude test battery (SAT) for selection into the UC system schools, in favor of knowledge-based achievement testing (for example, the SAT-II). Individual differences in level of relevant domain knowledge has been found to be at least equal in importance to broad aptitude measures in predicting success in graduate educational programs and beyond (see Willingham, 1974). Similarly, later occupational success has been found to be directly influenced by job-relevant knowledge, and only indirectly influenced by general intellectual ability (for example, see Hunter, 1983).

All these considerations suggest that educational systems need to place a greater degree of emphasis on developing domain knowledge. A generation of research in the field of artificial intelligence has shown that in many domains, expert knowledge is a far more critical determinant of success than high levels of abstract intelligence (for example, the contrast between expert systems and a general problem solver). The fundamental proposition is that it is far easier and more effective for an individual either to recall the solution to a problem directly, or transfer current knowledge to new, but related problems, and far more difficult and less effective to derive a solution to a real-world problem from only a set of general critical thinking skills. The corollary to this proposition is that the capabilities of older, non-traditional students, as measured by the SAT and other general aptitude tests, are substantially underestimated when considered in the context of the levels of their respective domain-specific knowledge structures. Educational selection procedures that increasingly focus on knowledge, in comparison with intelligence, are expected to yield substantially greater utility in terms of predicting academic success. Abstract reasoning and problem solving tests are much better assessments of "maximal" intelligence, but there is a lack of alignment between predictor and criterion when such measures are used to predict typical performance (such as academic grades). In contrast, knowledge measures are clearly more highly related to "typical" levels of intellectual investment than are measures of reasoning and abstract problem solving (for example, see Ackerman, 1994; Goff and Ackerman, 1992). Knowledge measures can be expected to provide a much better match between the predictor domain and the criterion domain – in line with what has been referred to as Brunswik Symmetry (see Wittmann and Süß; 1999).

Trait-Trait Interactions

Over the past thirty years, the aptitude-treatment interaction rubric has been viewed as failing to deliver a comprehensive framework for instructional design. However, work by Snow and his colleagues (see Snow, 1989, 1996 for reviews) and our own research have suggested that interactions among multiple traits (that is, trait-trait interactions) may provide a more powerful heuristic basis for instructional design and educational interventions. From a prediction perspective, it appears that assessment of trait complexes that are impeding for domain-knowledge development may be useful in identifying students at risk for academic failure. Future educational interventions might be constructed at many different stages along the educational lifespan of the individual. However, such interventions will probably need to focus not just on aptitude development, as traditional interventions, or on development of academic self-efficacy, but rather on the entire complex of traits that are indicators of an avoidance of domain-knowledge acquisition. The concept that underlies this perspective is that in order to interrupt a "low-achievement" cycle of

abilities→interests→personality→self-concept→knowledge,

one probably needs a multiple-pronged intervention that addresses most or all of these traits.

IMPLICATIONS FOR SOCIETY

One major impetus for the PPIK theory was the historical bias of some intelligence researchers *against* the notion that intellect can increase as young adults develop into middle age and beyond (see Ackerman, 2000, for a review). That is, intelligence-theory perspectives that univocally identify intelligence as Gf or g (as exemplified by working memory tests or tests of abstract reasoning) regard intelligence as a trait that increases in level up to the early twenties and then declines rather precipitously with increasing age. Our view of intelligence is that the trait can more usefully be considered as representing "what an individual can do" in a way that encompasses both the solution of novel problems *and* the solution of problems with which the individual may have an extensive body of knowledge or developed expertise. Moreover, we believe that the vast majority of problem solving that is done by adults falls under the heading of application of developed knowledge (whether by direct recall of prior solutions, or by the employment of either near transfer or far transfer from long-term memory). The approach to adult intelligence that has been inspired by the PPIK theory has clearly demonstrated that as far as intelligence-as-knowledge is concerned, middle-aged adults are generally far better endowed, in comparison to college sophomores (with the exception of knowledge in some domains of the physical sciences and mathematics). When averaging across a wide battery of measures that represent Gf, Gc, and domain-specific knowledge, middle-aged adults can be considered, on average, to have greater overall levels of intelligence (for example, see Ackerman, 2000).

The obvious implication from this research is that traditional means of assessing adult intelligence (such as omnibus intelligence tests, like the Wechsler Adult Intelligence Scale; or aptitude tests, such as the SAT or the general Graduate Records Examination) yield results that substantially underestimate the intellect of adults. Therefore, predictions of educational or occupational success predicated on such traditional measures most likely result in both non-optimal selection decisions and in a built-in bias against non-traditional students or middle-aged employees. To better serve a meritocratic society, measures need to be developed that provide a more comprehensive assessment of what the individual can do – which means that assessments need to encompass domain knowledge and expertise, in addition to abstract problem solving.

Although our results provide very encouraging news about the nature of adult intellectual development and provide a much more favorable comparison between middle-aged and younger adults, our findings regarding gender differences suggest that there is a great need to understand the etiology of gender differences in knowledge acquisition across the lifespan. It is too early to tell at this point in the research program, but gender differences in supportive and impeding trait complexes appear to partially account for a large portion of these gender differences in knowledge (for example, Ackerman et al., 2001). Understanding how such differences arise, and understanding whether it is possible to remediate gender differences in domain knowledge are important scientific questions. Whether remediation should be recommended, so that women attain levels of performance similar to those of men on domain-specific knowledge measures, is a broader societal question that cannot be easily answered. It may be, however, that such differences in domain knowledge are causally related to the differences in educational attainment by women and men – where women obtain 55.6 percent of the bachelor's level degrees in the United States, but only 40.8 percent of the doctoral degrees (Chronicle of Higher Education Almanac, 2000–2001).

References

Ackerman, P. L. (1988). Determinants of individual differences during skill acquisition: Cognitive abilities and information processing. *Journal of Experimental Psychology: General, 117(3)*, 288–318.

Ackerman, P. L. (1994). Intelligence, attention, and learning: Maximal and typical performance. In D. K. Detterman (Ed.), *Current Topics in Human Intelligence; Volume 4: Theories of Intelligence*, pp. 1–27. Norwood, NJ: Ablex.

Ackerman, P. L. (1996). A theory of adult intellectual development: Process, personality, interests, and knowledge. *Intelligence, 22*, 227–257.

Ackerman, P. L. (1997). Personality, self-concept, interests, and intelligence: Which construct doesn't fit? *Journal of Personality, 65(2)*, 171–204.

Ackerman, P. L. (2000). Domain-specific knowledge as the "dark matter" of adult intelligence: Gf/Gc, personality and interest correlates. *Journal of Gerontology: Psychological Sciences, 55B*, P69–P84.

Ackerman, P. L., Bowen, K. R., Beier, M. E., & Kanfer, R. (2001). Determinants of individual differences and gender differences in knowledge. *Journal of Educational Psychology, 93*, 797–825.

Ackerman, P. L., & Heggestad, E. D. (1997). Intelligence, personality, and interests: Evidence for overlapping traits. *Psychological Bulletin, 121*, 219–245.

Ackerman, P. L., & Lohman, D. F. (in press). Education and g. To appear in H. Nyborg (Ed.), *The Scientific Study of General Intelligence – Tribute to Arthur R. Jensen*. Elsevier Science.

Ackerman, P. L., & Rolfhus, E. L. (1999). The locus of adult intelligence: Knowledge, abilities, and non-ability traits. *Psychology and Aging, 14*, 314–330.

Alexander, P. A., & Murphy, P. K. (1999). Learner profiles: Valuing individual differences within classroom communities. In P. L. Ackerman, P. C. Kyllonen, and R. D. Roberts (Eds.), *Learning and Individual Differences: Process, Trait, and Content Determinants* (pp. 413–436). Washington, DC: American Psychological Association.

Baltes, P. B., & Schaie, K. W. (1976). On the plasticity of intelligence in adulthood and old age: Where Horn and Donaldson fail. *American Psychologist, 31*, 720–725.

Barrett, G. V., Alexander, R. A., & Doverspike, D. (1992). The implications for personnel selection of apparent declines in predictive validities over time: A critique of Hulin, Henry, and Noon. *Personnel Psychology, 45*, 601–617.

Bayley, N. (1949). Consistency and variability in the growth of intelligence from birth to eighteen years. *Journal of Genetic Psychology, 75*, 165–196.

Beier, M. E., & Ackerman, P. L. (2001). Current events knowledge in adults: An investigation of age, intelligence and non-ability determinants. *Psychology and Aging, 16*, 615–628.

Beier, M. E., & Ackerman, P. L. (in press). Determinants of health knowledge: An investigation of age, gender, abilities, personality, and interests. To appear in *Journal of Personality and Social Psychology*.

Brainard, J. (2001, February 19). U. of California's President Proposes Dropping the SAT Requirement. *Chronicle of Higher Education, 47*.

Bryan, W. L., & Harter, N. (1899). Studies on the telegraphic language: The acquisition of a hierarchy of habits. *Psychological Review, 6*, 345–375.

Carroll, J. B. (1982). The measurement of intelligence. In R. J. Sternberg (Ed.), *Handbook of human intelligence* (pp. 29–120). New York: Cambridge University Press.

Carroll, J. B. (1993). *Human cognitive abilities: A survey of factor-analytic studies.* New York: Cambridge University Press.

Cattell, R. B. (1943). The measurement of adult intelligence. *Psychological Bulletin, 40*, 153–193.

Cattell, R. B. (1957). *Personality and motivation structure and measurement.* Yonkers-on-Hudson, NY: World Book Company.

Cattell, R. B. (1971/1987). *Intelligence: Its structure, growth, and action.* (Revised and reprinted from *Abilities: Their structure, growth, and action*, Boston: Houghton- Mifflin). Amsterdam: North Holland.

Chronicle of Higher Education Almanac, 2000–2001. Washington, DC: Author.

Cole, N. S. (1997). *The ETS gender study: How females and males perform in educational settings.* Princeton, NJ: Educational Testing Service.

Cronbach, L. J. (1949). *Essentials of psychological testing.* New York: Harper.

Cronbach, L. J. (1957). The two disciplines of scientific psychology. *American Psychologist, 12*, 671–684.

Cronbach, L. J. (1975). Beyond the two disciplines of scientific psychology. *American Psychologist, 30*, 116–127.

Ericsson, K. A. (1996). The acquisition of expert performance: An introduction to some of the issues. In K. A. Ericsson (Ed.), *The road to excellence: The acquisition of expert performance in the arts and sciences, sports and games* (pp. 1–50). Mahwah, NJ: Lawrence Erlbaum.

Ericsson, K. A., & Charness, N. (1994). Expert performance: Its structure and acquisition. *American Psychologist, 49(8)*, 725–747.

Ericsson, K. A., & Kintsch, W. (1995). Long-term working memory. *Psychological Review, 102(2)*, 211–245.

Ericsson, K. A., Krampe, R., & Tesch-Römer, C. (1993). The role of deliberate practice in the acquisition of expert performance. *Psychological Review, 100(3)*, 363–406.

Ericsson, K. A., & Lehmann, A. C. (1996). Expert and exceptional performance: Evidence of maximal adaptation to task constraints. *Annual Review of Psychology, 47*, 273–305.

Gardner, H. (1999). *Intelligence reframed: Multiple intelligences for the 21st century.* New York: Basic Books.

Gleick, J. (1992). *Genius: The life and science of Richard Feynman.* New York: Pantheon Books.

Goff, M., & Ackerman, P. L. (1992). Personality-intelligence relations: Assessing typical intellectual engagement. *Journal of Educational Psychology, 84*, 537–552.

Holland, J. L. (1959). A theory of vocational choice. *Journal of Counseling Psychology, 6(1)*, 35–45.

Holland, J. L. (1973). *Making vocational choices: a theory of careers.* Englewood Cliffs, NJ: Prentice Hall.

Honzik, M. P., MacFarlane, J. W., & Allen, L. (1948). The stability of mental test performance between two and eighteen years. *Journal of Experimental Education, 17,* 309–324.

Horn, J. L., & Cattell, R. B. (1966). Refinement and test of the theory of fluid and crystallized general intelligences. *Journal of Educational Psychology, 57(5),* 253–270.

Horn, J. L., & Donaldson, G. (1976). On the myth of intellectual decline in adulthood. *American Psychologist, 31,* 701–719.

Horn, J. L., & Donaldson, G. (1977). Faith is not enough: A response to the Baltes-Schaie claim that intelligence does not wane. *American Psychologist, 32,* 369–373.

Hulin, C. L., Henry, R. A., & Noon, S. L. (1990). Adding a dimension: Time as a factor in the generalizability of predictive relationships. *Psychological Bulletin 107,* 1–13.

Hunter, J. E. (1983). A causal analysis of cognitive ability, job knowledge, job performance, and supervisor ratings. In F. Landy, S. Zedeck, & J. Cleveland (Eds.), *Performance measurement and theory.* Hillsdale, NJ: Erlbaum.

Hunter, J. E., & Hunter, R. F. (1984). Validity and utility of alternative predictors of job performance. *Psychological Bulletin, 96,* 72–98.

James, W. (1890/1950). *The principles of psychology* (Vol. 1). New York: Dover Publications.

Jensen, A. R. (1998). *The g factor: The science of mental ability.* Westport, CT: Praeger.

Kanfer, R., & Ackerman, P. L. (1989). Motivation and cognitive abilities: An integrative/aptitude-treatment interaction approach to skill acquisition. *Journal of Applied Psychology Monograph, 74(4),* 657–690.

Kyllonen, P. C., & Christal, R. E. (1990). Reasoning ability is (little more than) working-memory capacity?! *Intelligence, 14,* 389–433.

Lin, P. C., & Humphreys, L. G. (1977). Predictions of academic performance in graduate and professional school. *Applied Psychological Measurement, 1,* 249–257.

Moffitt, T. E., Caspi, A., Harkness, A. R., & Silva, P. A. (1993). The natural history of change in intellectual performance: Who changes? How much? Is it meaningful? *Journal of Child Psychological Psychiatry, 34(4),* 455–506.

Peterson, P. L. (1976). *Interactive effects of student anxiety, achievement orientation, and teacher behavior on student achievement and attitude.* Unpublished doctoral thesis, Stanford University, Palo Alto, CA.

Porteus, A. W. (1976). *Teacher-centered vs. student-centered instruction: Interactions with cognitive and motivational aptitudes.* Unpublished doctoral thesis, Stanford University, Palo Alto, CA.

Rolfhus, E. L., & Ackerman, P. L. (1996). Self-report knowledge: At the crossroads of ability, interest, and personality. *Journal of Educational Psychology, 88,* 174–188.

Rolfhus, E. L., & Ackerman, P. L. (1999). Assessing individual differences in knowledge: Knowledge structures and traits. *Journal of Educational Psychology, 91,* 511–526.

Simonton, D. K. (1988). *Scientific genius: A psychology of science.* New York: Cambridge University Press.

Snow, R. E. (1963). *Effects of learner characteristics in learning from instructional films.* Unpublished doctoral dissertation, Purdue University, Lafayette, IN.

Snow, R. E. (1976). *Research on aptitudes: A progress report.* Stanford University Aptitude Research Project, Technical Report No. 1. Palo Alto, CA: Stanford University.

Snow, R. E. (1989). Aptitude-treatment interaction as a framework for research on individual differences in learning. In P. L. Ackerman, R. J. Sternberg, & R. Glaser (Eds.), *Learning and individual differences. Advances in theory and research* (pp. 13–59). New York: W. H. Freeman.

Snow, R. E. (1996). Aptitude development and education. *Psychology, Public Policy, and Law, 2,* 536–560.

Spearman, C. (1904). "General intelligence," objectively determined and measured. *American Journal of Psychology, 15,* 201–293.

Spearman, C. (1914). The theory of two factors. *Psychological Review, Vol. 21(2),* 101–115.

Spearman, C. (1927). *The nature of "intelligence" and the principles of cognition.* London: Macmillan and Co.

Spearman, C. E. (1938). Measurement of intelligence. *Scientia, Milano, 64,* 75–82.

Spearman, C. (1939). "Intelligence" tests. *Eugenics Review, 30,* 249–254.

Sternberg, R. J. (1996). Costs of expertise. In K. A. Ericsson (Ed.), *The road to excellence: The acquisition of expert performance in the arts and sciences, sports and games* (pp. 347–354). Mahwah, NJ: Lawrence Erlbaum.

Watson, J. B. (1926). What the nursery has to say about instincts. In C. Murchison (Ed.), *Psychologies of 1925* (pp. 1–34). Worchester, MA: Clark University Press.

Watzman, H. (2000, January 21). Israeli colleges will begin using an alternative to national admissions tests. *Chronicle of Higher Education, 46,* A53.

Willingham, W. W. (1974). Predicting success in graduate education. *Science, 183,* 273–278.

Willingham, W. W., & Cole, N. S. (1997). *Gender and fair assessment.* Mahwah, NJ: Lawrence Erlbaum.

Wittmann, W. W., and Süß, H.-M. (1999). Investigating the paths between working memory, intelligence, knowledge, and complex problem-solving performances via Brunswik symmetry. In P. L. Ackerman, P. C. Kyllonen, & R. D. Roberts (Eds.), *Learning and individual differences: Process, trait, and content determinants* (pp. 77–108). Washington, DC: American Psychological Association.

2

Intelligence as Adaptive Resource Development and Resource Allocation:

A New Look Through the Lenses of SOC and Expertise

Ralf T. Krampe and Paul B. Baltes

The psychology of intelligence has undergone major changes in theoretical orientation and in its empirical approach since its early days close to a hundred years ago (Sternberg, 1990; Sternberg and Detterman, 1986). For the pioneers of intelligence testing, most notably Binet and Stern, the concept of intelligence captured relatively stable, interindividual differences in general abilities and capacities that were relevant to acquiring new skills and learning in novel situations. The idea of adaptation in the sense of mastering the challenges of a changing environment was constituent for the concept of intelligence in its earliest forms. In the minds of the general public until today, having a high IQ was synonymous with being smart and having a large potential for successfully coping with all kinds of professional and everyday challenges.

Due to these underlying theoretical ambitions the construction of intelligence tests in the decades following the pioneering stages faced no less than the triple challenge (1) to identify basic capacities that (2) reflected stable interindividual differences, and (3) that were general in terms of their relevance for all kinds of real-life competencies and skills. In response to these challenges extant psychometric tests have narrowed down the conceptual scope of the intelligence concept quite considerably. Implicit in the psychometric approach to intelligence is a focus on measurement (as opposed to understanding the causes, contexts, and functions of intelligence) and the view that intelligence reflects a collection of fairly static or dispositional abilities that characterizes a person (as opposed to a dynamic system of contextualized and adaptive cognitive functions that individuals continue to acquire throughout their life course). As a consequence, the psychometric intelligence literature

31

has zoomed in on two general ways to define its content: (a) presumably content-free measures of basic cognitive functioning (for example, processing speed, abstract reasoning, spatial abilities in figural transformation tasks) and (b) content that was overlearned where differences in level, therefore, would indicate "talent" differences. The typical instances were separate measures of general verbal knowledge and rule-based problem solving of the logical type, such as inductive reasoning or numerical performance. Arguably, however, these abilities reflect a rather limited set of abilities related to academic performance for the most part. And most certainly, the resulting tests did not capture the rather varied contents and skills that form the life experiences of adults.

Over the last decades the climates of the scientific inquiry about intelligence have shifted from the IQ-based tradition to more broadly based inquiries about the contextual and functional aspects of intelligence (Dixon and Baltes, 1986). From our point of view, four areas of empirical study have added critical momentum to this theoretical evolution: (1) lifespan approaches to the structure and function of psychometric intelligence, (2) the investigation of the interplay between cognitive and sensorimotor functioning in multi-task situations, (3) studies on age-differential plasticity in the acquisition of new skills, and (4) research on the long-term development of expertise. Each approach has revealed certain limitations of the psychometric approach to intelligence testing with respect to understanding the adaptive processes inherent to intellectual functioning. Our approach in this chapter is to use these shortcomings as a starting point for the development of a different vantage point that puts the concept of intelligence back into the context originally intended by its earliest protagonists: intelligence as a source of interindividual differences in the adaptive potential to cope with context-rich, real-life domains of psychological functioning.

One avenue we chose for this rejuvenation of a context-driven approach to intelligence is a focus on the specific contexts and tasks of adaptive competence in adulthood. To this end, we start out by describing a theoretical framework designed to conceptualize the mechanisms and processes underlying adaptive development, the SOC-Model of selection, optimization, and compensation (originally proposed by P. B. Baltes and M. M. Baltes, 1990) and we sketch our view of the triangular relations between SOC, psychometric intelligence, and expertise. We then highlight evidence from the four aforementioned areas of empirical investigation and we frame related findings from an SOC perspective. We conclude with an outlook on potential routes to the empirical study of adaptive components of intellectual functioning. To prevent a possible misunderstanding, we need to emphasize that the approach chosen is not based on our conception that SOC is the dominant frame within which intelligence is studied. Rather, we use this approach to present an exemplar of how research on intelligence is modified by a contextually and functionally driven line of inquiry. In our approach the typical "external validity of intelligence" question becomes a constituent part of the concept itself. A corollary implication is that the focus on the adaptive mastery of adult and aging tasks highlights the need to expand the structures and functions beyond those of the two traditional content territories of intelligence: educational and occupational performance.

ADAPTIVE DEVELOPMENT: THE TRIANGULATION OF SOC, INTELLIGENCE, AND EXPERTISE

The model of selection, optimization, and compensation was originally proposed as a theory of successful aging by Paul and Margret Baltes (1990). Since then it has been developed into a framework or meta-theory of lifespan development that attempts to define universal processes of developmental regulation, that is, the mastery of life (Freund and Baltes, 2000; Freund and Baltes, 2002; Marsiske, Lang, Baltes, and Baltes, 1995). The fundamental approach to developmental regulation is that individuals must continuously adapt to opportunities and constraints, both of which take different forms or change throughout the whole life course. The metaphor used in the SOC-Model for developmental opportunities and constraints is the amount and types of resources available to an individual. Such resources can be physical strength, intelligence, or the capacity to sustain challenging activities. However, the term resources is also used for cultural support structures like the educational and living opportunities provided by a society, the family context of an individual, or her income.

According to the SOC theory, adaptive development amounts to a resource development as well as a resource management and allocation process. Selection involves goals or outcomes, optimization relates to goal-relevant means such as practice, and compensation denotes the use of alternative means to maintain performance in the face of losses of means. The orchestration of these three processes is assumed to be central in achieving adaptive mastery and continued lifelong development.

Our goal in the present chapter is to highlight the kinds of conceptions of intelligence that emerge if one is committed to elaborating the interface between intelligence and the contexts of life in which intellectual functions operate. Aside from SOC as a general process of adaptive mastery and development, the concept of expertise (Ericsson, Krampe, and Tesch-Römer, 1993; Ericsson and Lehmann, 1996; Ericsson and Smith, 1991) is exploited for the purpose of explicating a new look at the structure and function of intelligence. Figure 2.1 gives an illustration of this sketch, which we labeled the *triangulation of SOC, intelligence*, and expertise*.

One cornerstone of our triangulation is SOC as a repertoire of adaptive mechanisms underlying developmental regulation. Individual

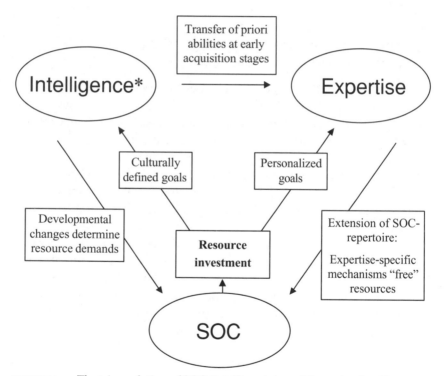

FIGURE 2.1. The triangulation of SOC, Intelligence*, and Expertise. Intelligence* refers to the concept of intelligence as implicitly defined by extant psychometric tests, like the primary mental abilities. SOC is conceived as a repertoire of adaptive mechanisms underlying developmental regulation. Developmental regulation amounts to resource investment through selection, optimization, and compensation into culturally defined (intelligence*) or personalized (expertise) domains of functioning. The relations between SOC, on the one hand, and expertise and intelligence, on the other, are reciprocal.

developmental trajectories emerge as a result of resource investments into culturally defined (intelligence*) or more personalized (expertise) goals. In this context we use the term "goals" in a broad sense denoting different domains of functioning rather than implying that individual resource allocation necessarily reflects conscious or even deliberate decisions.

We use the label intelligence* to refer to those abilities measured by extant psychometric tests (like the primary mental abilities), which, in our view, represent a limited set of what should be subsumed under the concept of intelligence. Following a line of thought originally proposed by George Ferguson (1954; 1965), we posit that interindividual differences in intelligence* represent the outcomes of individuals' adaptations in domains emphasized by a specific culture and its associated learning histories. Ferguson argued that stable interindividual differences in related abilities emerge as a result of individuals' efforts to optimize their functioning in these domains. From our developmental perspective of long-term resource investment, intelligence* abilities resemble *expertise-like capacities*. The critical differences between intelligence* abilities and expertises like chess or being a concert pianist are that all individuals in a given culture are expected to optimize their functioning in intelligence* domains and that trajectories toward "expertise" along with the necessary external resources in terms of coaching and known training methods are, in principle, available to most individuals. Society and culture direct individuals' resource investments (in terms of selection, optimization, and compensation processes) thereby organizing the "channeling" of individuals into related developmental trajectories.[1]

We distinguish between more universal (such as the primary mental abilities) and more individualized domains of expertise-like categories of intelligence (Baltes, Staudinger, and Lindenberger, 1999). We view

---

[1] We do not wish (and neither did Ferguson) to espouse a tabula rasa view of the development of primary mental abilities. Genetic endowment is a part of an individual's resources and it enters into the developmental regulation process as such. We believe that the emerging findings in modern molecular biology suggest that terms like "innate abilities" tend to obscure rather than elucidate discussions about adaptive development. Thus, we deliberately refrain from using this term here. It is important that the present treatment does not highlight the role of the nature-nurture issues associated with the developmental emergence of intelligence* or the putative different sources of determining factors of the cognitive mechanics and the cognitive pragmatics. In our triangulation approach intelligence* is NOT identical with cognitive mechanics. Rather, we treat intelligence* abilities, like the primary mental abilities, as *confounds* of mechanics and pragmatics, though with differential compositions (for example, vocabulary being closer to pragmatics or reaction time speed being closer to mechanics).

more individualized expertise development as different from the more general set of mental abilities, as a trajectory organized around more "personalized" goals, which are pursued by a subset of the members of a given society. Acquisition of more personalized expertises involves use of the more generally available abilities to some degree. However, the distinguishing process is the acquisition of expertise-specific mechanisms. Becoming an expert chess player or a concert pianist is a long-distance race during which individuals at each stage of development negotiate internal (for example, mental energy to sustain practice) and external (for example, availability of teachers and instruments) resource constraints with the goal of optimizing the outcomes of their resource investments (that is, their levels of performance). This view originates from the one espoused in the *deliberate practice* model proposed by Ericsson, Krampe, and Tesch-Römer (1993). Although the evidence is scarce at present, we suggest that findings from biographies and analyses of the daily routines of young athletes provide a good illustration for the SOC perspective on differential resource investment into intelligence* and expertise abilities that we propose here: Kaminski, Mayer, and Ruoff (1984) found that adolescents engaging in high-performance sports had a considerable need for private teaching to keep up with school requirements, presumably due to time demands imposed by training and competitions abroad (see also, Lerner, Freund, De Stefanis, and Habermas, 2001; Ruoff, 1981).

Following the deliberate practice perspective on expertise development we assume that expert individuals face a continuous quest for methods to overcome and push beyond limitations and weaknesses in their performance. Related problem solving skills involve the acquisition of domain-specific knowledge and mechanisms that are beyond the knowledge and mechanisms underlying intelligence* capacities. The degree of (non-)overlap between intelligence* abilities and those abilities defining expertise or specific skills is by itself subject to developmental change, both in the sense of aging and advancing performance levels in the context of skill or expertise development. This is most evident at extreme stages of expertise development. Attaining expert-level performance requires the mastery of an existing repertoire (as in music) and skills and the individual can rely on known training methods and role models in this context; transitions to eminence in domains like arts and sciences are marked by novel contributions or by excelling beyond the levels of peak performance at a given historical time (see, for example, a discussion in Krampe and Ericsson, 1995).

Although our view of intelligence* abilities as expertise-like capacities may seem counterintuitive, there exist theoretical propositions and empirical findings in the literature that speak to its heuristic potential. As an example, Simon and Chase (1973) compared chess masters' knowledge base, in terms of the different positions encountered and studied, with the size of the vocabulary acquired by an adult native speaker of English; the authors also drew parallels with respect to the necessary time to acquire both knowledge bases. Similar to intelligence* abilities, the types of abilities and the levels of performance characterizing expert individuals have changed over historical time and they also differ between cultures and societies. As an example, literacy, a rare form of expertise in the Middle Ages, is a basic intellectual requirement in modern societies. The standard repertoire to be mastered by an aspiring soloist musician and related technical skills, for instance, have changed dramatically since the days of Bach or Mozart, presumably leading to a differentiation into performing experts and composers in the field. Analyses of peak performances in various expertise domains (Ericsson, 1990; Schulz and Curnow, 1988) reveal dramatic changes in the levels of accomplishment necessary to attain expert status or eminence. From a cultural perspective, it is informative that chess, considered the *drosophila of expertise research* in the literature (Charness, 1989; Simon and Chase, 1973), used to be a subject at public schools in parts of Russia and several other countries of the former Soviet Union. Institutionalized instruction through master teachers and clubs is still far more common in those countries than in the United States or Canada (Charness, Krampe, and Mayr, 1996). One could argue that in several Eastern European countries, chess skills come close to "universal" intelligence* abilities, with a large part of the population participating in culturally organized trajectories toward expertise-like abilities.

Our attempt thus to reconceptualize intelligence as adaptive behavior in varying contexts of cultural practice makes use of both: the SOC concept as *one* framework that can comprise intellectual development in intelligence* abilities and the concept of expertise. In addition, we explore, based on lifespan considerations, the kinds of ecologies (contexts) in which individuals operate as they move through their lives from childhood into old age. To this end, we emphasize the reciprocal relations between SOC, on the one hand, and expertise and intelligence, on the other (see Figure 2.1).

In the following sections we review and reinterpret empirical findings from the aforementioned areas of investigation into intellectual

development to elaborate on the characteristics of these reciprocal relations. We start out by considering age-related changes in components of
intellectual functioning and how differences in developmental trajectories constrain and challenge the SOC repertoire of resource investment.
Throughout, to highlight the dramatic changes in contexts and adaptive demands of lifelong development, we draw on research typically
not seen as in the center of intelligence, that is, research on the role of
intelligence in the aging of sensorimotor behavior such as walking and
balance.

MECHANICS AND PRAGMATICS OF INTELLIGENCE
AS INDIVIDUAL RESOURCES

Our starting point is a dual-process model of intelligence proposed by
Baltes, Staudinger, and Lindenberger (1999; see also Baltes, 1987). This
model was developed as a follow-up on Hebb's (1949) differentiation between innate potentials for information processing (Intelligence A) and
the acquired level of performance and comprehension (Intelligence B).
It also extends the Cattell-Horn theory of fluid-crystallized intelligence
(Cattell, 1971; Horn, 1982). At the core of the model is a distinction
between two dimensions of intellectual functioning, the cognitive mechanics and the cognitive pragmatics.

The category of mechanics of intelligence, comparable to fluid intelligence, relates to basic information processing in the sense of cognitive primitives like being able to react to stimuli by simple motor
responses, rehearse information in working memory, or the ability to
learn associations from contingencies in the environment. So defined,
cognitive primitives in their ideal type are conceived as content-poor
because they can operate on all kinds of information (that is, content).
The speed, accuracy, and coordination of these elementary information
processes index the efficiency of mechanics. In contrast, the content-
rich dimension of pragmatics of intelligence refers to culture-based
knowledge and skills (factual and procedural) that are acquired through
cultural learning and experience. Prototypical examples of pragmatics
are being able to speak a natural language, to solve daily problems
(such as using the transportation system), or to acquire a professional
expertise.

One important aspect of the framework proposed by Baltes et al.
(1999) is that the mechanic and the pragmatic dimensions of intelligence
interact and overlap rather than form two fully separate entities within

the human system of adaptive capacities. On the one hand, this view is consistent with Cattell's developmental investment theory of Gf into Gc. On the other hand, the focus is on concurrent interactions that are operative when intellectual resources collaborate in the generation of intellectual products.

The relation between the mechanics and pragmatics can be illustrated by considering their conceptual relation to the human hardware, that is, the brain. It is assumed that the mechanics are predominantly pre-programmed by the neurophysiological architecture of the mind as it evolved during biological evolution and that it unfolds under relatively minor conditions of specific environmental support during early individual ontogenesis. The development of the pragmatics, on the other hand, is impossible without extensive and structured learning within an environmental and cultural context. In fact, the pragmatics are the most direct expression of experience and culture-based learning. This conceptual distinction does not imply that the functionality of cognitive primitives (that is, mechanics) cannot be altered through training, especially during the early stages of life. It is well known that performance in even the simplest cognitive-motor tasks like visual search for an object, simple reaction time, or repetitive finger tapping benefit considerably from practice (Gottlieb, Corcos, Jaric, and Agarwal, 1988). However, the lifespan model of intelligence espoused by us suggests that the malleability of the cognitive mechanics decreases with age (see also, Li, 2001). Likewise we do not argue at all that the pragmatic functions of intelligence do not rest on the neurophysiological functions of the brain. On the contrary, the mechanics are a necessary condition for pragmatic functioning. The key concept we wish to promote here is that adaptive, intelligent functions differ to the degree at which their development throughout the lifespan is constrained (both in the sense of limitation and enrichment) by biological functions and/or culture.

The usefulness of the mechanic-pragmatic distinction to the understanding of lifespan intellectual development was demonstrated in two recent studies. S.-C. Li, Lindenberger, Prinz, Baltes, and Team (2000) conducted a large-scale cross-sectional study using a lifespan sample covering the first to the eighth decades of life. Participants were tested for their intellectual functioning with respect to mechanics (perceptual speed, memory, and reasoning) as well as to pragmatic components (verbal knowledge and fluency). The authors observed differential lifespan trajectories for the two dimensions. Relative to the pragmatics, the mechanics showed an earlier rise in efficiency with age; however, there was also an earlier and sharper drop during later adulthood. S.-C. Li and her colleagues argued that the early rise of mechanics reflects rapid brain maturation during childhood until young adult ages, while the later decline is due to losses in biological functioning during late adulthood. In contrast, culture-based pragmatics has a later onset because the accumulation of related knowledge and skills takes considerable time for acculturation and learning. At the same time, pragmatics decline in old age is less pronounced because the environment continues to provide or even extend its supportive context for the maintenance of pragmatic functions. Likely, it is only in advanced old age, where due to age- and brain illness-associated losses the cognitive mechanics fall below a level that permits efficient learning of new skills and new subject matter (Baltes and T. Singer, 2001; Lindenberger and Baltes, 1997).

In this vein, there is also evidence for age-related changes in cognitive mechanics (including sensory primitives) and cognitive pragmatics. Whereas as we age, most of us continue to have considerable resources for the maintenance or even improvement of pragmatic intelligent functions, the quantity and quality of the pool of resources decreases. For instance, the reduction of efficiencies in the mechanics of intelligence puts specific constraints on adult development and their amelioration. Because cognitive mechanics evince major decline, it will be more and more difficult to nurture the pragmatics.

One underlying assumption of this chapter is the proposition that the structure and function of intelligence – when placed into the contexts of life including adult development and aging – needs to consider tasks that are not part of traditional tests of intelligence. Locomotion is such an example of everyday intellectual functioning. We maintain that its general "intellectual" significance in old age is comparable to the role of school and work in earlier periods of life. In the next section we discuss studies that provide evidence for our proposition by demonstrating the workings of SOC mechanisms in ecologically relevant settings.

COGNITIVE-MOTOR PERFORMANCE: AN EXEMPLAR OF A LIFESPAN CHANGE IN ADAPTIVE RESOURCE ALLOCATION OF INTELLIGENCE

Everyday observation suggests that older adults must invest more resources (like attentional effort) in sensorimotor functions than young adults for whom tasks like walking or maintaining their balance and upright stands appear almost automatic. For instance, when hiking in difficult terrain and facing an obstacle, older adults are likely to interrupt an ongoing conversation and only resume it after they have navigated the obstacle. Younger people seem to show lesser effects of that kind.

We argue that this anecdotal example points to two phenomena that have their empirical equivalences in the research literature: first, older adults have smaller amounts of overall cognitive resources (here in the sense of fluid intelligence or cognitive mechanics) available than younger adults; second, at advancing ages, more and more cognitive resources are needed to coordinate sensorimotor behavior. For reasons of biological aging, the tasks of walking or balancing one's body, for instance, become more and more difficult. The first phenomenon is well documented in the literature of age-related changes in the mechanics of intelligence (see for an overview, Baltes et al., 1999). With respect to the second phenomenon, several groups of investigators have proposed that the pronounced interference observed for older adults between sensorimotor and cognitive tasks in dual-task paradigms is due to higher attentional or "cognitive-mechanic" demands for the support of balance or walking in older adults (Brown, Shumway-Cook, and Woollacott, 1999; Maylor, Allison, and Wing, 2001; Maylor and Wing, 1996; Teasdale, Bard, LaRue, and Fleury, 1993).

There is a third aspect to our everyday example, which relates to the multiple-task characteristics of the described situation. Everyday life for the most part consists of settings in which multiple sensory inputs are relevant or in which concurrent tasks must be coordinated: examples are walking while trying to memorize a shopping list, steering your car in heavy traffic while picking up important information from the radio, or maintaining one's balance on the bus while trying to read an advertisement on the other side of the road. Experimental cognitive aging research has indeed found some evidence for higher dual-task costs in older compared with younger adults (Anderson, Craik, and Naveh-Benjamin, 1998; McDowd and Craik, 1987). In our view, the laboratory tasks used had little ecological validity because they were of little relevance to older participants and their daily lives.

Different from these earlier dual-task studies we propose that – as was true for studying cognitive development of children in the context of school-related cognitions – a refined approach to adaptive, intelligent behavior in later phases of life must consider the interplay of sensorimotor and cognitive functions that matter in everyday life. In short, in the same way as language, logical thinking, and knowledge of arithmetics are constituent to the development of cognitive pragmatics in children, the regulation of locomotor behavior is an important ingredient to old-age intelligence. And furthermore, as Cattelian investment Gf-Gc theory suggests an investment of the fluid cognitive mechanics into school-based cognitive performances, lifespan theory suggests a continuous redistribution of investment of cognitive mechanics into the cognitive pragmatics that are salient at different ages. One key example is the age-associated increase of investment into locomotion and other sensorimotor functions.

The SOC framework can be used to design experimental studies that approach older adults' performances in everyday multi-task situations from the perspective of adaptive development and ontogenetic transformations of intelligence-relevant investments. Figure 2.2 sketches the implications of a SOC perspective for a situation in which young and older participants simultaneously perform a sensorimotor task (walking) and a cognitive task (thinking). The circles represent the hypothetical amounts of general intellectual processing resources available to young and older individuals, respectively. The different sizes of the circles for young and older adults reflect the smaller amounts of overall resources older individuals can devote to each task. The segments

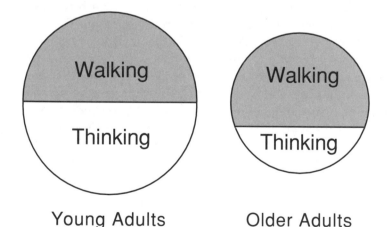

FIGURE 2.2. The SOC-Model's predictions regarding resource allocation to thinking and walking in young (left circle) and older (right circle) adults. Compared with younger adults, older adults allocate relatively more resources to walking than to thinking.

within each circle indicate the allocation of resources to master performance constraints in the thinking and the walking (shaded areas) tasks. For older participants, the model predicts that a relatively larger share of resources goes into the mastery of the walking task. These predictions arise from three assumptions:

- the age-related reduction in overall intelligence resources available
- the relative increase in resource demands for the walking task in older adults due to age-related biological decrements in sensorimotor functioning
- the higher ecological relevance of the walking task for older compared to younger adults (objective risk and subjective fear of falling, higher costs in terms of resulting physical impairment for older adults)

As a result, intelligence operates differently in young and older adults. In the terminology of the SOC-Model, older adults should select the walking task over the cognitive task (prioritization in resource allocation) when related performance constraints arise simultaneously in a dual-task context.

Two recent studies from our laboratory (K. Li, Lindenberger, Freund, and Baltes, 2001; Lindenberger, Marsiske, and Baltes, 2000) have put these predictions to a test by simulating everyday multi-task situations in experimental settings. Participants' task in these studies was to walk a narrow track while memorizing a list of words simultaneously presented over wireless earphones. The basic approach in both studies was to train participants in component tasks (walking, memorization) and then to contrast performances under single-task and dual-task conditions (memorizing while walking). The critical measures were the dual-task costs, which were calculated as the decrement in performance under dual-task conditions relative to single-task performance for each task. If our SOC-related expectations are correct, older adults should invest a larger share of their "intelligence" into walking (selection) and also use compensatory strategies (such as a handrail) to be successful.

Lindenberger et al. (2000) compared three age groups with the described dual-task paradigm. They found that dual-task costs for both walking and memorization increased with age suggesting that in older adults balance and gait are in increasing need of attentional "intellectual" resources. Even more direct evidence for this interpretation came from the finding that participants tended to slow down in walking during the eight seconds immediately following the presentation of a

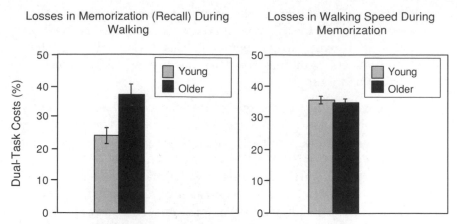

FIGURE 2.3. Dual-task costs for memorization (left panel) and walking (right panel) in young and older adults. Data are losses in performance under dual-task conditions expressed in percentages of single-task performance. Older adults show higher losses (number of words recalled) in the memorization task than younger adults do. Relative losses under dual-task conditions in walking performance (walking speed) are similar for young and older adults. The SOC-interpretation is that older adults protect their walking performance at the cost of performance in the memorization task (loss-based selection). (Figure adapted from data from the study by Li, Lindenberger, Freund, and Baltes [2001]. Adapted with permission from *Psychological Science, 12,* 2001; Taylor & Francis Ltd., http://www.tandf.co.uk/journals.)

to-be-memorized item. In continuation of this line of work, K. Li et al. (2001) conducted a twenty-five-session experiment in which participants were first trained to their individual asymptotic performance levels (testing-the-limits approach) in single-task conditions before being tested under dual-task conditions.

Figure 2.3 shows that our expectations were supported. There were dual-task age losses in memory but not in walking. Significantly, older adults showed higher losses than young adults did in memory performance when simultaneously walking the track (left panel). At the same time young and older adults did not differ with respect to dual-task costs exerted by memorization on the walking task. This means that older adults "protect" their balance and gait functioning at the cost of reduced resource allocation to the cognitive task. This was especially true when the walking task was made more difficult by the presence of potentially dangerous obstacles. Note in this context that the asymmetric pattern of dual-task costs does not signify failure to multi-task on the part of older adults but rather reflects intelligent, adaptive behavior in response to changes in older adults' everyday contexts and their ecology (namely the increased risks and negative consequences of falling). At a general level we consider this strong evidence for systematic age-related changes in the dynamics of investment linking basic internal capacities (the fluid cognitive mechanics) to pragmatic outcomes.

The second prediction of the SOC theory, that older adults should make use of compensatory aids to compensate for losses and declines in specific domains of functioning, was also supported. In the K. Li et al. (2001) study, participants were allowed to use a handrail to support their balance and gait performance as well as a button-box that enabled them to extend memorization periods. Overall, older adults made more frequent usage of the handrail and those who did manifested higher performance in the walking task. The reverse pattern – more frequent and effective use of the memory aid – was obtained for younger adults.

Our scenario of adaptive transformations of the investment of intelligence resources in general, as well as the age-associated progressive utilization of cognitive resources for the maintenance of bodily functions, has many implications for a lifespan perspective on the role of intelligence in skill acquisition and the maintenance of real-life expertise. For instance, the question emerges, how much reserve capacity in both mechanics and pragmatic functions of intelligence remains available to older individuals and whether such a reduction in plasticity constrains the acquisition of new skills. We turn to these questions, all of which relate to the dynamic interplay of the mechanics and pragmatics, in the next section.

INTELLIGENCE AND PLASTICITY IN ACQUIRING NEW SKILLS

A central implication of our work on the dual-process theory of mechanical Gf pragmatic Gc theory is the concurrent and developmental interaction between the two components.[2] We have already mentioned

---

[2] For our line of argument we will rely on a distinction between skill acquisition and expertise. These two concepts are not systematically distinguished in the literature and they can only be loosely associated with different research traditions. Studies on expertise and skill acquisition differ not only with respect to their empirical approaches and their choices of topics but also in their underlying theoretical assumptions, many of which are only implicit in the related literature. At a descriptive level, skill and expertise are traditionally distinguished with respect to three aspects. First, the inherent complexity of a real-life expertise is higher than that of a skill, that is, expertise comprises more

Cattell's original contribution to this interaction by highlighting the investment consequence of the fluid mechanics into the crystallized pragmatics. Are there reverse consequences and reciprocal relations? In our past work we have often underplayed this dual-process specificity and collaboration. Rather, we joined in discussions aimed at pushing the general notion of plasticity as the core of adaptive functioning. In the long run, we need to clarify whether plasticity is largely synonymous with the operation of cognitive mechanics or whether it is inherently the joint expression of mechanical and pragmatic components. Learning-to-learn, for instance, will be a pragmatic facet of plasticity.

For instance, the central concept motivating extensive skill acquisition and training studies with older adults was the notion of plasticity. At the neural level, the concept of plasticity refers to the capacity of the brain to change cortical representations as a function of experience. At the behavioral level, plasticity denotes the (reserve) capacity to extend the behavioral repertoire by acquiring new skills or behaviors through experience or practice (Baltes and Schaie, 1976; Baltes and T. Singer, 2001; Buonomano and Merzenich, 1998; Lerner, 1984; T. Singer and Lindenberger, 2000; W. Singer, 1995). Over the last decades cognitive aging research has generated much optimism by showing that older adults in their sixties and seventies continue to profit from learning and can clearly improve their performances even to some degree in psychometric tests of fluid intelligence (Baltes and Willis, 1982; Baltes and Lindenberger, 1988; Baltes, Dittmann-Kohli, and Kliegl, 1996). Likewise, neuropsychological studies (for example, Cotman and Nieto-Sampedro, 1984; Kaas, 1991; Karni et al., 1995; Wang, Merzenich, Sameshima, and Jenkins, 1995) support the view that brain plasticity extends into later adulthood and may be considered a lifelong phenomenon. Plasticity in late adulthood is not limited to the acquisition of knowledge-based skills. Playing a musical instrument increases the cortical representation of the hand and single fingers and the size of the effect correlates to the years of training (Elbert, Pantev, Wienbruch, Rockstroh, and Taub, 1995). Plasticity of related brain areas has also been demonstrated for

different capabilities and task constraints to be mastered. Second, expertise is by definition attributed to but a small number of people who excel in a given domain, whereas the capabilities and accomplishments associated with the concept of real-life skills are believed to be within the reach of every normal individual. Third, skills and expertise differ with respect to the presumed durations of their acquisition processes: a skill can be acquired within weeks or even days, while attaining expert level performance takes years or decades.

older adults who take up playing the violin or intensify their practice regime later in life (Elbert, Sterr, and Rockstroh, 1996).

That behavioral plasticity is intimately connected with the fluid mechanics is supported by the fact that the amount of reserve capacity or the degree of plasticity is subject to age-related changes. Compared with younger adults, older adults tend to benefit less from performance enhancing training programs (at least after initial stages), need more cognitive support during training, and their ultimate levels of performance attained after training is below that of younger adults (Baltes and Baltes, 1997; Camp, 1998; Verhaeghen, Marcoen, and Goosens, 1992). The latter point is most evident from studies applying the testing-the-limits paradigm (Baltes, 1987; Kliegl and Baltes, 1987). Reinhold Kliegl, Paul Baltes, and their colleagues extensively trained healthy young and older adults with a mnemonic technique (the method of loci). Although older adults' performance after training clearly surpassed that of younger adults prior to the intervention, age-effects after training were magnified: After thirty-eight sessions of training there was almost no overlap of the distributions of young and older participants and none of the older adults reached the mean level of final performance of young adults (Baltes and Kliegl, 1992; Kliegl, Smith, and Baltes, 1989; Kliegl, Smith, and Baltes, 1990).

One implication of these findings is that the more one approaches peak performance range, the more it becomes evident that older adults' potential for high levels of functioning is reduced relative to younger adults. The most radical evidence for such reductions in cognitive plasticity and learning potential comes from a study with very old individuals recently conducted by T. Singer, Lindenberger, and Baltes (2001). These authors conducted memory training with a large sample of adults ranging in age between 75 and 105. Not all participants in this group of the oldest-old (which did not include persons with diagnosed dementias) were able to profit from the instruction with the mnemonic technique. Moreover, following the basic initiation to the method, even most of those who had benefited from instruction failed to further improve their performance. In contrast, young adults continuously improved their performance through continued training. Such marked losses in cognitive or behavioral plasticity in old age are further magnified when brain pathologies, such as dementias, join the normal process of aging (Baltes and Baltes, 1997; Camp, 1998).

Two other age-related limitations in older adults' learning potential became evident from recent training and intervention studies: (1)

older adults' failure to optimize learning benefits to the level of flaw-less performances in certain tasks, and (2) older adults' increasing need for specific tutoring, feedback, and training methods. Kliegl, Krampe, Mayr, and Liebscher (2001) trained episodic learning of word lists in healthy young and older adults using the Method-of-Loci technique. The authors found that after massive training both young and older participants reached flawless performances in a condition where to-be-learned items were different between lists, although older adults took considerably more training to achieve this end. However, a specific age-differential deficit in asymptotic accuracy for older adults emerged in a condition with difficult to discriminate context cues (proactive inter-ference). This specific disadvantage of older adults was reliable across forty sessions of testing.

The second characteristic typical of older adults' limitations in ac-quiring new skills emerged from a series of intervention studies focus-ing on face recognition. Everyday problems with recognizing faces is among the top complaints in healthy older adults and several experi-ments failed to demonstrate substantial training benefits in laboratory tasks even with older adults who were from the top percentiles of their age-graded distributions in fluid intelligence (Kliegl, Phillipp, Luckner, and Krampe, 2001b). In their intervention study of face-place mem-ory, Kliegl, Krampe, Philipp, and Luckner (in prep.) used a cognitive-engineering approach based on the concept of deliberate practice pro-posed by Ericsson, Krampe, and Tesch-Römer (1993). Older participants were not only trained in a mnemonic skill, but were given extensive tutoring in elaborating memory cues specific to the trained materi-als (that is, details in the pictures of faces presented and associative cues for the landmarks). A noticeable difference from earlier labora-tory studies was that participants could repeatedly work on the same lists, thereby optimizing their encoding strategies using computers for practice at their homes. The authors observed a clear positive interven-tion effect after such extensive coaching. However, the levels of perfor-mance achieved by older participants were still considerably below that typical of younger adults after much less practice and limited tutoring conditions.

These findings indicate that continued everyday experiences with a task and even repeated exercise under laboratory training conditions are not sufficient to mobilize older adults' reserve capacities. Compensating for age-related declines in episodic encoding of visuospatial materials through the acquisition of a mnemonic skill clearly requires extensive deliberate efforts on the part of older individuals. At the same time, the outcome falls short of what young adults can achieve with far less effort. Kliegl et al. (in prep.) proposed that perfecting certain everyday skills in older adults might involve as much effort and training as required from a young individual who starts to learn a musical instrument. This metaphor directly relates to our view of skill acquisition in late adulthood from an SOC perspective: Transformations or investments (Cattell, 1971) from mechanics into pragmatic forms of intelligence appear to be more difficult for older adults and lead to less optimal results.

In our triangulation approach (Figure 2.1) we argued that certain forms of expertise and skill involve specific, more individualized developmental trajectories compared to the more universally controlled trajectories leading to interindividual differences in intelligence* abilities. That is to say, lifespan development includes the advancement of skills or expertises that result from long-term resource investments into specific abilities as opposed to more general abilities. That is to say, most individuals in a given culture attain "expert" status in speaking their native language. The result at the level of an individual's capacities is a diversification and specialization of abilities. In this context, correlational analyses and studies of transfer between intelligence* abilities and skill level are informative. Typically, little transfer to other tasks or real-life skills is observed from successful training in fluid (Baltes et al., 1996; Baltes and Lindenberger, 1988) as well as pragmatic components of intelligence (Kliegl et al., 2001b). However, the investment of fluid mechanics is not fixed and static. Rather, the pragmatic components during skill acquisition and refinement draw on different mechanical components and, at higher levels of accomplishment, take on a "causal" life on their own. Several studies demonstrated, for instance, that the correlational patterns between psychometric components of intelligence and performance change across different stages of skill development (Ackerman, 1988; Fleishman, 1972; Labouvie, Frohring, and Baltes, 1973). Most notably, general intelligence (g) appears to be a factor at early stages of skill acquisition, when understanding the nature of the task is a critical requirement. Later stages and performance after practice tends to be less correlated with g, but to show substantial relations to interindividual differences in factors closer to the skill under investigation (for example, perceptual speed correlated with post-training performance in Ackerman's air traffic control task).

The relation between psychometric markers of intelligence* and performance in specific abilities is also a central question in another line of inquiry that we consider of interest in explicating the conceptual and developmental connection between intelligence as adaptive capacity and SOC as a general theory of adaptive development: the long-term acquisition and maintenance of expertise. In the following sections we briefly discuss the critical assumptions underlying the expertise approach, and we explore to what degree there is a fundamental association between intelligence and expertise. Subsequently, we use the SOC framework to describe how this association undergoes a process of developmental emergence and transformation. Our claim is that, in the context of expertise development, the processes of SOC produce changes in intellectual functioning – for instance, by dividing individuals into trajectories generating and refining bodies of factual knowledge and procedural skills. At the same time, SOC as an individualized system of adaptive repertoires benefits from the intellectual and expertise-related reservoirs emerging with expertise development in a reciprocal manner.

INTERINDIVIDUAL DIFFERENCES IN LEVEL OF EXPERTISE

Although expertise research is rooted in a different research tradition from that of psychometric intelligence testing, it shares with the latter field the focus on stable interindividual differences. Aside from the predominant focus on the long-term – and usually experience-based – acquisition of interindividual differences, one critical difference is that expertise is associated with much more specific domains and areas of functioning and performance. Probably the most general characteristic of expertise in all kinds of domains is the apparent ease with which experts perform in their specific domains. This phenomenon has nurtured the specific "talent"-associated view that experts are not constrained by those presumably natural limitations in available processing resources that restrict the performances of most individuals in the normal population (for a discussion of different viewpoints see Howe, Davidson, and Sloboda, 1999, and the commentaries on their paper). We address the relation between resources invested in more general abilities and skills, like those reflected in intelligence* in our triangulation sketch, and those invested in the development of expertise-specific knowledge and mechanisms that we consider a crucial facet that needs to be added to concepts of lifespan intelligence.

In principle, there appear to be three alternative possibilities why individuals having reached expert levels of accomplishment enjoy relative freedom from normal limitations: One explanation is that the experts have always been superior in the relevant abilities or necessary resources such that their advantages could be attributed to interindividual differences with long-term stability (including status on dimensions of intelligence such as the primary mental abilities) that already existed prior to expertise acquisition. We call this the *priori disposition account*.[3] A second possible explanation is that the process of expertise acquisition involves an individual's gradual improvement in those abilities that constrain normal performance. One important implication of this account is that long-term expertise development should yield positive transfer to broad intelligence[*] capacities, that is, experts should be superior in some, though not necessarily all, relatively broad abilities that show a correlation with novice performance. We refer to this second explanation as the *expertise-driven broad abilities account*. The third account of how experts escape the normal limitations is that experts have acquired mechanisms that permit them to circumvent the specific limitations in general processing resources in those tasks or activities relevant to their domains (Chase and Ericsson, 1982; Ericsson and Charness, 1994; Salthouse, 1991). According to this view, expertise development amounts to a long-term process resulting in maximum adaptation to specific task constraints (Ericsson et al., 1993; Ericsson and Lehmann, 1996). Certain more general functions might well benefit from long-term training in a specific expertise (as single-finger-tapping rate could benefit from practicing the piano or typing). However, the critical sources of interindividual differences should be found in more specific mechanisms. We label this third account the *expertise-driven specific abilities account*.

All three accounts – though with differences in emphases – employ the notion of constraints arising from task characteristics or individuals' limitations in available processing resources and they consider the ultimate level of expert performance as a reflection of individuals'

---

[3] In related discussions (see for example, Salthouse, 1991) the term "innate" is occasionally used to refer to interindividual differences existing prior to intense learning experiences. Again, we deliberately refrain from using this term here. In our view, the outcomes of such intricate interactions of biological propensities (the development of some of which might well relate to genetic dispositions) and environmental influences preceding the engagement in expertise-related practice are not properly described as innate dispositions.

adaptations to or mastery of these constraints. It is this two-fold theoretical perspective, (a) the distinction among abilities differing with respect to their domain-specificity and (b) the emphasis on the time course (lifespan development) of individual adaptation processes in terms of resource investment, that we highlighted in our triangulation approach. In the following section we discuss evidence related to the generality versus specificity dimension of the abilities constituting expertise. Then we focus specific adaptive mechanisms underlying skilled performance that speak to our SOC perspective on expertise. Finally, we consider evidence related to the time-course perspective of the adaptation processes accompanying expertise development and highlight the reciprocal relations between SOC and expert abilities.

General and Specific Abilities in Expert Performance

In certain areas of expertise that heavily rely on domain-specific knowledge, like chess or medical diagnosis, an explanation based on priori dispositions is unlikely to turn out a primary account. The level of chess expertise is only weakly correlated to performance in psychometric IQ tests (Doll and Mayr, 1987). Arguably, the priori disposition account has more plausibility in domains of expertise that have strong sensorimotor or physiological components, like athletic sports, typing, or playing musical instruments. The assumption that interindividual differences in basic cognitive-motor functions are natural precursors to or contribute to interindividual differences in expert performance can be found in the literature (for example, Keele and Hawkins, 1982). Given that these basic components also overlap with fluid intelligence as measured by psychometric tests, an argument can be made that interindividual differences in psychometric intelligence or relatively broad abilities are causally linked to the ultimate level of performance achieved.

Correlational findings from several studies appear in line with related assumptions. As an example, maximum finger tapping rate is correlated with overall typing speed (Book, 1924; Salthouse, 1984) or level of accomplishment in pianists (for example, Keele, Pokorny, Corcos, and Ivry, 1985; Krampe and Ericsson, 1996; Telford and Spangler, 1935). However, related results speak equally to the expertise-driven broad abilities account and they could also reflect limited transfer as hypothesized by the expertise-driven specific abilities account. Given age-related changes in intelligence* abilities, age-comparative studies with individuals differing in levels of expertise provide a special route to further disentangle these issues through systematic comparisons of interindividual differences in broad intelligence* components and more specific expertise-related functions.

Age-comparative studies with individuals differing in their levels of expertise have been conducted in such diverse domains as typewriting (Bosman, 1993; Salthouse, 1984), chess (Charness, 1981a; Charness, 1989), GO playing (Masunaga and Horn, 2001), air-traffic control and piloting (Morrow and Leirer, 1997; Morrow, Leirer, Altieri, and Fitzsimmons, 1994), mastermind (Maylor, 1994), crossword-puzzle solving (Rabbitt, 1993), management skills (Walsh and Hershey, 1993), and piano playing (Krampe and Ericsson, 1996). The general picture emerging from these studies supports the notion of a developmental separation of more person-general from more person-specific trajectories of intellectual functionality. Older experts show "normal" (that is, similar to non-expert controls) age-graded decline in general measures of processing speed, intelligence* abilities, and performance on unfamiliar materials. At the same time, older experts show reduced, if any, age-related declines in the efficiencies or the speed at which they perform skill-related tasks. The evidence from age-comparative expertise studies thus clearly speaks for the *expertise-driven specific abilities account* rather than supports the expertise-driven broad abilities account. Consequentially, models of expertise have departed from the assumption that the same set of abilities that underlie performance in psychometric intelligence tests can also account for the ultimate level of expertise attained or the level of expertise maintained in later adulthood. We need to acknowledge, however, that long-term (ideally, longitudinal) experimental studies are lacking that would be necessary to reach a final conclusion; especially since we need to consider the possibility that intensive investment of time and effort into specific expertises may reduce (due to negative transfer or practice deficits) levels of performance in more general cognitive abilities.

We proposed that expertise is the outcome of a developmental trajectory organized around individuals' resource investments into optimizing specific abilities. In this process, the orchestration of SOC components likely plays a critical role, because expertise acquisition is dependent on such factors as elective selection (for example, goal commitment), loss-based selection (for example, changes in goal structures), optimization (for example, deliberate practice) as well as compensation (for example, the use of task-specific strategies or cognitive mechanisms to counteract losses in basic mental speed). Given the cross-sectional design of age-comparative expertise studies, they are susceptible to the criticism of different selection criteria for young and older experts. For instance, there is a fair chance that older expert participants are the survivors of an age-graded selection process during which individuals with stronger age-related declines in relevant capacities or those less motivated to continuously invest in the development of their skills have dropped from their fields of expertise. For these reasons we now take a closer look at the interaction of basic cognitive-motor abilities and expert-specific mechanisms at different stages of development. We apply the SOC-Model to integrate the expertise notion of circumventing normal processing limitations into our triangulation approach and thus enrich it.

Evidence for SOC-like Mechanisms in Expert Performance

Donald Gentner's (1988) work on typing can be viewed as a classic example of decomposing expert performance into basic cognitive-motor processes and more complex specific mechanisms. We use it here to illustrate how changes in processing mechanisms underlying skill acquisition can be interpreted from an SOC perspective.

In his studies of typists Gentner showed that beginning and expert typists show very distinct patterns of transition times (inter-key-stroke intervals) for successive key strokes. The fastest transitions in novice typing are repetitions of identical letters typed with the same finger, whereas the slowest (and most error-prone) transitions emerge for successive letters typed with different fingers. For expert typists, the pattern is reversed, with repetitive key strokes being the slowest and hand alternations yielding the fastest transitions. From analyses of high-speed video films of typists' performances Gentner was able to identify the critical processes underlying this change in performance characteristics. Skilled typists launch key strokes with different fingers or hands almost simultaneously or with very short time delays, thereby minimizing the resulting inter-key-stroke intervals. Gentner termed this phenomenon advance preparation. He conceived of the process of skill acquisition in typing as a gradual optimization of those cognitive processes that support advance preparation such that the ultimate level of performance is maximally adapted to peripheral factors (that is, keyboard layout).

Similar findings were reported by Salthouse (1984; 1991) in his study with typists from a large age range. He found that across age groups basic components of movement proficiency, like the rate of repetitively typing the same letter, showed a relatively modest relation to overall typing speed, accounting for 42 percent of the variance and this was also true for other broad speed measures for intelligence* capacities. In contrast, measures reflecting complex expertise-related mechanisms, like the speed of typing letters with alternate hands or the eye-hand span, accounted for more than 70 percent of the interindividual differences in overall typing speed. Salthouse argued that the successful maintenance of typing skills in his older expert typists relies on cognitively complex mechanisms, extensive anticipation or advance preparation, as illustrated by older skilled typists' longer eye-hand spans (that is, the number of letters they looked ahead to prior to executing the actual key strokes).

The study by Salthouse broke new ground in that it suggests that older experts attain the same level of performance as young experts either by means of different mechanisms, or at least by differentially relying on different component processes (see also, Bosman, 1993). This clearly supports our argument that in older adults, expertise-specific mechanisms can free performance from abilities and resources that are subject to age-related decrements in the normal population. In our triangulation context this amounts to an extension of the SOC repertoire of adaptive skills through expertise development. However, it is not possible from these data to determine whether older individuals deliberately adopt compensatory mechanisms in response to aging, or whether their performance at younger ages was already superior and associated mechanisms were better preserved due to a slower age-related decline or deliberate activities to maintain these critical capacities.

The same perspective applies to another pioneering study on age and chess expertise conducted by Charness (1981a; 1981b). He found that the quality of the chess moves subjects selected for an unfamiliar chess position was unrelated to age and closely linked to skill level (current chess rating). Detailed analysis of think-aloud protocols revealed that older experts engaged in less extensive search (that is, they had slower rates of retrieving potential moves and retrieved fewer moves in a move-selection task) than their younger counterparts did, but they nonetheless came up with moves of comparable quality. One is tempted to conclude that older players compensate for age-related declines in search and retrieval speed with more refined knowledge-based processes related to move selection. However, such a specific SOC-related interpretation is tentative.

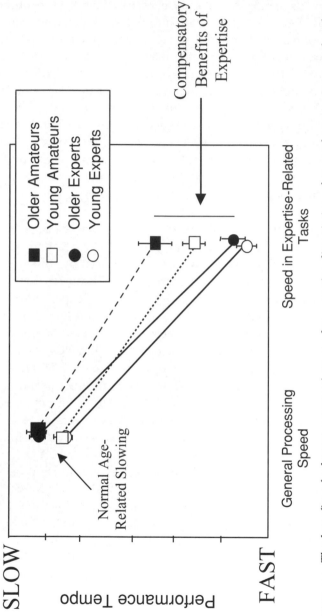

FIGURE 2.4. The benefits of advance preparation: age by expertise dissociation of general processing speed and speed in expertise-relevant tasks in pianists. The SOC-interpretation is that as a result of selective optimization, older professional pianists have largely freed their expert performance from general factors increasingly constraining normal and amateur performance in older age. (Figure adapted from Krampe and Ericsson [1996].)

Our triangulation approach implies that individuals maintaining their levels of expert performance into later adulthood are on developmental trajectories of lifelong resource investment into specific abilities. This presumes that selection, optimization, and compensation processes operate not only at the level of task-related cognitive processes but also should be found at the larger scale of time investment into means and activities designed to optimize performance. Investing time in deliberate practice is such a means, that is, an instance for optimization in the sense of the SOC-Model. A study that provides several hints about the workings of SOC-related mechanisms at the level of cognitive processing as well as at the level of resource investment into critical activities was more recently conducted by Krampe and Ericsson (1996). The authors studied expert and amateur pianists of different age groups with a combination of experimental and psychometric methods of ability assessment, along with self-report and diary data measuring the time investment into deliberate practice and other activities. The expertise-related abilities tested comprised skills related to virtuosity like maximum repetitive tapping and speeded multi-finger sequencing tasks, and non-speeded tasks like memorization of sequences and (rated) expressive musical interpretation.

In line with the results on typists and chess experts Krampe and Ericsson (1996) found that older professional pianists showed normal age-related declines in intelligence* capacities (that is, measures of general processing speed like choice reaction time and digit-symbol substitution rate). Age effects in expertise-related measures of multiple-finger coordination speed were similar to the above pattern in the amateur group, but reduced or fully absent in the expert sample. Taken together, these findings led to an age-by-expertise dissociation of mechanism-supporting general processing and expertise-specific processing (see Figure 2.4).

Krampe and Ericsson (1996) argued that this dissociation reflects older experts' selective maintenance of acquired, expertise-specific, mechanisms of advance preparation of movements. Their selective maintenance interpretation rests on data on older experts' deliberate amounts of practice invested at different stages of expertise development. Consistent with this view, the authors showed that the degree to which levels of performance in speeded expertise tasks was maintained depended on the amounts of deliberate practice invested at the later stages of expertise development, in the fifth and sixth decades of life. Note that measures of general processing speed did not relate to the interindividual differences in levels of maintained expertise in the expert group. In contrast, however, such measures of intelligence* abilities correlated with performance in the amateur group. In our view, this is another instance where, with expertise acquisition, the process decouples itself from a primary investment dependency on the basic system of cognitive mechanics or fluid intelligence.

In a similar vein Charness, Krampe, and Mayr (1996) found that chess tournament performance in a large sample of rated players twenty to eighty years in age depended on amounts of deliberate practice far more than on chronological age. The effects of deliberate practice were even more pronounced in the older players, again pointing to the continued need to selectively regulate performance in later adulthood by processes of selection, optimization, and compensation.

Evidence for Reciprocal Relations Between Expertise and SOC

Life-long investment of resources into expertise abilities makes older experts to a large degree more independent of the intelligence* abilities and age-related declines in related resources. At the phenotypic level of expression, it appears as if there were a process of decoupling of the cognitive mechanics and the cognitive pragmatics. At a very general level of reciprocal relations between SOC and expertise, this enables older experts to continue making a living with their skills and to support external resources in all domains of intellectual functioning.

There is some evidence that expertise abilities as such differ with respect to the amounts and the nature of optimization efforts necessary to sustain positive development into later adulthood or at least to delay negative developments in older age. As an example, Krampe and Ericsson (1996) found that age effects were absent in amateur pianists' musical interpretations of a piece with few challenges in terms of speed or technical virtuosity. This latter finding suggests that expertise abilities resting more on specialized knowledge than on technical performance might be easier to maintain, or that their maintenance benefits from physically less challenging activities. The prominent role of pragmatic knowledge as compared to physical exercise is also one potential explanation for the relatively small negative age effects in the sample of rated chess players studied by Charness et al. (1996). One intriguing finding in this study was that the number of chess books owned by participants significantly contributed to accounting for rated performance in a regression model over and above the effects of age and amounts of deliberate practice. At the level of reciprocal SOC-expertise relations, the specific combination of maintained skills might determine professional decisions or changes in life goals, like a shift from a soloist performer of music to a career as a chamber musician.

The SOC framework opens an additional perspective that relates to experts' adaptive allocation at the level of daily activities. Related evidence can be found in diary data collected in the aforementioned age-comparative study with expert and amateur pianists (Krampe, 1994). Older experts were found to engage in even more professional activities (working sixty and more hours a week) than their young counterparts. However, a relatively smaller portion (18 percent) of older experts' total professional activities were deliberate practice efforts (young experts: 47 percent). Typical for their age group, older experts spent more time on health care and maintaining bodily functions than young experts did. At the same time older professional pianists had less leisure time than their young counterparts, a finding quite atypical for age-comparative studies of young and older professionals. Our interpretation is that older experts compensate for the increased resource (time and energy) requirements from age-related changes in bodily functions and professional requirements (teaching, organization) by reducing their leisure time. At this level, freeing time for maintenance practice can be viewed as another process of selective optimization that has compensatory implications.

SOC AND AGE-ASSOCIATED TRANSFORMATIONS IN RESOURCES REVISITED

We started out pointing to the similarities between the original concept of intelligence on the one hand, and a common theme in four diverse areas of empirical study of individual differences on the other. The four areas we discussed were lifespan development in intellectual functioning, mastery of everyday multi-task situations, the acquisition of new skills in later adulthood, and the maintenance of real-life expertise. The common theme in these diverse research areas centers on notions of adaptation to changing performance constraints and the idea of successful management of internal and external resources.

We argued that extant psychometric intelligence tests measure (in contrast to explaining) interindividual differences in a limited set of (mostly academic) abilities which we labeled "intelligence*" abilities. These abilities we consider to be the outcome of the investment of basic elementary cognitive resources (fluid intelligence) in a fairly universal and highly practiced set of knowledge and culture-based functions (crystallized pragmatics). Extant measures of intelligence are confounds of both, some being closer to mechanics (retrieval speed for novel information), others closer to the pragmatics (vocabulary).

We also argued that the expertise literature identifies other domains of functioning that are more person-specific and that reflect more idiosyncratic bodies of factual and procedural knowledge. It makes explicit also how the mechanics and pragmatics undergo systematic shifts in investment and degrees of coupling.

To highlight this lifelong process of coupling and uncoupling as well as age-related changes in allocation (investment) of resources into mechanical versus pragmatic operations, we use the theory of SOC as an overarching framework. Thus, the resulting focus is shifting toward general mechanisms of intellectual development. Our specific proposal is a triangulation of SOC as a general repertoire of adaptive mechanisms, intelligence* as reflecting universally available and highly practiced components of intelligence emphasized by a given culture, and domain-specific (expert) abilities. This triangulation was inspired by Ferguson's (1954; 1965) original proposal for an *integrate theory* of learning and interindividual differences. Empirical research in the four domains we discussed revealed some potential but also strong limitations of extant psychometric concepts of intelligence. We tried to illustrate how the core mechanisms of the SOC-Model, selection, optimization, and compensation, can be used to understand the larger context of long-term development and interindividual differences in these domains.

We documented that mechanic and pragmatic components of intelligence show different developmental trajectories in adulthood. Correlational evidence (Lindenberger and Baltes, 1994; 1997) supports the idea of general integrity of the nervous system as a larger base of support for all kinds of adaptive behavior, and it points to a strong connection between bodily functioning and intellectual abilities at older ages. This arena of research makes the lifespan shifts in investment and allocation of cognitive resources explicit enough that they could serve as research models. In this vein, the thinking and walking dual-task studies directly reveal the relevance of bodily functions for understanding intellectual abilities and their changing investments. Based on the SOC framework we argue that the preference for sustaining sensorimotor functioning we observed in older adults is the result of adaptation processes during long-term everyday experiences. At the same time this example illustrates how the SOC framework can inform experimental studies that are at the intersect of developmental research with an ecological view on adaptive intelligence and basic questions raised in the cognitive neurosciences.

Taken together with findings from expertise research, most notably age-comparative approaches and investigations of expertise development trajectories, the implication is that intelligence* abilities as measured by extant psychometric tests are but a weak reflection of the *overall* resources available to an individual as a pool of investments, nor are they general constraints that delimit the developmental potential at ultimate levels of a specific expertise. In our view, this is what the circumvention of "normal" processing limitations through expertise boils down to, unless we want to exclude a large range of adaptive behaviors from the notion of intelligence. Only in very old individuals does declining mechanics of intelligence, a high prevalence of dementia, and a considerable need of cognitive resources for the maintenance of bodily functions constrain functioning to a degree that health status, perceptual acuity, or psychometric speed components of intelligence become good proxies of developmental plasticity.

At the same time, we need to acknowledge that, as is the case for bodily functions, the universally practiced mental abilities nevertheless operate as a limiting resource because they undergo age-related changes. Deliberate practice is an effective and powerful means to improve and maintain mental and bodily functions. However, deliberate practice takes much time and effort, resources that, if spent on practicing specific skills, are no longer available for the maintenance of other, more general abilities. This SOC perspective informing our triangulation approach provides a theoretical frame for understanding the shifts in expert pianists' daily activities and related changes in life goals. An illustration of related phenomena comes from the case of the world-famous pianist Wilhelm Kempff, who decided to give up public performances when he felt his finger dexterity deteriorating and his memory becoming less reliable. At this point in his career he was no less than eighty-five years old, suggesting that adaptation (plasticity and deliberate practice) goes a long, but not infinite way.

We are cognizant that our effort at triangulating conceptions of intelligence, expertise and SOC is a first step fraught with many uncertainties and speculations. This is work in progress. We conclude our effort presenting relevant evidence with an outlook extending the work on locomotion and memory. We do this because this work, in our assessment, makes most apparent the notion of lifespan changes in relocation or reinvestment of cognitive resources and the fact that SOC-related mechanisms are involved in the maintenance of expertise, in this case the – in adulthood fairly automatic – co-occurrence of walking and thinking. The work also highlights the significance of intelligence for non-academic subject matters.

Future Perspectives

Throughout this chapter we have argued for a strong connection between bodily functioning and intellectual potential in older ages. There is a far-reaching assumption implicit in our interpretation of reciprocal relations between intellectual abilities and SOC mechanisms regulating resource demands for bodily and cognitive functioning: We argue that in older adults, bodily functions permanently block resources that, in turn, are no longer available for cognitive tasks, including the acquisition of new or the maintenance of existing skills through focused practice. Multiple-task paradigms reveal these phenomena. We assume, however, that the effects pertain to many other everyday and laboratory situations as well. More recently, it was demonstrated that interventions based on physical exercise (for example, aerobics and taking walks) can improve the level of functioning in components of the mechanics of intelligence (Kramer et al., 1999).

From our triangulation perspective physical exercise can be seen as a means to optimize bodily functions and to thereby compensate for their increased resource requirements at the cost of higher cognitive functions. As a concrete example, if older adults' attention in reaction-time experiments or while completing psychometric tests is reduced by invading thoughts about bodily conditions, the digestion of the last meal, or the reachability of the nearest available rest room, both psychometric tests and experiments with little ecological relevance will underestimate older adults' intellectual capacities and their adaptive potentials. A similar argument could be made for children with attention deficits or physical health problems. We strongly feel that more research along these lines is necessary.

In conclusion, we argued for a revised, contextualized view of intelligence that focuses on the mechanisms of and the interindividual differences in adaptive potential. In our view, such a perspective on intelligence must comprise developmental changes in many more domains of the mind-body interface than have been traditionally the focus of the study of intelligence – including bodily functions, the acquisition of skills, and expertise development. With respect to incorporating intellectual abilities related to expertise into a revised notion of intelligence, we find similar proposals in recent writings of one of the pioneers of psychometric intelligence testing (Horn and Masunaga, 2000a; Horn and Masunaga, 2000b; Masunaga and Horn, 2001). Only a combined approach of properly designed experiments and psychometric measures can provide the basis for asking related questions. Our call for a combination of psychometric and experimental approaches to intelligence is echoed in recent commentaries on the future of intelligence research (for example, Sternberg, 2001).

References

Ackerman, P. L. (1988). Determinants of individual differences during skill acquisition: Cognitive abilities and information processing. *Journal of Experimental Psychology: General, 117*, 288–318.

Anderson, N. D., Craik, F. I. M., & Naveh-Benjamin, M. (1998). The attentional demands of encoding and retrieval in younger and older adults: 1. Evidence from divided attention costs. *Psychology and Aging, 13*, 405–423.

Baltes, M. M., & Baltes, P. B. (1997). Normal versus pathological cognitive functioning in old age: plasticity and testing-the-limits of cognitive/brain reserve capacity. In F. Forette, Y. Christen, & F. Boller (Eds.), *Démences et longévité* (pp. 77–101). Paris: Fondation Nationale de Gérontologie.

Baltes, P. B. (1987). Theoretical propositions of life-span developmental psychology: On the dynamics between growth and decline. *Developmental Psychology, 23*, 611–626.

Baltes, P. B., & Baltes, M. M. (1990). Psychological perspectives on successful aging: The model of selective optimization with compensation. In P. B. Baltes & M. M. Baltes (Eds.), *Successful aging: Perspectives from the behavioral sciences* (pp. 1–34). Cambridge: Cambridge University Press.

Baltes, P. B., Dittmann-Kohli, F., & Kliegl, R. (1996). Reserve capacity of the elderly in aging-sensitive tests of fluid intelligence: replication and extension. *Psychology and Aging, 1*, 172–177.

Baltes, P. B., & Kliegl, R. (1992). Further testing of limits of cognitive plasticity: Negative age differences in a mnemonic skill are robust. *Developmental Psychology, 28*, 121–125.

Baltes, P. B., & Lindenberger, U. (1988). On the range of cognitive plasticity in old age as a function of experience: 15 years of intervention research. *Behavior Therapy, 19*(3), 283–300.

Baltes, P. B., & Schaie, K. W. (1976). On the plasticity of intelligence in adulthood and old age: Where Horn and Donaldson fail. *American Psychologist, 31*, 720–725.

Baltes, P. B., & Singer, T. (2001). Plasticity and the ageing mind: An exemplar of the biocultural orchestration of brain and behaviour. *European Review, 9,* 59–76.

Baltes, P. B., Staudinger, U. M., & Lindenberger, U. (1999). Lifespan psychology: Theory and application to intellectual functioning. *Annual Review of Psychology, 50,* 471–507.

Baltes, P. B., & Willis, S. L. (1982). Plasticity and enhancement of intellectual functioning in old age: Penn State's Adult Development and Enrichment Program (ADEPT). In F. I. M. Craik & S. E. Trehub (Eds.), *Aging and cognitive processes* (pp. 353–389). New York: Plenum Press.

Book, W. F. (1924). Voluntary motor ability of the world's champion typists. *Journal of Applied Psychology, 8,* 283–308.

Bosman, E. A. (1993). Age-related differences in the motoric aspects of transcription typing skill. *Psychology and Aging, 8,* 87–102.

Brown, L. A., Shumway-Cook, A., & Woollacott, M. H. (1999). Attentional demands and postural recovery: The effects of aging. *Journal of Gerontology: Medical Sciences, 54A,* M165–M171.

Buonomano, D. V., & Merzenich, M. M. (1998). Cortical plasticity: From synapses to maps. *Annual Review of Neuroscience, 21,* 149–186.

Camp, C. J. (1998). Memory intervention for normal and pathological older adults. *Annual Review of Gerontology and Geriatrics, 18,* 155–189.

Cattell, R. B. (1971). *Abilities: Their structure, growth, and action.* Boston, MA: Houghton Mifflin.

Charness, N. (1981a). Aging and skilled problem solving. *Journal of Experimental Psychology: General, 110,* 21–38.

Charness, N. (1981b). Search in chess: Age and skill differences. *Journal of Experimental Psychology: Human perception and Performance, 7,* 467–476.

Charness, N. (1989). Expertise in chess and bridge. In D. Klahr & K. Kotovsky (Eds.), *Complex information processing: The impact of Herbert A. Simon* (pp. 183–208). Hillsdale, NJ: Erlbaum.

Charness, N., Krampe, R. T., & Mayr, U. (1996). The role of practice and coaching in entrepreneurial skill domains: An international comparison of life-span chess skill acquisition. In K. A. Ericsson (Ed.), *The road to excellence: The acquisition of expert performance in the arts, sciences, sports, and games* (pp. 51–80). Mahwah, NJ: Erlbaum.

Chase, W. G., & Ericsson, K. A. (1982). Skill and working memory. In G. H. Bower (Ed.), *The psychology of learning and motivation* (Vol. 16, pp. 1–58). San Diego, CA: Academic Press.

Cotman, C. W., & Nieto-Sampedro, M. (1984). Cell biology of synaptic plasticity. *Science, 225*(4668), 1287–1294.

Dixon, R. A., & Baltes, P. B. (1986). Toward life-span research on the functions and pragmatics of intelligence. In R. J. Sternberg & R. K. Wagner (Eds.), *Practical intelligence: Nature and origins of competence in the everyday world* (pp. 203–235). New York: Cambridge University Press.

Doll, J., & Mayr, U. (1987). Intelligenz und Schachleistung-eine Untersuchung an Schachexperten [Intelligence and achievement in chess – A study of chess masters]. *Psychologische Beitraege, 29,* 270–289.

Elbert, T., Pantev, C., Wienbruch, C., Rockstroh, B., & Taub, E. (1995). Increased cortical representation of the fingers of the left hand in string players. *Science, 270*, 305–307.

Elbert, T., Sterr, A., & Rockstroh, B. (1996). Untersuchungen zu corticaler Plastizität beim erwachsenen Menschen: Was lernt das Gehirn beim Geige spielen? [Studies of cortical plasticity in adults: What does the brain learn from playing the violin?]. *Musikphysiologie und Musikmedizin, 3*, 57–65.

Ericsson, K. A. (1990). Peak performance and age: An examination of peak performance in sports. In P. B. Baltes & M. M. Baltes (Eds.), *Successful aging: Perspectives from the behavioral sciences* (pp. 164–196). New York: Cambridge University Press.

Ericsson, K. A., & Charness, N. (1994). Expert performance: Its structure and acquisition. *American Psychologist, 49*, 725–747.

Ericsson, K. A., Krampe, R. T., & Tesch-Römer, C. (1993). The role of deliberate practice in the acquisition of expert performance. *Psychological Review, 100*, 363–406.

Ericsson, K. A., & Lehmann, A. C. (1996). Expert and exceptional performance: Evidence on maximal adaptations on task constraints. *Annual Review of Psychology, 47*, 273–305.

Ericsson, K. A., & Smith, J. (1991). Prospects and limits of the empirical study of expertise: An introduction. In K. A. Ericsson & J. Smith (Eds.), *Toward a general theory of expertise: Prospects and limits*. New York: Cambridge University Press.

Ferguson, G. A. (1954). On learning and human ability. *Canadian Journal of Psychology, 8*, 95–112.

Ferguson, G. A. (1965). On transfer and the abilities of man. *Canadian Journal of Psychology, 10*, 121–131.

Fleishman, E. A. (1972). On the relation between abilities, learning, and human performance. *American Psychologist, 27*, 1017–1032.

Freund, A. M., & Baltes, P. B. (2000). The orchestration of selection, optimization, and compensation: An action-theoretical conceptualization of a theory of developmental regulation. In W. J. Perrig & A. Grob (Eds.), *Control of human behavior, mental processes, and consciousness* (pp. 35–58). Mahwah, NJ: Erlbaum.

Freund, A. M., & Baltes, P. B. (in press). Life-management strategies of selection, optimization, and compensation: Measurement by self-report and construct validity. *Journal of Personality and Social Psychology*.

Gentner, D. R. (1988). Expertise in typewriting. In M. T. H. Chi, R. Glaser, & M. J. Farr (Eds.), *The nature of expertise* (pp. 1–21). Hillsdale, NJ: Erlbaum.

Gottlieb, G. L., Corcos, D. M., Jaric, S., & Agarwal, G. C. (1988). Practice improves even the simplest movements. *Experimental Brain Research, 73*, 436–440.

Hebb, D. O. (1949). *The organization of behavior*. New York: Wiley.

Horn, J. L. (1982). The theory of fluid and crystallized intelligence in relation to concepts of cognitive psychology and ageing in adulthood. In F. I. M. Craik & E. Trehub (Eds.), *Ageing and cognitive processes: Advances in the study of communication and affect* (pp. 237–278). New York: Plenum Press.

Horn, J. L., & Masunaga, H. (2000a). New directions for research into aging and intelligence: The development of expertise. In T. J. Perfect & E. A. Maylor (Eds.), *Models of cognitive aging* (pp. 125–159). Oxford: Oxford University Press.

Horn, J. L., & Masunaga, H. (2000b). On the emergence of wisdom: Expertise development. In W. S. Brown (Ed.), *Understanding wisdom: Sources, science, & society* (pp. 245–276). Philadelphia, PA: Templeton Foundation Press.

Howe, M. J. A., Davidson, J. W., & Sloboda, J. A. (1999). Innate talents: Reality or myth? *Behavioral and Brain Sciences, 21*, 399–442.

Kaas, J. H. (1991). Plasticity of sensory and motor maps in adult mammals. *Annual Reviews of Neuroscience, 14*, 137–167.

Kaminski, G., Mayer, R., & Ruoff, B. A. (1984). *Kinder und Jugendliche im Leistungssport [Children and adolescents in high-performance sports]*. Schorndorf, Germany: Hofmann.

Karni, A., Meyer, G., Jezzard, P., Adams, M. M., Turner, R., & Ungerleider, L. G. (1995). Functional MRI evidence for adult motor cortex plasticity during motor skill learning. *Nature, 377*, 155–158.

Keele, S. W., & Hawkins, H. L. (1982). Explorations of individual differences relevant to high level skill. *Journal of Motor Behavior, 14*, 3–23.

Keele, S. W., Pokorny, R. A., Corcos, D. M., & Ivry, R. (1985). Do perception and motor production share common timing mechanisms: A correlational analysis. *Acta Psychologica, 60*, 173–191.

Kliegl, R., & Baltes, P. B. (1987). Theory-guided analysis of mechanisms of development and aging through testing-the-limits and research on expertise. In C. Schooler & K. W. Schaie (Eds.), *Cognitive functioning and social structure over the life course* (pp. 95–119). Norwood: NJ: Ablex.

Kliegl, R., Krampe, R. T., Mayr, U., & Liebscher, T. (2001a). *Context memory deficit constrains asymptotic recall accuracy*. Potsdam, Germany: University of Potsdam.

Kliegl, R., Krampe, R. T., Philipp, D., & Luckner, M. (in prep.). *Where have I seen that face before? Face memory skill acquisition*. Potsdam, Germany: University of Potsdam.

Kliegl, R., Phillipp, D., Luckner, M., & Krampe, R. T. (2001b). Face memory skill acquisition. In N. Charness, D. C. Park, & B. A. Sabel (Eds.), *Communication, technology and aging: Opportunities and challenges for the future* (pp. 169–186). New York: Springer.

Kliegl, R., Smith, J., & Baltes, P. B. (1989). Testing-the-limits and the study of adult age differences in cognitive plasticity of a mnemonic skill. *Developmental Psychology, 25*, 247–256.

Kliegl, R., Smith, J., & Baltes, P. B. (1990). On the locus and process of magnification of adult age differences during mnemonic training. *Developmental Psychology, 26*, 894–904.

Kramer, A. F., Hahn, S., Cohen, N. J., Banich, M. T., McAuley, E., Harrison, C. R., Chason, J., Vakil, E., Bardell, L., Boileau, R. A., & Colcombe, A. (1999). Aging, fitness and neurocognitive function. *Nature, 400*, 418–419.

Krampe, R. T. (1994). *Maintaining excellence: Cognitive-motor performance in pianists differing in age and skill level*. Berlin, Germany: Edition Sigma.

Krampe, R. T., & Ericsson, K. A. (1995). Deliberate practice and elite musical performance. In J. Rink (Ed.), *The practice of performance: Studies in musical interpretation* (pp. 84–104). Cambridge, UK: Cambridge University Press.

Krampe, R. T., & Ericsson, K. A. (1996). Maintaining excellence: Deliberate practice and elite performance in young and older pianists. *Journal of Experimental Psychology: General, 125,* 331–359.

Labouvie, G. V., Frohring, W. R., & Baltes, P. B. (1973). Changing relationship between recall performance and abilities as a function of stage of learning and timing of recall. *Journal of Educational Psychology, 64,* 191–198.

Lerner, R. M. (1984). *On the nature of human plasticity.* New York: Cambridge University Press.

Lerner, R. M., Freund, A. M., De Stefanis, I., & Habermas, T. (2001). Understanding developmental regulation in adolescence: The use of the selection, optimization, and compensation model. *Human Development, 44,* 29–50.

Li, K. Z. H., Lindenberger, U., Freund, A. M., & Baltes, P. B. (2001). Walking while memorizing: A SOC study of age-related differences in compensatory behavior under dual-task conditions. *Psychological Science, 12,* 230–237.

Li, S.-C. (in press). Aging mind: Facets and levels of analyses. In N. J. Smelser & P. B. Baltes (Eds.), *International encyclopedia of the social and behavioral sciences.* Oxford, UK: Elsevier Science.

Li, S.-C., Lindenberger, U., Prinz, W., Baltes, P. B., & Team, C.-M. R. (2000). *A lifetime from differentiation to dedifferentiation: The fall and rise of covariations between intelligence, information processing, and sensory functioning across the lifespan.* Berlin: Max Planck Institute for Human Development and Education.

Lindenberger, U., & Baltes, P. B. (1994). Sensory functioning and intelligence in old age: A strong connection. *Psychology and Aging, 9,* 339–355.

Lindenberger, U., & Baltes, P. B. (1997). Intellectual functioning in old and very old age: Cross-sectional results from the Berlin Aging Study. *Psychology and Aging, 12,* 410–432.

Lindenberger, U., Marsiske, M., & Baltes, P. B. (2000). Memorizing while walking: Increase in dual-task costs from young adulthood to old age. *Psychology and Aging, 15,* 417–436.

Marsiske, M., Lang, F. R., Baltes, M. M., & Baltes, P. B. (1995). Selective optimization with compensation: Life-span perspectives on successful human development. In R. A. Dixon & L. Bäckman (Eds.), *Compensation for psychological defects and declines: Managing losses and promoting gains* (pp. 35–79). Hillsdale, NJ: Erlbaum.

Masunaga, H., & Horn, J. (2001). Expertise in relation to aging changes in components of intelligence. *Psychology and Aging, 16,* 293–311.

Maylor, E. A. (1994). Ageing and the retrieval of specialized and general knowledge: Performance of masterminds. *British Journal of Psychology, 85,* 105–114.

Maylor, E. A., Allison, S., & Wing, A. M. (in press). Effects of spatial and non-spatial cognitive activity on postural stability. *British Journal of Psychology.*

Maylor, E. A., & Wing, A. M. (1996). Age differences in postural stability are increased by additional cognitive demands. *Journal of Gerontology: Psychological Sciences, 51B,* 143–154.

McDowd, J. M., & Craik, F. I. M. (1987). Effects of aging and task difficulty on divided attention performance. *Journal of Experimental Psychology: Human Perception and Performance, 14,* 267–280.

Morrow, D., & Leirer, V. (1997). Aging, pilot performance and expertise. In A. D. Fisk & W. A. Rogers (Eds.), *Handbook of human factors and the older adult* (pp. 199–230). New York: Academic Press.

Morrow, D., Leirer, V., Altieri, P., & Fitzsimmons, C. (1994). When expertise reduces age differences in performance. *Psychology and Aging, 9*, 134–148.

Rabbitt, P. M. A. (1993). Crystal quest. A search for the basis of maintenance of practised skills into old age. In A. Baddeley & L. Weiskrantz (Eds.), *Attention: Selection, awareness, and control* . Oxford, UK: Clarendon Press.

Ruoff, B. A. (1981). *Psychologische Analysen zum Alltag jugendlicher Leistungssportler: Eine empirische Untersuchung (kognitiver Repräsentationen) von Tagesabläufen [Psychological investigations of everyday lives in adolescent top-performance athletes: Empirical studies of cognitive representations of daily routines].* Munich, Germany: Minerva.

Salthouse, T. A. (1984). Effects of age and skill in typing. *Journal of Experimental Psychology: General, 113*, 345–371.

Salthouse, T. A. (1991). Expertise as the circumvention of human processing limitations. In K. A. Ericsson & J. Smith (Eds.), *Toward a general theory of expertise: Prospects and limits* (pp. 286–300). New York: Cambridge University Press.

Schmidt, L. R. (1971). Testing the limits im Leistungsverhalten: Möglichkeiten und Grenzen. In E. Duhm (Ed.), *Praxis der klinischen Psychologie* (Vol. 2, pp. 9–29). Göttingen: Hogrefe.

Schulz, R., & Curnow, C. (1988). Peak performance and age among superathletes: Track and field, swimming, baseball, tennis and golf. *Journal of Gerontology: Psychological Sciences, 43*, 113–120.

Simon, H. A., & Chase, W. G. (1973). Skill in chess. *American Scientist, 61*, 394–403.

Singer, T., & Lindenberger, U. (2000). Plastizität. In H.-W. Wahl & C. Tesch-Römer (Eds.), *Angewandte Gerontologie in Schlüsselbegriffen* [Applied gerontology in keywords] (pp. 39–48). Stuttgart: Kohlhammer.

Singer, T., Lindenberger, U., & Baltes, P. B. (2001). *Plasticity of memory for new learning in very old age: A story of major loss?* Berlin: Max Planck Institute for Human Development.

Singer, W. (1995). Development and plasticity of cortical processing architectures. *Science, 270*, 758–764.

Sternberg, R. J. (1990). *Metaphors of mind: Conceptions of the nature of intelligence.* New York: Cambridge University Press.

Sternberg, R. J. (2001). How much money should one put into the cognitive parking meter? *Trends in Cognitive Sciences, 5*, 190.

Sternberg, R. J., & Detterman, D. K. (1986). *What is intelligence?* Norwood, NJ: Ablex.

Teasdale, N., Bard, C., LaRue, J., & Fleury, M. (1993). On the cognitive penetrability of posture control. *Experimental Aging Research, 19*, 1–13.

Telford, C. W., & Spangler, H. (1935). Training effects in motor skills. *Journal of Experimental Psychology, 18*, 141–147.

Verhaeghen, P., Marcoen, A., & Goosens, L. (1992). Improving memory performance in the aged through mnemonic training: A meta-analytic study. *Psychology and Aging, 7*, 242–251.

Walsh, D. A., & Hershey, D. A. (1993). Mental models and the maintenance of complex problem solving skills in old age. In J. Cerella, J. Rybash, W. Hoyer, & M. Commons (Eds.), *Adult information processing: Limits on loss* (pp. 553–584). San Diego: Academic Press.

Wang, X., Merzenich, M. M., Sameshima, K., & Jenkins, W. (1995). Remodelling of hand representation in adult cortex determined by timing of tactile stimulation. *Nature, 378*, 71–75.

3

Developing Childhood Proclivities into Adult Competencies

The Overlooked Multiplier Effect

Stephen J. Ceci, Susan M. Barnett, and Tomoe Kanaya

In this chapter, we tackle a problem that has been at the heart of the debate over the relative influence of genes and environments in producing cognitive competencies. Our goal is to attempt to reconcile the disparate claims of behavior genetics researchers who stress the prepotency of genes in producing intellectual competence (for example, Bouchard, Lykken, Tellegan, and McGue, 1998) with those whom Scarr (1997) refers to as "socialization theorists" because of their stance on the crucial role of the social and material environment in shaping developmental outcomes.

Our means of making this reconciliation is to describe recent efforts by diverse scholars to explain cognitive growth in terms of theories, models, and metaphors that are inherently multiplicative, more so than prior ones. We do not intend to delve into a comparative analysis of the strengths and weaknesses of each model or metaphor, as that is not our goal, but instead we want to make the point that various researchers, coming from very different orientations, have found the need to postulate similar types of multiplier effects to account for cognitive growth across a wide range of attainments (reading, intelligence, mathematics, motoric).

In the treatment that follows we use the terms "proclivities," "penchants," and "abilities" interchangeably, to refer to basic, underlying "resource pools" that are undoubtedly biologically based. Thus, we speak of a newborn's penchant, ability, or proclivity to stare, attend, remember, and process the perceptual world. In this usage, abilities are not the full-blown cognitive attainments they are usually seen as, such as mathematical or spatial reasoning skills, but the initial biological resources that allow children to attend, focus, remember, and so forth. With experience, these initial biological abilities or resources will be instrumental in attaining adult academic skills, here referred to as "competencies." So, we use the term competence to refer to adult attainments that are the result of gene-environment interactions and correlations, as well as main effects.

We use the term *expertise* here to refer to a very high degree of competence, and like all competencies, the result of genes and environments.[1] None of this nomenclature is meant to argue against other uses of the terms ability, competence, and expertise; our definitions merely alert readers that this chapter deals with how biological resources that may not even be cognitive (for example, attention, intrinsic motivation, vigilance) trigger a series of experiences to ultimately foster adult cognitive competencies.

Our model of the development of competencies is inherently multiplicative, as will be seen. It is this feature that we offer as a means of reconciling past disputes about the roles of biology and experience in producing competencies. As Dickens and Flynn (2001) recently demonstrated, without such a multiplicative approach, there is the risk of underestimating the power of environmental inputs and overestimating the magnitude of genetically based variance.

Most research on cognitive competencies has focused on the level of the individual's ability, identifying specific time-locked factors that may be responsible for the conversion of initially underlying genetically endowed abilities into full-blown adult competencies. Thus, early

---

[1] We reject the idea that expertise, defined this way, is simply a hypertrophied response to the environment, absent any special biologically based ability. Many individuals who possessed extreme levels of expertise (Beethoven, Toscanini, Ramanujan, and similar others) had siblings who lacked the same expertise, despite being reared in environments that were somewhat similar. We adhere to the view that such manifestations of extreme talent depend on a statistically rare combination of polygenic systems (Jensen, 1997), which is a precondition for the environment to crystallize the expertise. Without the requisite environment, such expertise will not crystallize. On the other hand, simply randomly assigning the identical environment to all individuals will not result in a flood of Beethovens, or Bernsteins, because most individuals lack the genetic proclivities of these rare experts. Examples of cognitive expertise in persons with low IQs are probably cases in which the competence in question does not depend on rare combinations of polygenic systems because the type of cognition itself is unmediated, untransformed or simple, for example, memorization of long strings of digits, calendar "counting," and so forth, none of which may require transformation of the nominal stimulus). We are not claiming that performance cannot be elevated by massive practice; merely that the extreme forms we focus on require as a precondition a genetic basis.

intervention programs that provide cognitive and linguistic enrichment have their effectiveness assessed in terms of subsequent growth in cognitive competencies such as changes in IQ, reasoning scores, and so forth (Lazar and Darlington, 1982). The problems with such approaches are well known. It is very difficult to pinpoint the precise causes of cognitive growth, if they even occur. And attenuation of cognitive gains over time is common. Finally, the magnitude of such gains are nevertheless commensurate with high levels (50 percent or greater) of heritability (Ceci, 1996). To those outside this area of research, it is perplexing that large mean gains in cognitive competencies (gains have been reported on the order of .2 to .5 SDs as a result of smaller classes in math, scientific reasoning, and reading; see Ehrenberg, Brewer, Willms and Gamoran, 2001) are compatible with large heritability, leading to the view that the environment is unable to account for much in the way of differences in competencies.

Missing from the traditional way we estimate the effects of genes and environments is a consideration of both individual and group-level factors that may amplify changes in cognitive competencies through a series of progressively more complex and differentiated interactions that occur over longer periods of time (Bronfenbrenner and Ceci, 1994; Ehrenberg et al., 2001). The reason for this omission is understandable because until Dickens and Flynn (2001) provided their recent solution, individual and societal factors that operate over time have been difficult to dissociate from factors that are tied to a specific period of time. As a result, even when main effects are observed in response to some factor at time 1 (for example, some preschool intervention to boost cognitive performance), there is often substantial evidence of heritability – the weakest may gain from exposure to the intervention, but the strongest may gain as well, sometimes even more, thus limiting the factor's role in accounting for the variance in individual differences. For example, much of the research on the effects of early educational television programs such as *Sesame Street* found that the children at the top of the ability distribution benefited more than the low ability children, thus increasing the gap between them (Cook, Appleton, Conner, Shaffer, Tamkin, and Weber, 1975). Similarly, computer interventions to learn arithmetic resulted in widening gaps between the top and bottom students (Hativa, 1988).

It has been argued that environment, and especially shared environment, has only a small effect on the level of cognitive competencies. For example, some scholars have opined that with the exception of those statistically rare cases in which a child's environment is so aberrant as to lie outside the normal species range, environmental interventions are doomed: "environments that most parents provide for their children have few differential effects on their offspring [p. 3] . . . it is not easy to intervene deliberately in children's lives to change their development, unless their environments are outside the normal species range" (Scarr, 1992, p. 16). Consistent with this gloomy opinion are those studies of the IQs of identical twins raised apart, which routinely show heritability increasing as twins age (Loehlin, Horn, and Willerman, 1997; McClearn et al., 1997). Such studies report heritability estimates that show shared environmental factors accounting for roughly 25 percent of variance in IQ during the twins' childhood. Yet those same shared environmental factors subsequently fade away to account for almost zero variance by late adolescence, causing a rise in heritability with age (for example Loehlin, Horn, and Willerman, 1997) that tapers off in adulthood (McClearn et al., 1997).

From this increase in heritability and decrease in shared environmental potency over time it is assumed that intervention efforts are largely fruitless. However, Petrill, Plomin, Berg, Johansson, Pedersen, Ahern, and McClearn (1998) have reported that among very old twins the relationship among discrete cognitive abilities (speed, spatial, verbal, and memory) differs from that observed among children and younger adults, particularly for perceptual speed, which has a g-loading for older adults higher than the g-loading for verbal ability that is highest among younger persons. In this study, genes appeared responsible for the similarities among adults' abilities but the environment influenced the differences. Hence, although genetic factors are the driving force behind the substantial g-factor loadings of specific cognitive abilities, nonshared environmental factors account for their independence.

Flynn (2001) has shown that notwithstanding this alleged lack of environmental potency among younger persons, IQ has been increasing dramatically over the last 100 years (five to nine points per decade). Such increases have taken place in the absence of obvious changes in the gene pool, presumably due to environmental factors such as better nutrition, more and better schooling, smaller families (more resources per child), better educated parents, and more complex visual environments (computers, educational toys, television, and so forth). This leaves the puzzling gap between the presumed strong effect of the environment in increasing average cognitive competence across generations, and the apparently weak power of shared environmental effects on individual differences at any given point within a generation. A new breed of so-called multiplier models has offered a way out of this conundrum. We describe below five types of multiplier models that, although differing in their motivations and details, converge on the notion that small gene–environment correlations can cascade over time to produce very large differences easily misclassified as direct genetic effects.

DICKENS AND FLYNN'S MULTIPLIER EFFECTS MODEL

Scarr (1997) and her colleagues have argued that within the range of species-normal environments, differences among people arise mainly from genetically based differences in the experiences to which they are attracted and which they evoke from their environments (Scarr and McCartney, 1983). Of particular interest here are active gene–environment correlations caused by self-selection of environments by children due to their genetic predispositions. In Scarr's words:

Genotype-environment correlations are ubiquitous, non-random associations between one's personal characteristics and one's environment [p. 6].... The everyday world for most people consists of choices about what to listen to and look at, what to ignore, where to be and with whom. People expose themselves differentially to opportunities for experience. These are g-e correlations. (Scarr, 1997, p. 37).

In their recent mathematical model, however, Dickens and Flynn (2001a) revisit the claim that gene–environment correlations are a major force in cognitive competence. They ask how environment can be potent enough to cause massive IQ gains over time when kinship studies (on a given population at a particular time) give such high h^2 estimates – without resorting to the absurd notion of a factor X.[2]

The Dickens and Flynn model shows that we can posit h^2 estimates as high as we like, and nevertheless still show how environmental factors could produce huge between-group IQ differences – without resorting

---

[2] A *Factor X* is an unknown, but absurdly implausible explanatory mechanism. For example, high h^2 estimates seem to show either: (1) that environmental factors operating *within* generations are so feeble that if they were operative *between* generations, you would have to posit a 3 SD environmental gap between the generations – which means the last generation had an average environment that was worse than 99 percent of the present generation – implausible to say the least; or (2) that a factor X operates between the generations that is uniform in its effects within generations (and therefore does not show up in the calculation of h^2 estimates). Most scholars view such uniformity of effect as absurdly implausible, begging the question.

to a factor X and without altering IQ variance over time from its observed levels (which would suggest some other mechanisms at work). These authors hypothesize that the often observed increase in heritability with age occurs because genes have both a direct effect on brain physiology and their influence is simultaneously magnified by a social interaction process, called a "multiplier." In their view, the fact that initial genetic proclivities select for specific environments leads to the erroneous assignment of subsequent environmental variance to genes. Small genetic advantages for an individual can be multiplied by the environment, but traditional behavior genetic models will attribute the resulting within-cohort changes to genes (that is, a multiplier due to g–e correlations that result from self-selected environments).

Dickens and Flynn argue that in heritability calculations such environmentally mediated effects are somewhat misleadingly attributed to genes because they go along with genetic differences and the matched environments are genetically loaded, thus boosting heritability estimates. The proximal cause, however, is clearly environmental, despite the fact that variability in this aspect of the environment within a population may be initially driven by genetic factors. If these environmentally mediated effects are large, the environment can be a potent factor in development, even when heritability coefficients are very high, suggest Dickens and Flynn. Although each occurrence may be a minor factor, active genetic effects on the environment may multiply because the small environmental result of the initial genetic effect would change the child's competencies and lead to further environmental self-selections, which would subsequently change the child's competence further, and so on.

Consider the example of an individual born with a genetically based slight physical superiority (that is, somewhat above average) for eye-hand coordination, forearm strength, and reflexes. Initially, this individual may take satisfaction in doing slightly better at baseball than his schoolyard peers because he possesses slightly better coordination, strength, and reflexes. This satisfaction may lead such an individual to practice more, search more aggressively for others willing to play after school and on weekends, try out for teams (not just school teams but also summer league teams), get professional coaching, watch and discuss televised games, and so forth. Such an individual is likely to become matched with increasingly enriched environments for baseball skills. If one assessed the influence of any environmental factor at a specific time, it would be weak (for example, watching x number of hours more televised baseball would not account for superiority in playing baseball). Factors cascade over time because they multiply the effects of earlier, seemingly weak, factors.

Analogous to this hypothetical baseball player with the slight genetic advantage is the individual with a slight genetic superiority for a type of academic competence. Such a person may do slightly better in the early grades, get satisfaction from teachers' and classmates' praise, study harder, visit the library more often, be encouraged to enroll in honors-level classes, apply for scholarships to elite universities, engage in cognitively demanding activities and strive toward cognitively complex careers. Static, time-locked models will not reveal the potency of the environment, however, according to Dickens and Flynn (2001b).

In both the above examples, the interaction between genetically influenced skill and the environment serves as a type of "multiplier." Each increase in competence is matched to a better environment, and, in turn, the better environment will be expected to further enhance their competence. This notion of a multiplier explains how a slight genetic advantage can snowball into a very large difference in competency. It also explains why genes appear to possess an unwarranted potency in heritability studies, driving a powerful interaction process. In Flynn's words,

From early childhood, separated identical twins, thanks to their genetic identity, tend to match with similar environments despite their separation. Their autonomy in early childhood is limited by their differing home environments, but as they mature and escape the influence of home for school, peers, and the wider world, they seize control and the non-random environment portion of IQ variance steadily declines. All the kinship studies pick up is the eventual similarity of their IQs. They do not reveal that genes seem so potent only because they have been credited with both their direct influence and the enormous potency of environment – the latter masked by the fact that environmental differences have become correlated with genetic differences. (Flynn, 2001, p. 14).

The powerful effect of multipliers does not mean that skill/environment interactions become the slave of genes. When comparisons are made between cohorts, the impetus for the multiplier can be a wider social change that raises the average competence of society by a tiny amount. This small improvement will initiate a feedback loop to enhance each individual's performance, due to the benefit of interacting with a more motivated and demanding group and the increase in availability of environmental support. This small increase in individual performance in turn enhances the quality of the group environment. In contrast to within-generation analyses, between-generational changes are captured by steady environmental trends and these trends thereby multiply their effects and produce substantial gains in IQ across time periods. The very interaction process that makes genes so potent in kinship analyses, when individuals compete with one another at a specific place and time, also makes environment potent when it lifts the mean IQ of an entire population over time. This is what Dickens and Flynn (2001a) refer to as the social multiplier effect.

However, although both the within-generation self-selection multiplier and the between-generation social multiplier share the same characteristics of feedback and a cascading change prompted by a small initial impetus, they are different in other ways. Most important, the former is initiated by a genetic individual difference whereas the latter is initiated by a global environmental change over time. There is also the possibility of a combination of the two, for example, if the context changed between cohorts, due to TV or other media, such that engaging in demanding conversations with smart kids was considered to be desirable rather than "nerdy," then children might choose to participate without the genetic attribute previously necessary to seek out such productive stimulation, an attribute, perhaps, such as an indifference to social stigma. Thus, a change in context could influence the way a gene–environment correlation might operate, to avail the benefit, previously selected only by the genetically privileged few, to others.

Other Multiplier-Based Approaches

Dynamical Systems Models

The notion of a social multiplier that amplifies a trait via successive interactions finds a counterpart in other models. The large and growing body of work on dynamical systems models or so-called chaos models is a case in point (see Gleick, 1987; Smith and Thelen, 1993; Thelen and Smith, 1994). Chaos models are predicated on the insight that development is dynamic, with small inputs accumulating in nonlinear ways.[3] Dynamical systems modelers approach this from a slightly different perspective, that of general mathematical modeling, but nevertheless arrive at some of the same interesting conclusions. Basically, if a model includes nonlinearity and feedback and looks at the changes

---

[3] Neural nets and connectionist models share the same basic insight, nonlinearity and dynamic feedback.

in a system over time, the model can show "sensitive dependence on initial conditions," the hallmark of chaos models, which is exactly what Dickens and Flynn (2001a,b) are talking about: "Tiny differences in input could quickly become overwhelming differences in output" (Gleick, 1987). This effect has been termed the "butterfly effect" after Edward Lorenz, who presented a paper at the annual meeting of the American Association for the Advancement of Science discussing the question of whether the flapping of a butterfly's wings in Brazil could set off a tornado in Texas (Gleick, 1987).

In the case of developmental psychology, the feedback comes from the interaction of the child and the environment: "Positive feedback loops, of the sort that sponsor the development of novel or emergent system properties, serve to amplify differences between initial and obtained states ... by promoting exchanges with the environment" (Chandler and Boutilier, 1992, p. 125). And a small difference in that environment could have a major effect on the outcome for the child:

A dynamic view provides theoretical legitimacy to the rampant variability of development, both among contexts and among individuals. Because dynamic systems are fluid and nonlinear, components may assemble in qualitatively different configurations even when changes in the participating elements are small. Thus, barely perceptible differences in the organism or in the task environment may produce dramatic, and sometimes unpredictable, outcomes. This essential nonlinearity also helps us to understand the generation and maintenance of individual differences. As individuals explore and select solutions to functional tasks, small differences at the confluence of the organism and the task may have reverberating and cascading effects, so that the developmental trajectory becomes channeled into one of several possible pathways. (Thelen, 1992, p. 191).

Thus, the effect of a small ability difference, leading to a small difference in environmental self-selection, such as might be provided by different cohorts or created by intervention efforts could have dramatically differing consequences for the individual's competence in different contexts.

Researchers adopting this approach have focused more on motor development than intellectual attainment, but the reasoning applies equally to examining cognitive questions, provided the necessary detailed longitudinal data are available. One attempt to model a cognitive phenomenon dynamically is Van Geert's (1991) work on word learning. Employing a dynamic systems approach, he attempted to reanalyze several sets of data on word learning in infancy and other examples of intellectual growth. Van Geert built mathematical equations combining relevant variables (learning rate, feedback delay, maximum capacity, and so forth) in an intuitively plausible fashion, and set parameters to fit them to the data. His work clearly demonstrates the wide range of interesting and unexpected patterns of development, including qualitatively different stage phenomena, that can be generated by a combination of nonlinear equations.

Although applying the ideas of dynamical systems theory to the issues we are discussing in this chapter may be tough to do with the mathematical precision of Van Geert, the approach certainly highlights the weaknesses of existing static, linear models, such as the traditional behavior genetics paradigm. It is unfortunate that this insight has taken so long to filter through to the interpretation of twin and adoption studies. Given "sensitive dependence upon initial conditions," it is easy to see that little changes are capable of snowballing into big consequences under certain conditions and not show much of an effect under other conditions, just as Dickens and Flynn (2001a,b) suggest.

Bio-ecological Models

According to a bio-ecological framework, an organism begins life with a set of biologically based "resource pools" or abilities that constrain basic processing efficiencies (attention, memory, perceptual speed, and so forth). These resources are deployed in response to environmental events, and the result is learning and the development of competencies. The specific environmental events that engage these underlying ability resources are varied and age-based: For example, they may initially include caregiver vocal elicitation of the newborn's attention; for the preschool-aged child, they may be interactive games, objects, and events in the environment (Bronfenbrenner and Ceci, 1994). With time, important environmental events include such factors as classroom size, teacher credentials, peer values, and so forth. None of this is new and all these factors have been studied as influences on the emergence of cognitive competencies. The problem is that this has been accomplished by examining their influence in time-locked linear models in which variance in such factors is linked to variance in the competency at that time. Absent from such models is the effect of the prior interactions.

In their bio-ecological theory, Bronfenbrenner and Ceci (1993, 1994) describe a construct they term "proximal processes," which they use to refer to the successively differentiated and complex process that unfolds over time between the developing organism and persons, objects, and events in the environment. In their model, genotypic proclivities may get amplified by successively more differentiated interactions with, say, a caregiver. When this happens, the proclivity develops into a high level of competency in much the same way that Dickens and Flynn posit for their multiplier effects. Two expectations arise from this formulation, each given a preliminary empirical test by Bronfenbrenner and Ceci: 1) proximal processes serve as the engine for the development of competency, not SES or global aspects of the environment, and 2) it is under conditions of high proximal process that bio-ecological theory predicts the highest heritability for a competency. If a student has the genetic potential to learn, say, Greek, but the school she attends does not teach Greek, then her potential remains dormant and she will fail to become all she is capable of becoming. In such cases, both competence and heritability are low. It is only under conditions of high proximal process that proclivities will fully crystallize into competencies and heritability will be high.

As an example of the evidentiary base of this theory, Riksen-Walraven (1978) studied 100 nine-month-old infants living in a Dutch city with their working-class parents. She was specifically interested in the effects of "enhancing the amount of stimulation provided by parents to their infants" (p. 111). Groups of 25 infants were randomly assigned to one of four conditions: 1) the responsive group mothers received a workbook stressing the idea "the infant learns most from the effects of its own behavior" (p. 113). These mothers were advised not to direct their child's activities but instead give the child a chance to discover things on his or her own, praising the child's efforts and responding to his or her interactive initiatives; 2) the stimulation group mothers were instructed in the importance of providing their infants a great deal of perceptual experience of all kinds. Specifically, these mothers were told to speak a lot to their infants and name objects and people in the environment. Group 3 was a combination of the first two groups and group 4 was an untreated control.

As expected, the mothers did what they were told and an observation in their homes after three months showed they were still conforming to their group instructions. Infants of those mothers who had been instructed to be responsive were more exploratory, exhibited greater novelty preference, and learned more quickly in a contingency task. Thus, a proximal process (reciprocal interaction between the infant and mother over time) led to higher levels of cognitive competence three months later. It would be fascinating to know how enduring this effect was, but unfortunately no such follow-up data were provided by Riksen-Walraven (1978).

An implication of the foregoing is that genes (here used as a surrogate for "ability") do have a significant influence on the development of cognitive competence, though probably their impact is neither so direct nor so potent as has been assumed by behavior geneticists' heritability studies.

Abilities are akin to potential muscles: without exercise the genetic potential will not become actualized. Someone with less genetic potential for muscular development may actually develop more muscle because of the availability of a conducive environment coupled with the motivation to take advantage of this environment. So-called experts are examples of supremely motivated individuals. They may possess genetic advantages for specific competencies, but what leads to their expertise is the exceptional motivation to take advantage of relevant environmental factors associated with skill development. Although some experts (for example, Mozart) surely possessed a genetic advantage in the sense that most individuals subjected to the same environment would never reach the same level of expertise, this is not always clearly the case. Some experts appear to possess fairly unexceptional abilities, yet through sheer dint of effort they reach amazing levels of expertise. Autistic savants are a case in point: Howe (1989) has shown that their impressive memory feats in recalling perpetual calendars do not emanate from exceptional memories. Rather, the early praise they receive for simple memory feats is given a hypertrophied fixation by these individuals and eventually the multiplier effect takes it course. As noted in footnote 1, such cases of expertise do not appear to depend on rare combinations of polygenic systems that characterize expertise based on more complex cognitive abilities.

Matthew Effect Models

The idea that "the rich get richer and the poor get poorer" is a variant of the biblical aphorism attributed to the apostle Matthew, "For to him who has shall be given and he shall have abundance; but from him who does not have, even that which he has shall be taken away." This biblical metaphor seems related to the claim that initial genetic proclivities can mushroom over time into full-blown competencies via successive multipliers, whereas initial deficits also accentuate over time, creating what Stanovich (1986) calls a "fan spread" effect. In other words, not only will cumulative advantages lead to further advantages over time, but an initial disadvantage will lead to further disadvantages. Note the resemblance of this idea to the concepts of "proximal processes" in bio-ecological theory, to "sensitive dependence upon initial conditions" in dynamical systems theory, and to Dickens and Flynn's (2001a,b) "multiplier effect." All four of these concepts entail progressively cumulative interactions over fairly long periods of time between an initial small impetus, captured in gene–environment correlations within generations.

The idea of a Matthew Effect accounting for differences in reading competence was first put forward by Stanovich (1986). In his construal, there are two key concepts comprising a multiplier effect of initial differences in reading competence. One is the concept of "reciprocal relationships" or "reciprocal causation" in which individual differences in a particular process may cause different initial reading efficacy, but reading itself may also cause further individual differences in the process.

The very children who are reading well and who have good vocabularies will read more, learn more word meanings, and hence read even better. Children with inadequate vocabularies – who read slowly and without enjoyment – read less, and as a result have slower development of vocabulary knowledge, which inhibits further growth in reading ability. (p. 381)

Stanovich's (1986) second key concept is the principal of "organism [that is, genes]-environment correlation," (g-e) or that people are selectively exposed (or selectively expose themselves) to different environments. He describes two ways, active and evocative, g-e can effect competencies (in his case, reading). In an active g-e correlation, a person actively selects and shapes his or her environment whereas in an evocative g-e correlation, a person is affected by the environment's response to him- or herself:

Children who become better readers have selected (e.g., by choosing friends who read or choosing reading as a leisure activity rather than sports or video games), shaped (e.g., by asking for books as presents when young), and evoked (e.g., the child's parents noticed that looking at books was enjoyed or perhaps just that it kept the child quiet) an environment that will be conducive to further growth in reading. Children who lag in reading achievement do not construct such an environment. (Stanovich, 1986, p. 382).

There are a few empirical studies that have sought to test Stanovich's multiplier notion. One is a longitudinal study by Shaywitz et al. (1995), who failed to find a Matthew Effect on reading, as Stanovich proposed. Rather, their results indicated that children tend to remain close to their original reading levels over time. Shaywitz and his colleagues did, however, find a small Matthew Effect on children's WISC-R IQs. In their words, "a child with a mean IQ for Grades 1–5 of 80 would be expected to show a decrement of–1.1 per year, while a child with a 140 IQ would tend to show an increase of about 4.5 points a year" (p. 903).

More recently, Bast and Reitsma (1998) reported a Matthew Effect on word recognition skills from a three-year longitudinal study of a Dutch sample. Their results showed that initially poor readers remained poor readers, in terms of word recognition, but, what is important, the performance gap relative to good readers became larger over the three years. These researchers also found some evidence for interactive relationships between reading and attitude toward reading, which they hypothesize to be causes for the increased differences between readers.[4]

Expertise Models

The multiplier process is also similar to the mechanism proposed by researchers such as Ericsson (Ericsson, Krampe, and Tesch Roemer, 1993) and Howe (Howe, Davidson, and Sloboda, 1998) for the development of expertise. These researchers claim that repeated practice can have a similar effect on the development of competencies by causing a slight improvement in performance that in turn leads to a choice to participate in more demanding activities and surround oneself with more stimulating company:

In our framework, accumulated deliberate practice causes acquired skill and characteristics, which in turn cause performance, and some of these characteristics increase the maximal amounts of possible practice. (Ericsson et al., 1993, p. 390).

Thus, self-selection is operating but in the case of these expertise researchers it is not necessarily genetically driven but could be the consequence of a small initial difference in interest or ability, which may not be caused by genes but rather by exposure to experience. As we noted earlier, we suggest here that if the type of expertise involves cognitively complex behaviors (for example, mathematical reasoning) as opposed

---

[4] Parenthetically, Matthew Effects have also been reported for areas other than the development of competence, including the social reward system among scientists. A common theme in interviews with Nobel laureates shows that "eminent scientists get disproportionately greater credit for their contributions to science while relatively unknown scientists tend to get disproportionately little credit for comparable contributions" (Merton, 1968, p. 57). Likewise, institutions that are already well known get better perks such as better graduate students, better grants, and so forth. Detterman (2000) recently argued that elite institutions do not educate their students any better than state universities, in terms of gains on cognitive tests over the four years of college.

to low level ones such as rote memorization of strings of digits, then the expertise will be associated with some gene–environment correlations. However, regardless of whether the initial catalyst for expertise is genetic or environmental, the multiplier process takes off to deliver an environmentally caused extreme improvement in competence.

These expertise researchers argue that the amount of practice determines the eventual level of competence rather than innate talent. However, this does not completely rule out a role for the genes, as a distinction is made between innate talent – defined as a genetic superiority for the specific task – and other nonspecific genetic advantages, such as "general levels of activity and emotionality" (Ericsson et al., 1993), which they acknowledge might play a role. One could argue that referring to such an advantage as "talent" would be misleading, but nevertheless it may be genetic in origin.

IMPLICATIONS FOR THE ENHANCEMENT OF COGNITIVE COMPETENCE

All five of the above approaches argue that powerful multiplier effects can occur, through an iterative process of feedback between the organism and its environment. But what is new about this notion? After all, scholars have been writing about potent dynamic gene–environment correlations driving development for the past twenty years (for example, Scarr and McCartney, 1983). The concept of a multiplier is significantly new, however, holding implications for both theory and practice.

Past scholars have concluded that interventions were largely fruitless because the catalyst that jump-started the multiplicative process was genetic in origin, and thus immutable. For example, the fifteen-point gap in IQ between Blacks and Whites, which is equivalent to a full standard deviation, coupled with the typically weak estimate of the influence of environment on IQ (typically 0.33), leads ineluctably to the conclusion that, for the environment to explain the racial IQ gap, the gap between the environments of Blacks and Whites would have to be on the order of three standard deviations – a figure no serious scholar or policy maker entertains (that is, that the average White environment exceeds that of 99 percent of Blacks). Yet, it is precisely this type of reasoning that is sidestepped when the notion of a multiplier is introduced into the equation. This is because it avoids assigning all the environmental potency to genetic variance; it avoids assumptions based on weak environmentality coefficients while not disagreeing that genes may be kick starting the environmental effects.[5]

In doing all this, the multiplier concept opens possibilities for intervention that would be viewed as futile if such low environmentality figures as .33 are assumed in conjunction with such large racial gaps in IQ. This is one reason why the racial gap in achievement scores (which can be used as a proxy for general intelligence) converged during the 1980s (Williams and Ceci, 1997). This was a cohort of Black children whose parents a generation earlier had made disproportionately large gains in their own education, thus providing their children with an intellectual environment richer than their own had been. This led to a social multiplier effect wherein all these children of newly educated African American parents were themselves surrounded by peers from equally educated families, synergizing each other's achievements through more cognitively demanding interactions.

Another advantage of using the multiplier concept is that it reconciles a nagging inconsistency. Specifically, the current generation outscores the previous generation by between nine and twenty IQ points, depending on the measures used. The size and speed of these IQ gains strongly implicate an environmental explanation because genes just don't change that fast. Hardly anyone believes that the Dutch gain of twenty points between 1952 and 1982 is explicable in terms of genetic actions that had not existed prior to this cohort. The point of this example is that the potency of the environment is masked by high heritability estimates and very low environmentality estimates.

Even if a catalyst is a genetic predisposition for competence that leads to self-selection of stimulating environments, which in turn result in even larger individual differences in competence, this does not mean that the only possible catalyst to get the ball rolling has to be genetic. Scarr (1992) and Scarr and McCartney (1983) assume it does, and as a result of this assumption conclude that attributing the consequences to genes is appropriate. No proof is offered for this assumption, however. In drawing attention to this key assumption, we suggest it is a testable empirical question whether or not environmental interventions could also jump start the dynamic multiplier effect. And as far as we are aware, this has not been tested in an empirically adequate manner.

---

[5] It is worth noting, however, that even under conservative estimates of environmentality, only about 50 percent of cognitive variation can be attributed to genetic effects. Thus, there is a lot of room for intervention (even under the worst case scenario).

So where would one look for possible manipulable environmental catalysts? Presumably, the answer is not better parenting techniques and other similar interventions, as these aspects of the shared environment do not matter much, according to the behavior genetic studies mentioned earlier.[6] Assuming that the accepted estimates of heritability are correct as a worst case scenario (for interventionists), what does the possibility of a strong intercohort effect of environmental factors and a powerful intracohort effect of genetically driven self-selection of environments suggest can be achieved by an *environmental intervention, within* a cohort? A number of hypothetical possibilities are suggested.

One approach would be to examine the genetically driven catalysts that result in fruitful self-selection of environments, and consider which might conceivably be replicated by environmental factors, rather than continue the supposedly "ineffective" environmental changes that can be manipulated by parents and schools. Such an approach attempts to create the benefits currently possessed by genetic high-fliers for low-achieving children in order to spur development from their environments. Consider the hypothetical situation in which a genetically competent child usually obtains a better environment for cognitive development by seeking out other highly competent classmates who engage in demanding conversation. It is possible that the same consequence could be achieved by putting a child in an environment where there are more kids engaging in demanding conversations in general. A well-intentioned parent acting alone might attempt to prod his or her child to participate in such an environment but this might not have a multiplicative effect if the child does not choose to seek out the necessary conversation partners or if his or her classmates were not more competent as conversational partners. However, in an initial environment where many more conversations happened to be demanding (for example, by bussing a child to a magnet school), the child would be exposed to more challenging and abstract language without having to seek it out, thus enhancing his or her own competence and seeking out more such stimulation. Although the specific causal chain in this example is

---

[6] Stoolmiller's work (1998, 1999), however, suggests that the picture may not be so bleak as suggested, because the restriction of range in behavior genetic studies may be partly responsible for the findings of lack of shared environmental effect. His calculations suggest that the proportion of variance attributable to shared environmental effects would be considerably greater if less restricted samples were used, in which case promoting an extension of good parenting practices across the breadth of the population might be fruitful after all.

hypothetical, the idea that the overall quality of the social group can affect development has some support.

For example, Azmitia (1988) showed that five-year-old novice Lego builders, paired with same-aged experts, improved their performance on a building task. The improvement was sustained when they were subsequently tested alone on a similar task, as well as on a related transfer task. Working alone or with another novice did not show the same benefits. Similarly, Hamilton, Nickerson, and Owan (2001), studying the completely different environment of worker teams in a factory, found that teams benefited from having a high-ability worker as a member, either because it led to higher expectations within the team, or because the expert's superior skills got transmitted to the other members of the team through mutual learning. In some cases, median team performance was even better than the previous performance of the member with the highest ability. (However, it is worth noting that their study focused on team *production* rather than team *learning*, a distinction important to bear in mind; perhaps team membership did not actually affect the learning process itself.) Thus, such a change could potentially provide a genetically nonadvantaged child with an advantage previously only an option for the genetically privileged few.

Another approach to identifying intervention opportunities based on existing sources of multiplier effects might be to look for cohort effect differences in environmental factors that may also be driving multiplier effects. Examples of this include improving access to education or availability of books and other sources of intellectual stimulation. Such across-the-board changes are obviously very difficult and costly to accomplish, however, and the question of whether they result in the maximum outcomes for the money and time needs careful attention.

A third approach is a combination of the first two – a change in context between cohorts resulting in changing the environmental consequences of a given set of genes. This approach seeks to mimic ways in which between-cohort changes in context could alter the manner in which a g-e correlation process might work. As a hypothetical illustration, imagine that classes in schools have gotten smaller over time (between cohorts). Further, imagine that children who are better behaved for genetic reasons, select seats next to children who are also well behaved. Thus they are less distracted from their work and achieve greater competencies. This motivates such children and their neighbors to behave well in the future, so they do even better, and so on. If smaller classes provide fewer distractions than larger classes, then a child in a randomly chosen seat in a small class might function as well as a child in a seat surrounded by other well-behaved kids in a larger class. Thus, if class sizes were reduced, performance of the average child might improve due to environmental reasons, despite the fact that, in the current context, individual differences in outcomes correlate with genetic differences. Although this is a hypothetical example, there is some evidence that smaller classes do enhance cognitive competence in a manner that lasts at least five years after the intervention has terminated (Ehrenberg, Brewer, Gamoran and Willms, 2001). It is interesting that the advantage of smaller classes is greatest for those who need it most, the poorest performing students, in line with the hypothetical example above, and also possibly because they lack access to the same level of multipliers in their home environments.

How do these options relate to practical considerations? An initial step would be to figure out which dimensions of the environment self-selection is operating on, and whether the process can be influenced by external factors. In parallel, the study of long-term environmental changes would attempt to identify the contextual factors behind the cohort effect, and see whether any of these could be manipulable. Existing intervention efforts appear to be a combination of the above options. Preschoolers are often put temporarily into good environments at an age when they aren't capable of exerting much choice in the matter. Within these environments, educators attempt to jump-start competencies by inculcating changes in behaviors that will generate long-lasting consequences. Even though the direct boost in cognitive skills that children receive in many early intervention efforts appears to decay (Lazar and Darlington, 1982), if children's future self-selected choices can be affected, the intervention may nevertheless have long-lasting consequences.

For example, as part of the Consortium for Longitudinal Studies, Lazar and Darlington conducted a systematic analysis of a longitudinal follow-up on a group of eleven of the most rigorous educational early intervention programs started in the 1960s, several years after the end of the interventions. The interventions produced IQ gains that lasted for up to three or four years after the end of the programs, but these gains were not permanent and had dissipated by the last follow-up.[7] They

---

[7] However, in some intensive intervention programs cognitive differences may be more long lasting: "There appears to be a broad consensus that preschool Head Start-type programs – as have been implemented in the past – do not produce lasting improvements in

found, however, that significantly fewer children who had participated in the early intervention programs had been assigned to special education classes and fewer had been held back a grade. Perhaps this is due to lasting differences in achievement orientation and self-evaluation. Thus, successful interventions may include teaching self-selection skills that have multiplicative effects rather than directly creating permanent cognitive benefits.

We are not suggesting here that all the impact of the gene–environment correlations could be captured by multipliers set in motion by environmental interventions that are independent of genes. Genetic effects will clearly always exist and some multipliers will not be sustained, even if successfully initiated by environmental factors. We are merely suggesting that some of the effect of active g-e correlations that generates the strong individual differences observed in behavior genetic studies could possibly be set into motion by such catalysts, so that a portion of the gap between the genetically advantaged and the genetically disadvantaged would be closed. The intervention efforts discussed earlier offer a few hints how such processes might possibly work, and suggest the direction that future empirical work might profitably take.

CONCLUSIONS

In this chapter we have reviewed recent theoretical and empirical work on various classes of multiplier effects, arguing that these hold promise for explaining conundrums that have dogged psychologists for the past twenty years (such as the seeming paradox between behavior genetic findings within cohorts and strong environmental effects across cohorts). We have also attempted to redefine the challenge posed for interventionists. Instead of attempting to identify a powerful environmental factor that can boost competence (for example, early enrichment programs), the most enduring effects are to be accomplished by finding a powerful genetic factor to drive self-selection of environments that can be *proxied* by an environmental factor. In the course of doing this, we have tried to shift the search for successful intervention candidates from environmental factors to genetic factors. This counterintuitive notion is made sensible by the "sensitive dependence on initial conditions"

cognitive ability, unless they are extremely intensive. One such intensive program, however, is the Abecedarian Project, the results of which showed a five-point IQ difference in favor of the treatment group at age 15." (Reifman, 2000).

shown by the multiplier effects described here. The new work on multipliers strongly suggests that we will make more progress if we search for a catalyst to jump-start the process instead of a way to directly change the environment for the better. Thus, the child as a ball in Waddington's epigenetic landscape (Waddington, 1957) must be nudged off the side of the hill that provides proximal processes that continuously provide more differentiated and complex reactions to the child's own behaviors, rather than allowed to roll down the other side into a suboptimal outcome *or* be pushed, at great expense, into a better outcome at a later date.

References

Azmitia, M. (1988). Peer interaction and problem solving: When are two heads better than one? *Child Development, 59*, 87–96.

Bast, J. & Reitsma, P. (1998). Analyzing the development of individual differences in terms of Matthew effects in reading: Results from a Dutch longitudinal study. *Developmental Psychology, 34*(6), 1373–1399.

Bouchard, T. J., Jr., Lykken, D. T., Tellegan, A. C., & McGue, M. (1998). Genes, drives, environment and experience: EPD theory – revised. In C. P. Benbow & D. Lubinski (Eds.), *Psychometrics and social issues concerning intellectual talent* (pp. 141–173). Baltimore, MD: Johns Hopkins Press.

Bronfenbrenner, U., & Ceci, S. J. (1993). Heredity, environment, and the question "how." In R. Plomin & G. McClearn (Eds.), *Nature nurture & psychology* (pp 313–324). Washington, DC: American Psychological Association.

Bronfenbrenner, U., & Ceci, S. J. (1994). Nature-nurture in developmental perspective: A bioecological theory. *Psychological Review, 101*, 568–586.

Ceci, S. J. (1996). *On intelligence: A bio-ecological treatise on intellectual development* (2d ed.). Cambridge, MA: Harvard University Press.

Chandler, M. J., & Boutilier, R. G. (1992). The development of dynamic system reasoning. *Human Development, 35*, 121–137.

Cook, T. K., Appleton, H., Conner, R., Shaffer, A., Tamkin, G., & Weber, S. J. (1975). *Sesame Street revisited.* NY: Russell Sage Foundation Publication.

Detterman, D. K. (2000). Tests, affirmative action in university admissions, and the American way. *Psychology, Public Policy, and Law, 6*(1) 44–55.

Dickens, W.T. & Flynn, J. R. (2001a). Heritability estimates versus large environmental effects: The IQ paradox resolved. *Psychological Review, 108*(2), 346–69.

Dickens, W. T., & Flynn. J. R., (2001b, April 21). Great leap forward, *New Scientist, vol. 170*, no 2287, pp. 44–47.

Ehrenberg, R. E., Brewer, D. J., Gamoran, A., & Willms, J. D. (2001). Class size and student achievement. *Psychological Science in the Public Interest, 2*, 1–30.

Ericsson, K. A., Krampe, R. T., & Tesch Roemer, C. (1993). The role of deliberate practice in the acquisition of expert performance. *Psychological Review, 100*(3), 363–406.

Flynn, J. (2001). The history of the American mind in the 20th century: A scenario to explain IQ gains over time and a case for the irrelevance of *g*. Otago, New Zealand. Unpublished manuscript.

Gleick, J. (1987). *Chaos: Making a new science*. New York: Viking Penguin, Inc.

Hamilton, B. H., Nickerson, J. A., & Owan, H. (2001, April 19). *Team incentives and worker heterogeneity: An empirical analysis of the impact of teams on productivity and participation*. Organizational Behavior Workshop, Cornell University. Unpublished manuscript.

Hativa, N. (1988). Computer-based drill and practice in arithmetic: Widening the gap between high- and low-achieving students. *American Educational Review Journal, 25*, 366–397.

Howe, M. J. A. (1989). *Fragments of genius: The strange feats of idiots savants*. London: Routledge.

Howe, M. J. A., Davidson, J. W., & Sloboda, J. A. (1998). Innate talents: Reality or myth? *Behavioral and Brain Sciences, 21*(3), 399–442.

Jensen, A. R. (1997). The puzzle of nongenetic variance. In R. J. Sternberg & E. L. Grigorenko (Eds.), *Intelligence, heredity, and environment* (pp. 42–88). New York: Cambridge University Press.

Lazar, I., & Darlington, R. B. (1982). Lasting effects of early education: A report from the Consortium for Longitudinal Studies. *Monographs of the Society for Research in Child Development, 47*(2-sup-3), 1–151.

Loehlin, J. C., Horn, J. M., & Willerman, L. (1997). Heredity, environment, and IQ in the Texas Adoption Project. In R. J. Sternberg & E. L. Grigorenko (Eds.), *Intelligence, heredity, and environment* (pp. 105–125). New York: Cambridge University Press.

McClearn, G. E., Johansson, B., Berg, S., Pederson, N. L., Petrill, S. A., & Plomin, R. (1997). Substantial genetic influence on cognitive abilities in twins 80 or more years old. *Science, 276*, 1560–1563.

Merton, R. K. (1968). The Matthew effect in science. *Science, 159*, 56–63.

Petrill, S. A., Plomin, R., Berg, S., Johansson, B., Pedersen, N. L., Ahern, F., & McClearn, G. E. (1998). Genetic and environmental relationship between general and specific cognitive abilities in twins age 80 and older. *Psychological Science, 9*, 183–189.

Reifman, A. (2000). Revisiting The Bell Curve. *Psycoloquy, 11*.

Riksen-Walraven, J. M. (1978). Effects of caregiver behavior on habituation rate and self-efficacy in infants. *International Journal of Behavioral Development, 1*, 105–130.

Scarr, S. (1992). Developmental theories for the 1990s: Development and individual differences. *Child Development, 63*, 1–19.

Scarr, S. (1997). Behavior-genetic and socialization theories of intelligence: Truce and reconciliation. In R. J. Sternberg & E. L. Grigorenko (Eds.), *Intelligence, heredity, and environment* (pp. 3–41). New York: Cambridge University Press.

Scarr, S., & McCartney, K. (1983). How people make their own environments: A theory of genotype → environment effects. *Child Development, 54*, 424–435.

Shaywitz, B. A., Holford, T. R., Holahan, J. M., Fletcher, J. M., Steubing, K. K., Francis, D. J, & Shaywitz, S. E. (1995). A Matthew effect for IQ but not for reading: Results from a longitudinal study. *Reading Research Quarterly, 30*(4), 894–906.

Smith, L. B., & Thelen, E. (1993). *A dynamic systems approach to development: Applications.* Cambridge, MA: MIT Press.

Stanovich, K. E. (1986). Matthew effects in reading: Some consequences of individual differences in the acquisition of literacy. *Reading Research Quarterly, 21*(4), 360–406.

Stoolmiller, M. (1998). Correcting estimates of shared environmental variance for range restriction in adoption studies using a truncated multivariate normal model. *Behavior Genetics, 28*(6), 429–441.

Stoolmiller, M. (1999). Implications of the restricted range of family environments for estimates of heritability and nonshared environment in behavior-genetic adoption studies. *Psychological Bulletin, 125*(4), 392–409.

Thelen, E. (1992). Development as a dynamic system. *Current Directions in Cognitive Science, 1*(6), 189–193.

Thelen, E., & Smith, L. B. (1994). *A dynamic systems approach to the development of cognition and action.* Cambridge, MA: MIT Press.

Van Geert, P. (1991). A dynamic systems model of cognitive and language growth. *Psychological Review, 98*(1), 3–53.

Waddington, C. H. (1957). *The strategy of the genes.* Winchester, MA: Allen & Unwin.

Williams, W. M., & Ceci, S. J. (1997). Are Americans becoming more or less alike?: Trends in race, class, and ability differences in intelligence. *American Psychologist, 52*(11), 1226–1235.

4

The Search for General Abilities and Basic Capacities

Theoretical Implications from the Modifiability and Complexity of Mechanisms Mediating Expert Performance

K. Anders Ericsson

The search within the social sciences for stable, invariant, and quantifiable attributes of living organisms closely parallels historic investigations in the hard sciences in search of characteristics of physical phenomena. The revolutionary advances in physics in the sixteenth through eighteenth centuries allowed scientists to develop lawful relations between characteristics of objects such as weight, size, and velocity with their subsequent "behavior" (trajectories) under specified physical conditions (for example, collisions between objects). Similarly psychology, when it emerged as an independent science in the nineteenth century, approached its own quest to uncover laws of perception and memory under the guidance of pioneering scientists such as Hermann Ebbinghaus, with comparable scientific methods. Psychology's focus was not, however, on the characteristics of physical objects, but on the search for invariant processes and attributes of individuals that could be quantified and used to predict human behavior and achievement. These same theoretical frameworks were subsequently extended to describe individual differences in ability, and finally used to predict performance in schools and other everyday settings.

In this chapter I review the search for general ability and basic capacities. I begin by briefly sketching the history of the study of individual differences and the methods pioneering investigators employed to develop theoretical conceptions of ability and capacity. Most important,

This research was supported by the FSCW/Conradi Endowment Fund of Florida State University Foundation. The author gratefully acknowledges the thoughtful and constructive comments given by Ray Amirault for an earlier draft.

I discuss the historical arguments for the existence of ability and capacity, efforts to measure these quantities, and proposals for the biological mechanisms mediating the effects of ability and capacity on performance. I document how the study of extreme expressions of ability was viewed by pioneering investigators (such as Franz Joseph Gall [1758–1828] and Sir Francis Galton [1822–1911]) as the most promising source to find empirical evidence for the existence of underlying capacities. It was found that even the study of these eminent individuals made it difficult to identify the specific innate characteristics that mediated their superiority, encouraging Galton to develop compelling arguments to indirectly prove their existence. Galton's original arguments are still consistent with more recent theoretical approaches, and I have attempted to capture his fundamental assumptions about the nature of individual differences in abilities and capacities. These fundamental assumptions are discussed, along with a review of recent studies on expert and exceptional performance. The final portion of the chapter demonstrates how the theoretical framework of expert performance offers alternative perspectives on the structure and acquisition of ability, especially high levels of ability.

HISTORICAL BACKGROUND TO THE APPROACHES STUDYING ABILITIES AND CAPACITIES

The search for stable attributes of individuals to explain individual differences in behavior is a relatively recent endeavor. During the Middle Ages it was generally believed that God controlled the outcome of all events and actively guided the destiny of people and their actions. During this period, the desire to search for causes of behavior in the physical and biological attributes of individuals was considered blasphemous. In successive centuries, scientific advances revealed that our natural environment was governed by stable regularities, and that God influenced events, not with moment-to-moment interventions, but by the creation of natural laws. This "realization" permitted scientists the opportunity for careful observation and experimental analysis by which they were able to uncover these laws, and use such laws to accurately predict the "behavior" of objects.

Scientists and philosophers eventually applied these same types of analyses to human behavior in an attempt to discover the stable attributes of human beings. However, the everyday behavior of human adults, unlike the behavior of physical objects, varies considerably across situations as a function of motivation, and thus makes stable assessments of abilities difficult and controversial. It was therefore natural for the early investigators to seek out individuals with extraordinary abilities where the exceptional achievements were not questioned, therefore producing less controversial assessments of stable attributes of human beings.

Franz Joseph Gall and Phrenology

In the eighteenth century, Gall made the revolutionary claim that the size and shape of the brain determined individuals' personality and abilities. This theory is often described as the first major step toward a science of the brain (Young, 1970). Gall also proposed that the brain areas associated with certain abilities could be found by looking for "bumps" on the skulls of individuals with extreme manifestations of a certain attribute. According to Young (1970, p. 33, original italics but underlining added): "The main criterion was that it be manifested *independent* of other characteristics of the individual or the species. When he found men or animals with an <u>eminent talent or propensity</u> he examined the form of the head for a <u>cranial prominence. He collected</u> and compared as many such correlations as he could find." Gall's method was thus based on the assumption that when "some particular quality is manifested in a much higher degree of activity than the others, it is fundamental" (Gall, quoted by Young, 1970, p. 36).

Gall's initial efforts into examination of his theory provided cases that established new information about the structure of the brain, but as the number of cases kept coming in, a growing number of counterexamples began to arise as well (Young, 1970) even as they were argued away. One example of such a "counterexample" included the head shapes of statues of famous people with clear traits and abilities, which presented in the statue no obvious head bumps or cranial protrusions as predicted by Gall's theory. These cases were simply rejected, however, as incorrect renderings of the head by the sculptors. Other inconsistencies were explained away by arguing that the expected talent might have been lost to excesses or diseases. Eventually, more challenging counterexamples emerged. For example, "a young boy was found with remarkable calculating ability and a depression where the prominence for numbers should have been" (p. 43), and Descartes' skull was found to be very small in the regions where the rational faculties were predicted to be located. Although complex explanations could be generated to explain these counterexamples, it was becoming increasingly clear that the theoretical framework's ability to make precise predictions was flawed, and the approach eventually lost favor.

Sir Francis Galton and "Heritable Genius"

If Gall pioneered the search for biological markers of ability, then Sir Francis Galton provided the theoretical rationale and methodology to find the innate biological attributes and mechanisms that would explain eminent achievement and ability. In his famous book, *Heritable Genius*, Galton presented evidence suggesting the heritable influence on height and body size, and more important, an argument that *similar innate mechanisms must determine mental capacities*. Galton (1869/1979, pp. 31–32, underlining added) argues, "Now, if this be the case with stature, then it will be true as regard to every other physical feature – as circumference of head, size of brain, weight of grey matter, number of brain fibres, etc., and thence, a step on which no physiologist will hesitate, as regards mental capacity."

Galton (1869/1979) clearly acknowledged the need for training to reach high levels of performance in any domain. He argued, however, that improvements are rapid only in the *beginning* of training and that subsequent increases become increasingly smaller, until "maximal performance becomes a rigidly determinate quantity" (p. 15). According to Galton, *the relevant heritable capacities set the upper bound for the attainable level in physical and mental activities*. Once the training benefits have been attained through sufficient practice, then the immutable limit for performance is attained, "where he cannot by any education or exertion overpass" (p. 15), and the maximal performance is achieved that "his nature has rendered him capable of performing" (p. 16). Galton's immutable characteristics limiting performance must, by definition, have had an origin different from training, and thus, by inference, *must have been innately endowed*. Galton's argument for the importance of innate factors in elite performance is highly compelling, and thus has had a lasting impact on researchers. I critically review this argument's fundamental assumptions later in this chapter.

It is important to note that Galton never was able to pinpoint which *specific* attributes or biological mechanisms determined "heritable" differences in various capacities. Nevertheless, he pioneered the methodology of measuring individual differences in mental performance. He also developed the correlation coefficient as a measure of how closely related different variables and factors are for a given sample of subjects.

The Inductive Search for Mental Abilities and Capacities

Toward the beginning of the twentieth century, numerous investigators collected data on the relation between performance and mental tests measuring basic cognitive functions of memory, attention, and perception. However, the patterns of correlation between tests measuring similar basic functions were not consistent across studies, and gave the appearance of being spurious (Anastasi, 1988; Brown and Thomson, 1921; Spearman, 1904). Much of the large variability could be attributed to the testing of school children who differed greatly in age, or the use of small samples of adults. However, when Wissler (1901) tested basic mental processes on over 150 college students, the correlations were low, and most not reliably different from zero. The correlation between these mental tests and the students' grades in different academic subjects were in the 0.0 to 0.3 range, even though the correlation between grades was mostly in the 0.5 to 0.7 range. Successful replications of Wissler's findings led Aikens, Thorndike, and Hubbell (1902) to argue that the tests measuring "speed of association" were not reliably correlated, and ability differences in the quickness of association of ideas was a myth. Other studies showed that performance on these types of tests could be improved with practice, but that these improvements were remarkably specific and did not transfer to other tests and types of stimulus materials (see Woodworth and Thorndike, 1901, for a pioneering study).

In a very influential paper, Charles Spearman (1904) proposed how one could use statistical techniques for controlling for factors contaminating the influence of intelligence, such as participants' age and relevant experience, and to correct for observational errors and lack of test reliability. Spearman initiated a research tradition that developed methods for analyzing the full matrix of correlations between a large number of psychometric tests to identify latent factors that could account for the pattern of covariance. He found evidence for clusters of correlated tests in the same domain that could be explained by relevant experience and basic domain-specific abilities. Most important, he found evidence for a general factor, referred to by the simple letter g, that "explains the correlations that exist between even the most diverse sorts of cognitive performance" (Spearman, 1923, p. 5). Spearman found it difficult to conceive what such a general mechanism might be, and speculated: "the factor was taken, pending further information, to consist in something of the nature of an 'energy' or 'power' which serves in common the whole cortex (or possibly, even the whole nervous system)" (p. 5). In later books, Spearman (1937) argued that g should "supplant all current determinations of 'mental age' or 'general intelligence'" (p. 241) and that its suggested innate nature would revolutionize the social sciences.

The complex statistical procedures used by Spearman and others to extract general latent variables such as g from the massive bodies of data and patterns of correlations across large populations of individuals made it impossible to study and capture these phenomena in individual subjects. Most investigators, however, accepted Spearman's proposed procedures to separate general capacities from domain-specific cognitive skills and knowledge, and the idea of *neural hardware* (discussed later) had an important influence on subsequent research on individual differences.

From Associative Learning to Information Processing Models of Human Cognition

During the reign of behaviorism (c. 1920 through c. 1950), the focus of research in general psychology was on mechanisms mediating learning of simple associations in long-term memory (LTM). Consequently, the research of learning never encountered the need to propose limits on processing capacity and associated interindividual differences. It was only when researchers became interested in contrasting the speed of human performance to that of machines and computers that investigators found it appropriate to describe human performance as limited by channel capacities. When scientists in the 1950s started to address complex cognitive processes such as *concept formation, problem solving*, and *decision*, they saw important parallels between computers and humans in that *both could be viewed as instances of information-processing systems*. Newell and Simon (1972) proposed a theory explicating a set of specified information-processing constraints for humans and described how human information-processing models could be designed for a wide range of cognitive tasks. These models could be implemented as completely specified models in the form of computer programs that could produce performance on laboratory tasks that matched the observable behavior and performance of humans.

The computer as metaphor for human cognition suggests a distinction between software and hardware. Humans can typically easily acquire new knowledge and skills, which is roughly comparable to the ease of exchanging and revising software (that is, computer programs and an operating system) on a computer. In fact, the observable behavior and performance of humans on a wide range of laboratory tasks can be reproduced by information-processing models implemented as computer programs. On the other hand, the hardware of the computer with its central processor and internal and external memories is *fixed*, and such hardware components determine the available memory capacity and overall processing speed. In a similar manner, the basic parameters of the nervous system and the brain in adult humans were typically believed to be fixed and thus not modifiable by experience and training. Hence, the neural "hardware" would seem a very plausible locus for innate differences between individuals in basic memory capacity and speed of elementary processes that would influence the performance in most tasks in differing degrees. Ever since George Miller's (1956) classical paper on the magical number of seven, the limits of short-term memory (STM) have been seen as quantifiable capacity of human cognition and a critical bottleneck for processing a possible source of individual differences. Newell and Simon (1972, p. 865) write that "Differences in the capacity of STM, for example, probably play a large role in the functional difference between the very young and the mature, and between those we consider intellectually sub-normal and those we consider normal." In the subsequent three decades, investigators have become interested in the related ideas of limits of working memory and/or attention as likely sources of individual differences in processing capacity and general ability (Miyake and Shah, 1999).

Some Fundamental Assumptions in the Search of Basic Capacities and General Abilities

My historical sketch shows that eminent psychologists have taken for granted that individual differences – especially those of outstanding individuals – can be explained by some measurable underlying mechanism that has a biological and innate basis, much as we know that the length of bones determine height and body size in a very heritable manner (compare Galton's suggestive analogy). If the neurological mechanisms have innately determined limits (like the length of most bones in our bodies), these limits cannot be improved by training and, by inference, individual differences in maximal performance are innately fixed.

Rather than simply accepting this inference, I review the empirical evidence on the modifiability of performance and its mediating biological mechanisms as a result of extended practice. My review will show that *the mediating biological mechanisms and the observable performance can be improved substantially even when individuals are highly experienced*. I also reject Galton's hypothesis that performance after practice has removed all trainable aspects, and thus becomes rigidly constrained by fixed innate capacities. Drawing on the research on expert performance, I will review evidence demonstrating that *expert performance is mediated by complex modifiable representations that allow experts to exhibit faster speed, superior selection of actions, and more precise motor execution*.

In the third and final section, I discuss the major challenges to any account of individual differences based primarily on acquisition. What are the processes that mediate the construction of complex mechanisms, and why do only a small fraction of individuals in a domain reach the highest levels? My conclusion will discuss the theoretical implications of the structure of an expert's acquired superior performance for the current practice of "quantifying" latent variables – such as capacities and abilities – that are hypothesized to determine individual differences in performance.

THE MODIFIABILITY OF PERFORMANCE AND ITS MEDIATING MECHANISMS

If psychometric tests measure basic nonmodifiable capacities and processes, then one would predict that this performance should be highly reliable across multiple test occasions. In particular, Galton's hypothesis would predict increased stability of performance and greater range of individual differences with opportunities for practice.

In my introductory review, I remark that investigators in the beginning of the twentieth century found substantial practice effects with laboratory tasks designed to measure simple mental functions. Even psychometric tests were shown to have a similar problem with practice effects. Greene (1937) found that college students' performances on a large number of psychometric tests improved substantially after they had taken the tests several times. Some psychometric tests, such as Koh's cube design and Minnesota space relation tests, showed between

50 percent and 100 percent improvement. Other tests, such as auditory digit span, showed intermediate improvement in a range around 10 percent. Some tests measuring speed of movement and sensory discriminations showed negligible gains. However, one should not infer from Greene's study that sensory judgments could not be improved by practice. In an extensive review Gibson (1969) showed that when the amount of practice with feedback increased, improvements on sensory discrimination and other types of perceptual tasks were large.

Large Practice Effects after Extended Practice

One of the most striking and reproducible processing constraints for humans concerns the limited capacity of their STM (Miller, 1956). In the 1960s and 1970s, investigators repeatedly demonstrated college students' inability to repeat correctly more than around nine presented digits – roughly a phone number with an unfamiliar area code. Would it be possible to increase the capacity of STM, commonly believed to be the primary constraint on information processing?

Bill Chase and I (Chase and Ericsson, 1982; Ericsson, 1988; Ericsson, Chase, and Faloon, 1980) recruited college students to be repeatedly tested on the standard test of STM – the digit span – for an hour every other day for many weeks and months. When we tested their STM before the start of the training, their recall performance was normal and limited to around seven digits. All the trained students increased their memory performance by 200 percent to over twenty digits after around fifty hours of practice on this task. After two hundred to four hundred hours, two of them improved their recall by more than 1000 percent (over eighty digits). Experimental analyses showed that the students had acquired a memory skill for rapid retrievable storage in LTM, and Ericsson and Kintsch (1995) showed that the same mechanisms of long-term working memory (LTWM) mediate reading and comprehension – skills attained by all educated adults. Furthermore, memory experts and expert performers are shown to acquire related LTWM mechanisms to improve their ability to expand their functional working memory (Ericsson and Lehmann, 1996). For example, these LTWM mechanisms allow chess masters to plan out possible move sequences mentally while selecting moves to a degree that they are able to play blindfold chess, that is, to play chess without a visible chess board.

The effects of specialized training are by no means limited to memory and other cognitive capacities. With specific practice, speed of performance increases considerably, and even physiological capacities can be markedly improved (Ericsson, Krampe, and Tesch-Römer, 1993). For example, Astrand and Rohdahl (1977) reported that the ability to sustain powerful activity could increase by over 5000 percent in some group studies. Let me also give one striking example of the effects of practice for a familiar activity often used to assess physical fitness where the improvements are far greater than most people believe possible. Physically fit adults, such as college students in a physical education class can make around twenty push-ups in a row, with a range from eight to thirty-two. However, in 1966 one individual was able, after extended practice, to achieve a new record for consecutive push-ups and completed over six thousand in a row. This record did not last long and has been broken again and again. The current record is over twenty-six thousand and is limited to the number of push-ups completed within twenty-four hours. This amounts to an improvement of push-up performance of 100,000 percent or an average of a completed push-up every three seconds for twenty-four hours straight. The possibility of changes in performance on tasks originally designed to measure stable capacities, such as anaerobic fitness, boggles the mind.

The Applicability of the Hardware versus Software Distinction for Biological Systems

When extended practice is permitted, the modifiability of the human body and its nervous system differs greatly from that of computers and other types of machines. Humans and other biological systems are able to change their "hardware," that is, their cells and organs. In contrast to machines, humans are able to heal wounds and broken bones, as well as build their organs to assist the body in adapting to repeated strain induced by practice and performance. Humans do not wear out from performing repetitive action (as long as the actions do not seriously injure tissue, and sufficient recuperation periods are allowed to avoid repeated stress injuries). Animals and humans are able to adapt over time, and will increase efficiency of repetitive actions (Bernstein, 1996). For example, it is well documented that adults have to engage in intense aerobic exercise to improve aerobic fitness. Specifically, young adults have to exercise at least a couple of times each week for at least thirty minutes per session with a sustained heart rate that is 70 percent of their maximal level (around 140 beats per minute for a maximal heart rate of 200). Similarly, improvements of strength and endurance require that individuals strain themselves on a weekly basis and each training session push the associated physiological systems outside the comfort zone, stimulating physiological growth and adaptation (Ericsson, 2001a, 2001b).

When the human body is put under exceptional strain, a whole range of extraordinary physiological processes are activated. For example, when an adult donates a kidney, the remaining kidney is insufficient to perform the clearance of waste products from the body. This insufficiency leads to a chemical reaction that signals the remaining kidney to grow in size to make up for the lost functioning of the missing kidney. During a period of a few weeks, the remaining kidney grows by around 70 percent to handle the increased load. Similar adaptations occur when individuals start training for long-distance running. Sustained running causes an oxygen deficiency in the affected muscles, which results in physiological strain that causes capillaries to grow and develop around the muscles within the first few weeks of regular training to permit muscle growth and development. Drawing on similar types of mechanisms, specific changes in various areas of the brains of animals have been induced by different types of physical activity (Black, Isaacs, Anderson, Alcantara, and Greenough, 1990). In fact, recent reviews (Buonomano and Merzenich, 1998; Kolb and Whishaw, 1998) show that the function and structure of the brain is far more adaptable to experience, especially early and extended experience, such as the effects of early practice by expert musicians (Elbert, Pantev, Wienbruch, Rockstoh, and Taub, 1995; Schlaug, Jancke, Huang, Staiger, and Steinmetz, 1995).

Adults are able to generate demanding, exceptional situations for their bodies by engaging in vigorous practice with a regular frequency and gradually increased intensity over extended time. The long-term responses to these physiological challenges allow elite athletes to transcend the typical physiological capacities necessary for everyday life. When we include all the evidence for training-related changes in the size of hearts, thickness of bones, and allocation of cortical areas in the brain, we see that virtually all aspects of humans' bodies and nervous systems are modifiable, with the exception of height and body size (Ericsson, 2001a, 2001b).

These and other examples raise doubt that fixed innate capacities limit an individual's ability to reach the highest levels of performance. Reviews of expert performance (Ericsson, 1996; Ericsson and Lehmann, 1996) have uncovered no evidence of characteristics that are critical to expert performance that cannot also be altered or circumvented with extended practice. There are some well-documented exceptions to this general principle, such as physical height and body size. (There is an obvious advantage to being a taller player in basketball and a shorter participant in gymnastics, and there is no known practice activity that can increase the length of bones and the associated height of humans.) When one excludes height-related characteristics, however, recent reviews (Ericsson and Lehmann, 1996; Howe, Davidson, and Sloboda, 1998) have not found any accepted evidence that innate characteristics are required for healthy adults to attain elite performance. When appropriately designed training is maintained with full concentration on a regular basis for weeks, months, or years, there appears to be no firm empirical evidence for innate capacities besides physical size that limits the attainment of high level performance. Consequently, height and body size appear to be qualitatively different from other anatomical and physiological characteristics, and rather than being typical examples of a general rule, as Sir Francis Galton suggested, the characteristics appear to be rare exceptions.

Perhaps the best evidence against a well-defined upper bound for individuals' capacity to perform is found in professional domains, where experienced individuals have repeatedly shown that they are able to increase their attained stable performance when they are sufficiently motivated (Ericsson et al., 1993). Similar increases in performance at the highest levels can be inferred from the improvements of performance across long periods of time. The best evidence for the value of current training methods and practice schedules comes from historical comparisons (Ericsson et al., 1993; Lehmann and Ericsson, 1998). Historically, very dramatic improvements in the level of performance are found in the sports domain. In competitions such as the marathon and swimming events, many serious amateurs of today could easily beat the gold medal winners of the early Olympic Games. For example, after the fourth Olympic Games in 1908, the Olympic committee almost prohibited double somersault dives because these dives were thought to be dangerous and could not be controlled. Today, divers have not only mastered double somersaults, but dives of far greater complexity.

This remarkable adaptability at the level of physiological, behavioral, and cognitive systems presents a major challenge to the view that nonmodifiable capacities and characteristics limit the attainable performance of individuals. On the other hand, these findings raise new questions, such as *what is the structure of skilled performance that allows it to be gradually changed and improved?*

THE COMPLEXITY OF THE MECHANISMS MEDIATING
THE SUPERIOR PERFORMANCE OF EXPERTS

In my historical sketch, I describe Galton's compelling argument for why superior performance after sufficient experience would be constrained by general capacities that could not be modified. In light of the demonstrated modifiability of human performance after extended practice, however, we now face the challenge of identifying the detailed mechanisms that allow individual experts to keep improving and eventually attain and exhibit vastly superior performance.

Ericsson and Smith (1991) proposed that, in order to describe these mechanisms, we need to identify and examine individuals who are able to perform repeatedly at a higher level than others. It would be reasonable, too, to identify experts within a *wide variety* of domains and study their superior performance in these differing areas. Finding individuals with superior performance turned out to be surprisingly challenging, because experts in many domains, such as investing, auditing, and clinical therapy, have not been found to perform at a level superior to other experienced individuals on representative tasks in their domains (see Ericsson and Lehmann, 1996, for a review). For example, highly experienced psychotherapists are not more successful in treatment of patients than novice therapists (Dawes, 1994) and stock market experts and bankers are not able to forecast stock prices reliably better than university teachers and students (Stael von Holstein, 1972). Consequently, Ericsson and Smith (1991) argued that the scientific study of expert and exceptional performance *must be restricted to individuals with reliably superior performance characteristics.* Once we have found individuals who can repeatedly perform at an exceptional level, then we should attempt to capture and reproduce their performance in the laboratory so we can use standard process tracing and experimental techniques to assess the structure of the mechanisms mediating their exceptional performance.

In many domains there have evolved procedures for fair measurement of superior performance. Over time, methods of measuring performance have become extremely precise, and a tenth or a hundredth of a second may distinguish the winner in swimming and sprinting events. In many sports, the conditions of competition are highly standardized so that it is common to use an individual's best performance at local and regional competitions to assess his or her qualifications to participate in national and international competitions.

Competitions in music, dance, and chess have a similar long history of attempting to design standardized situations that allow fair competition between individuals. In all these domains, elite individuals reliably outperform less accomplished individuals. Expert performers can reliably demonstrate their performance any time when required during competitions and training, and are thus also capable of reproducing their superior performance under controlled laboratory conditions.

Recent reviews (Ericsson, 2001a, 2001b; Ericsson and Lehmann, 1996) have shown that the performances of experts have been successfully reproduced in the laboratory, where methods of process tracing, such as analysis of think-aloud protocols and eye movements have been applied to assessing mechanisms that mediate experts' superior performances. In this chapter I briefly discuss three general characteristics of distinguishing expert performance: *the ability to select superior actions, the ability to generate rapid reactions,* and *the ability to control movement production.*

The Ability to Select Superior Actions

Most of us have had the experience of facing a superior opponent in chess or other competitive games. Whatever move we select, the expert has already anticipated the move, seemingly remaining several steps ahead of our strategy. In his pioneering work on chess expertise, de Groot (1946/1978) was the first to repeatedly reproduce this type of superior performance in the laboratory. He instructed good and world-class chess players to think aloud while they selected the best move in a set of unfamiliar chess positions taken from games of chess masters. The superior quality of the moves that the world-class chess players selected were closely associated with their higher chess skill, and later research validated the move-selection task as the best available assessment of chess skill (Ericsson and Lehmann, 1996; Ericsson, Patel, and Kintsch, 2000). Verbal report evidence revealed that all of the chess players first perceived, then interpreted, the chess position in order to retrieve potential moves from memory. Promising moves were then evaluated by mentally planning out the consequences of sequences of move exchanges. During this evaluation, even world-class players were able to discover better moves. Hence, *the performance of experts is mediated by increasingly complex control processes.* Although chess experts can rapidly retrieve appropriate actions for a new chess position (compare Calderwood et al., 1988 and Gobet and Simon, 1996), their move selection can be further improved by planning, reasoning, and evaluation (Ericsson et al., 2000). The superior ability of highly skilled players to plan out consequences of move sequences is well documented. In fact, chess masters are able to play blindfold, without a visible board showing the current position, at a relatively high level (Karpov, 1995; Koltanowski, 1985). Experiments show that chess masters are able to follow chess games in their head when the experimenter reads a sequence of moves from a chess game, and are also able to retrieve any aspect of the position when probed by the experimenter (see Ericsson and Oliver's studies described in Ericsson and Staszewski, 1989). Highly skilled players can even play several simultaneous games mentally, thus maintaining multiple chess positions in memory (Saariluoma, 1991).

The same paradigm has been adapted to study other types of expertise where experts have been presented with representative situations, such as simulated game situations, and asked to respond as rapidly and accurately as possible. Recent reviews (Ericsson, 1996; Ericsson and Kintsch, 1995) show that expert performers have acquired refined mental representations to maintain access to relevant information and to support flexible reasoning about an encountered task or situation. In most domains better performers are able to rapidly encode and store relevant information for representative tasks in memory so that they can efficiently manipulate the information mentally. For example, with increased chess skill, chess players are able to plan more deeply, generate longer mental sequences of chess moves, and evaluate the associated consequences. Similar evidence for mental representations has been shown for motor-skill experts such as snooker players and musicians (Ericsson and Lehmann, 1996).

The Ability to Generate Rapid Reactions

It is a common belief that athletes are able to hit fast balls or pucks because they can see better (superior vision) and exhibit greater quickness (faster reactions). However, expert athletes cannot be distinguished from their less skilled peers by superior basic abilities or faster speed on simple RT tasks. The superior performance of such athletes has been shown to reflect specialized perceptual skills, and not superiority on standard tests of visual ability (Williams, David, and Williams, 1999).

The rapid reactions of athletes, such as hockey goalies and tennis players, have been found to reflect acquired skills involving the anticipation of future events. For example, when highly skilled tennis players are preparing to return a serve, they study the movements of the opponent leading up to contact between the ball and the racquet to identify the type of spin and general direction of the ball. Given the ballistic and bio-mechanical nature of a serve, it is often possible for skilled players to anticipate outcomes far better than chance can explain. Thus, the advantage of expert athletes reflects primarily anticipatory skills rather than an innate neural speed advantage over their less accomplished peers (Abernethy, 1991).

Mediating cognitive representations can similarly account for the superior speed of expert typists and the faster rate of their typing movements. The key to the expert typists' advantage involves the ability to look beyond the word they are currently typing (Salthouse, 1984). By looking further ahead they are able to acquire skills to prepare future key strokes in advance, moving relevant fingers toward their desired locations on the keyboard. This finding has been confirmed by analysis of high-speed films of expert typists and experimental studies in which expert typists have been prevented from looking ahead. It is important to note that novice typists use an entirely different strategy and usually type only a small group of letters at a time in a piecemeal fashion. The perceptual skill to prepare sequences of typing movements in advance to allow continuous typing at a high speed must have been acquired later at a more advanced level of skill.

The Ability to Control Movement Production

Expert performers often confront unfamiliar situations where they have to generate complex sequences of movements. For example, when expert musicians perform unfamiliar music, a technique called *sight reading*, such experts demonstrate their ability to mentally plan how their fingers will strike the keys to retain control and minimize interference between fingers (Drake and Palmer, 2000; Lehmann and Ericsson, 1993, 1996; Sloboda, 1984; Sloboda, Clarke, Parncutt, and Raekallio, 1998). Evidence for the mental representation of pieces of music comes from studies showing that expert pianists retain control over their motor performance even after a piece of music has been memorized. In laboratory studies expert pianists have been able to perform music without additional practice under changed conditions, such as a different key or a slower tempo (Lehmann and Ericsson, 1995, 1997).

At a higher level of expertise, musicians attain a higher level of control than novices and can repeatedly reproduce a given musical performance with its subtle variations in tempo and volume (Ericsson et al., 1993). Similarly, elite athletes, such as highly skilled golfers, are able to perform the same action, such as putt or drive, several times more consistently than less skilled athletes (Ericsson, 2001a). More generally, empirical studies show that experts acquire mental representations that allow them to internally monitor and compare their concurrent performance with their desired goal, such as the intended musical sound or desired motor action, and thereby continue to improve their control over their performance.

Summary and Comments

When expert performance is studied with representative tasks, we find that the mechanisms that mediate the superior performance are not nonmodifiable basic capacities, but surprisingly complex mechanisms highly specific to the task domain. These experts have acquired mechanisms that transcend the limiting factors constraining a novice's performance. The novices' working memory problems are no longer relevant for experts who rely on acquired memory skills and LTWM to support their extensive working memory needs for planning, reasoning, and evaluation. The novices' problems with slow speed of cognitive and motor processes are made irrelevant with experts' acquired mechanisms mediating superior anticipation. The experts' need for higher consistency and control of motor actions is met with the development of more refined techniques tailored to the specific demands of the superior performance in the respective domain of expertise. As the principal mechanisms mediating experts' performance have not yet been acquired by novices, it is not surprising that the prediction by psychometric tests of individuals' ultimate expert performance has been so disappointingly poor (Ericsson et al., 1993; Ericsson and Lehmann, 1996).

EXPLANATION OF INTER- AND INTRA-INDIVIDUAL DIFFERENCES IN SKILLED PERFORMANCE

Expert performance was shown in the previous section to be mediated by complex mechanisms that allow the performers to increase speed, consistency, and memory capacity only for activities in a given domain of expertise. These findings strongly suggest that expert performance is primarily *acquired*, and that learning mechanisms account for vast improvements in the performance of each individual, because there is no possibility to change a given individual's genetic endowment and associated innate potential.

If skill acquisition can explain striking differences between the performances of the same individual at the introduction to the domain and as a mature elite performer (intra-individual differences), then one is faced with the challenge of accounting for how the same mechanisms could explain large differences in the final performances of adults (inter-individual differences). Traditional theories of skill acquisition in psychology (Fitts and Posner, 1967; Anderson, 1982) do not propose explanations for how expert performance is acquired. They propose mechanisms for how adults reach an acceptable level of performance in everyday and recreational activities, such as typing and playing golf. I will first describe these accounts for typical performance, and then discuss how the acquisition of expert performance differs from the typical.

THE ACQUISITION OF AMATEUR AND TYPICAL LEVELS OF PERFORMANCE

When individuals are first introduced to an activity such as driving a car or typing or playing golf, their primary goal is to reach a level of mastery that will allow them to perform everyday tasks or engage in recreational activities with their friends. During the first phase of learning (Fitts and Posner, 1967), novices try to understand the activity and concentrate on avoiding mistakes, as illustrated in the first part of the lowest curve in Figure 4.1. With more experience in the middle phase of learning, gross mistakes become increasingly rare, performance appears smoother, and learners no longer need to concentrate as hard to perform at an acceptable level. After a limited period of training and experience – frequently less than 50 hours for most ordinary activities, such as typing, playing tennis, and driving a car – an acceptable standard of performance is typically attained. As individuals adapt to a domain and their performance skills become automated, they may lose conscious control over execution of those skills and it may become difficult to intentionally modify the skills. Once the automated phase of learning has been attained, further experience will not markedly improve performance. Consequently, the correlation between amount of experience and performance will be low,

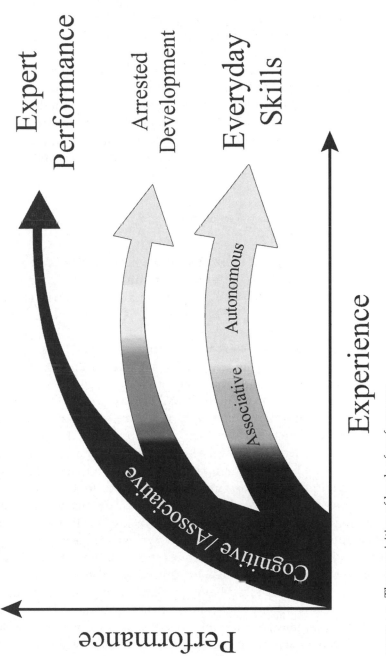

FIGURE 4.1. The acquisition of levels of performance.

and it is common to find recreational golfers, tennis players, and skiers who have not improved their performance after years, or even decades, of regular experience. Similarly, there is a weak relation between performance and length of experience after individuals have gained their initial experience during the first year (Ericsson and Lehmann, 1996). However, these stable levels of attained performance do not reflect a firm upper bound and when individuals are motivated to improve their current level of performance by training they are able to do so, and their performance can gradually be improved, often in a consistent manner (Ericsson et al., 1993).

The Acquisition of Expert Performance and Its Mediating Mechanisms

In contrast to the rapid stabilization of the performance in everyday and recreational activities, performance of future experts continues to improve with more experience for years and decades (Ericsson and Lehmann, 1996). The long preparation time is not an artifact due to the fact that the best performers start in their domains at early ages. Outstanding swimmers, tennis players, musicians, and chess players frequently start at very young ages. The average starting age for elite performers is around six years in many of the major domains (Ericsson et al., 1993). However, experts in most domains continue to improve even after full maturation of the body and brain, which typically happens around the late teens in industrialized countries. The expert performers typically reach their highest level of performance many years, or even decades, later. For example, in many vigorous sports, athletes attain top performance in their mid- to late twenties; for fine-motor athletic activities and the arts and sciences, it is a decade later, in the thirties and forties (Lehman, 1953; Schulz and Curnow, 1988). Furthermore, the most compelling evidence for the role of vast experience in expertise is that even the most "talented" individuals require around ten years of intense involvement before they reach an international level, and for most individuals it takes considerably longer. Simon and Chase (1973) originally proposed the *Ten-Year Rule*, showing that no modern chess master had reached the international level in less than approximately ten years of playing. Subsequent reviews show that the Ten-Year Rule extends to music composition, as well as to sports, science, and the arts (Ericsson et al., 1993). The striking difference between the development of elite and average performance appears unrelated to the overall duration of individuals' experience in the domain, but is rather reflected in the particular types of domain-related activities in which the future experts choose to engage.

The key challenge for aspiring expert performers is to avoid the arrested development associated with automaticity that is seen with everyday activities and instead acquire cognitive skills to support continued learning and improvement. The future expert performer actively counteracts the tendency toward automating performance by engaging in training activities. These training activities are specifically designed, typically with the help of teachers and coaches, to go just beyond the future experts' current reliable level of performance, referred to by Ericsson et al. (1993) as *deliberate practice*. These discrepancies between their actual and desired performance force the future expert performers to exert full concentration during practice, and "stretch" their performance by repeated attempts at higher performance levels. In addition, the raised performance standards cause experts to make mistakes. These failures force future expert performers to continuously refine their task representations so they continue regenerating the initial cognitive phase, as shown by the top curve in Figure 4.1. Experts continue to acquire and refine cognitive mechanisms that mediate continued learning and improvement. These mechanisms are designed to increase the experts' ability to monitor and control these processes (Ericsson, 1996, 1998, 2001a, 2001b). Most significantly, improvement in individuals' reproducible performance requires continued, often increased, levels of deliberate practice to change the mediating mechanisms. Without deliberate practice, the performer is likely to stagnate and prematurely automate his or her performance, as shown in the middle arm of Figure 4.1.

The acquisition of expert performance in most domains of expertise depends critically on access to training resources and follows a predictable course for most individuals. Many types of domains of expertise, such as music, figure skating, and ballet, involve mastering increasingly complex and challenging sequences of motor actions. In all these domains, guidance and instruction are crucial, and no performer reaches the elite levels without the help of coaches and teachers. International level performers start practice at very young ages, as young as three or four years of age, are given instruction by teachers, and are helped to engage in practice by their parents for their entire development cycle until adulthood (Bloom, 1985; Ericsson et al. 1993; Ericsson and Lehmann, 1996). The types of training activities (deliberate practice) that are necessary for development of mechanisms mediating expert performance differ for different domains and the experts' level of current mastery.

The Acquisition of Highly Technical Skills

In domains with long traditions of successfully trained expert performers (such as music and ballet), teachers over centuries have developed a consensus about how to present the techniques and knowledge of the domain in an organized sequence. Let me illustrate this in the domain of music. In the training of music students, the focus is on a gradual development of the skill of performing music in public. Students start by mastering simple pieces of music with a focus on accuracy of key strokes, but as they increase in mastery the teachers select more challenging pieces and have expectations for musical expression. When students repeatedly practice new and challenging pieces, their difficulties in mastering the pieces reveal weaknesses in their representations and technical skills. Depending on the type of problems, the teacher will recommend a specific type of deliberate practice to improve that aspect of the student's performance. Over the years many effective training methods have been devised to help musicians change their processes and representations. However, only the students themselves are able to address their own specific performance problems. Eventually, through problem solving, students can generate the specific modifications that, with extended practice, can be fully integrated with the complex representations that mediate their performance of complete pieces of music. The importance of solitary practice to master new pieces and techniques (deliberate practice) has been demonstrated by showing a close relation between the amount of deliberate practice accumulated during musicians' development and the level of attained music performance – even within groups of expert musicians (Ericsson, 2001b, for a review). The musicians in the most elite group were estimated to have spent over ten thousand hours in solitary practice by the age of twenty (Ericsson et al., 1993). Later studies have replicated the relation between attained level of skill and the amount of deliberate practice accumulated during the musicians' development (Krampe and Ericsson, 1996; Lehmann and Ericsson, 1996; Sloboda, 1996; Sloboda, Davidson, Howe, and Moore, 1996).

In other performance domains such as ballet, gymnastics, figure skating, and platform diving, there is a similar progression through increasingly difficult tasks, in which the guidance of a teacher is critical for success. Studies find that even in these domains, the level of attained performance is related to the accumulated amount of deliberate practice (Starkes, Deakin, Allard, Hodges, and Hayes, 1996). However, there are domains where large improvements in performance are regularly attained without teachers, where individuals can increase the level of difficulty by seeking out more challenging situations, such as skiing more difficult slopes, or playing with older or better players in tennis and soccer.

The Acquisition of Increased Performance Speed

The best insights into how speed of performance can be increased through deliberate practice are provided by extensive research on typing. The key finding is that individuals' typing speed is not completely fixed. It is possible for all typists to increase their typing speed by pushing themselves as long as they can sustain full concentration, which is typically about fifteen to thirty minutes per day for untrained typists. While straining to type at a faster speed – typically around 10 to 20 percent faster than their normal speed – typists seem to strive to anticipate better, possibly by extending their gaze ahead further. The faster tempo also serves to uncover key stroke combinations that are comparatively slow and poorly executed. By successively eliminating weaknesses, typists can increase their average speed and practice at a rate that is still 10 to 20 percent faster than the new average typing speed.

In domains where speed and efficiency of performance present the primary challenge to expert levels, it is possible to attain high levels of performance with less instruction than in the highly technical domains. Even in domains focusing on speed, there is evidence for the role of deliberate practice in attaining the highest levels of performance. Elite athletes are shown to spend more time in solitary practice and/or practice with their teammates (Helsen, Starkes, and Hodges, 1998; Hodges and Starkes, 1996; Starkes et al., 1996). An important aspect of expert performance in team sports, such as soccer and land hockey, concerns the selection of the correct actions in game situations.

The Acquisition of Superior Skills to Select Actions

The best insights into how it is possible to improve one's ability to generate superior plans and actions come from the study of chess expertise. Future chess experts spend as much as four hours a day studying games between chess masters (Ericsson et al., 1993). They play through the games one move at a time to see if their selected moves match the moves originally selected by the masters. If a chess master's move differed from their own selection, it would imply that their planning and evaluation must have overlooked some aspect of the position. Through careful, extended analysis, the chess expert is generally able to discover the reasons for the chess master's move. By spending a longer time analyzing the consequences of moves for a chess position, players can improve the quality of their future move selections. The amount of accumulated solitary study in chess is the best predictor of current chess performance. International chess masters accumulate around six thousand hours of solitary study during the first ten years of chess playing (Charness, Krampe, and Mayr, 1996).

Deliberate Practice and Expert Performance: General Comments

The acquisition of expert performance extends over years and even decades, but improvement of performance is not an automatic consequence of additional experience. Merely performing the same activities repeatedly on a regular daily schedule will not lead to further change once a physiological and cognitive adaptation to the current demands has been achieved. *The principal challenge for attaining expert performance is that further improvements require continuously increased challenges that raise the performance beyond its current level.* The engagement in these selected activities designed to improve one's current performance is referred to as *deliberate practice.* Given that these practice activities are designed to be outside the aspiring experts' current performance, these activities create mistakes and failures in spite of the performers' full concentration and effort – at least when practice on a new training task is initiated. Failing in spite of full concentration is not viewed as enjoyable and creates a motivational challenge (Ericsson et al., 1993). For example, it is understandable that musicians are reluctant to take on a difficult piece they cannot give musical expression to or that ice skaters hesitate to attempt new jumps that are likely to make them fall repeatedly on the hard ice. Recent observational studies (Deakin, 2001) show that sub-elite ice skaters spend more time on jumps that they have already mastered, whereas elite ice skaters allocate more time to the more difficult jumps, where failure rate is higher and the likelihood of improvement greater.

Once we conceive of expert performance as mediated by complex integrated systems of representations for the execution, monitoring, planning, and analyses of performance, it becomes clear that its acquisition requires an orderly and deliberate approach. Different forms of deliberate practice focus on improving specific aspects of performance while assuring that attained changes can be successfully integrated into representative performance. Hence, practice aimed at improving integrated performance cannot be performed mindlessly nor independent of the representative context for the target performance.

The early research on deliberate practice in music (Ericsson et al., 1993) showed that the engagement in deliberate practice is constrained. When music students start practicing, they average one hour per week, often split into fifteen to twenty minute sessions. The weekly amount of solitary practice increases over the next ten to fifteen years to around twenty-five to thirty hours per week for full-time students at the academy. The constraint on deliberate practice doesn't seem determined completely by developmental factors due to the young starting ages of future expert musicians, because a very similar gradual increase in practice has been seen for athletes who start practice in adolescence (Starkes et al., 1996). When expert performers engage in deliberate practice, they report that *full concentration* is necessary for improving their performance and that when concentration waned they stopped their practice (Ericsson, 2001a, 2001b; Ericsson et al., 1993). To maximize the time of full concentration, they tend to limit the duration of a single practice session and take short breaks after around an hour. They also tend to start early in the morning and frequently take a nap before resuming their demanding activity in the afternoon. When expert performers engage in deliberate practice on a daily basis, the available daily time with full concentration seems to limit the amount of deliberate practice for expert performers in all domains to around four to five hours. For example, world-class novelists work virtually exclusively in the morning and spend the rest of day recuperating, in order to prepare for the following day's writing session (Cowley, 1959; Plimpton, 1977).

In sum, the study of expert performance has uncovered a large number of factors associated with the acquisition of expert performance, such as an early start of involvement in domain-related activity, early start of training, and amount of relevant experience. More important, there is also an emerging body of necessary constraints for attaining expert levels of performance even among individuals regularly engaged in the activity, such as guidance and instruction by teachers and the regular engagement in deliberate practice. Even the most "talented" individuals need to engage in extended deliberate practice for many years to acquire the prerequisite mechanisms. Hence, the old assumption that expert performance is acquired virtually automatically by "talented" individuals has been replaced by the recognition of the complex structure of expert performance and the complexity of the necessary learning activities that build the required mediating mechanisms to support expert performance. Whether any healthy individual with appropriate body size who engages in the appropriate prerequisite deliberate practice will necessarily attain expert levels of performance in the associated domain is not currently known. So far, I am not aware of any confirmed exceptions to this notion. Regardless, the overwhelming importance of factors other than innate talent to reach an expert level of performance is likely to remain uncontested.

CONCLUDING REMARKS

Contemporary theoretical frameworks of human ability focus primarily on the relatively narrow range of achievement of school children and college students, where large samples of participants and sophisticated statistical models are necessary to analyze the pattern of correlations, often with small to medium statistical strength. These methods of analysis and the associated theoretical interpretations are motivated by several fundamental assumptions. My introductory historical sketch attempted to identify some of these assumptions. When these theories were originally proposed in the eighteenth and nineteenth centuries, they were empirically evaluated with analyses of exceptional and expert performers. To continue this tradition, my chapter has attempted to assess the validity of these assumptions by reviewing recent relevant research on expert levels of performance as well as the effects of extended training on expert performance.

Psychological scientists have always been inspired by the success of the natural sciences in uncovering general laws explaining the "behavior" of objects based on stable characteristics of uniform materials, such as hardness, volume, and weight, which can be quantified by objective measurement procedures. It is therefore reasonable for scientists working within the social sciences to attempt to explain the large individual differences in human performance in a similar fashion by attributing these performance differences to stable characteristics and mental capacities. As scientists should always look for the most general and parsimonious mechanism to explain observable patterns of results, it would seem reasonable to attempt to use individual differences in general basic capacities to explain consistent differences in ability and performance. However, the complex structure of human skills and performance raises questions about the stability and uniformity of any inferred capacities and characteristics. Mature human adults are *biological systems* that have developed from a single fertilized cell during a time period of around two decades. These developing systems are capable of remarkable changes and adaptations from large organic changes (such as increased kidney function) down to the individual cell level. From the perspective of developmental biology, the theoretical notion of basic general capacities that rigidly constrain the performance of adults is not simple, but requires explication in terms of specific genes and their timely expression to invariably influence the targeted anatomical structures. Until scientists have found the anatomical and physiological systems that implement these invariant basic capacities, along with plausible models for the specific genetic control of their differential development, these hypothesized capacities should not have priority among competing explanations of differences in human ability.

Because human characteristics are shown to be so modifiable after appropriate extended practice (with the exception of body size), scientists interested in performance limits need to search for a stable reproducible performance attained only after many years of deliberate practice designed to reach the highest levels. In the second section of this chapter, I outlined the compelling evidence that expert performance is mediated by complex mechanisms that anticipate, prepare, monitor, and evaluate its execution of actions. The highly reproducible performance of experts allows investigators to assess and validate the complex mechanisms at the level of each individual expert (Ericsson, in press). These complex mechanisms are not restricted to elite performers, and there is compelling evidence that the same types of mechanisms mediate skilled activities in all educated adults. [For example, there is a similar finding of advance anticipation of motor actions when adults read aloud: more skilled readers have a longer span between the words on which their eyes fixate and the words they concurrently vocalize (eye-voice span). Similarly, individuals who comprehend texts better also exhibit a larger functional working memory (LTWM) for the associated type of material (Ericsson and Kintsch, 1995; Kintsch, 1998).]

The complexity of the mechanisms that mediate skilled and expert performance presents a challenge to traditional theories of learning and skill acquisition. Ever since the seventeenth and eighteenth centuries, when associative learning was developed as an alternative account to the complex innate structure of the soul, the complexity of learning processes has been minimized by scientists. Learning based on simple processes, such as strengthening of associations, was preferred to avoid the introduction of the complexities associated with learning processes. In the third section of my chapter, I argue for the need for complex learning mechanisms and highly structured activities of practice *(deliberate practice)* to explain the extended acquisition of complex mechanisms that mediate expert levels of performance. Experts were shown to avoid the path taken by most novices where initial representations for performing the tasks were rapidly automated. Instead, experts were shown to keep building and refining their representations and the supporting working memory (LTWM) that supports *anticipation, planning,* and *decision making*. I have also demonstrated how deliberate practice can develop and refine the mediating mechanisms to allow aspiring experts to monitor and evaluate their performance to identify potential weaknesses that can be eliminated through problem solving and repetition (Ericsson, 2001b; in press).

The gradual development of complex mechanisms on the path toward high levels of performance has major implications for our current conceptions of ability. Although it is possible to assign quantitative metrics to a person's ability to play music, chess, or tennis, these numbers do not quantify any uniform capacity or ability to perform in the respective domains (see Mitchell, 1999, for a thorough critique of efforts to quantify individual differences in ability and capacity). For example, an international-level chess master does not simply have "two" times the units of chess ability of a strong club-level player, nor can we describe the difference as "one hundred" units of some uniform chess ability. The analyses of expert performers in domains such as chess, music, and tennis show a *qualitative* difference in the structure and complexity of the mediating mechanisms that such individuals use to progress to higher levels of performance. The steady development of the mediating mechanisms and the associated performance by aspiring expert performers makes it reasonable to describe successive levels of such performance by an ordinal, or rank-order, scale. More generally, similar rank-orders should be able to describe the stability of rank-orders across competitions for performers in a given domain.

In this chapter I try to raise doubts about the validity of the long-standing belief in stable innate capacities and any restraint such supposed innate capacities have on an individual's ultimate performance potential. The reviewed empirical evidence from the acquisition of expert performance contradicts this theory, and demonstrates that individuals gradually acquire increasingly complex mechanisms roughly ordered along an ordinal path leading to elite levels of performance.

These ordinal paths of development are far more consistent with Binet and Simon's (1915) descriptions of normal cognitive development along a defined path of discrete milestones of mastery for each age. Only future research will speak to the matter of how research on human ability can best be reconciled with the rapidly developing body of evidence on the structure and acquisition of expert and exceptional performance.

References

Abernethy, B. (1991). Visual search strategies and decision-making in sport. *International Journal of Sport Psychology, 22,* 189–210.

Aikens, H. A., Thorndike, E. L., & Hubbell, E. (1902). Correlations among perceptive and associative processes. *Psychological Review, 9,* 374–382.

Anastasti, A. (1988). *Psychological testing* (6th edition). New York: Macmillan Publishing Co.

Anderson, J. R. (1982). Acquisition of cognitive skill. *Psychological Review, 89,* 369–406.

Astrand, P.-O., & Rodahl, K. (1977). *Textbook of work physiology.* New York: McGraw-Hill.

Bernstein, N. A. (1996). Dexterity and its development. In M. L. Latash and M. T. Turvey (Eds.), *Dexterity and its development* (pp. 1 244). Mahwah, NJ: Erlbaum.

Binet, A., & Simon, Th. (1915). *A method of measuring the development of the intelligence of young children.* Chicago: Medical Book.

Black, J. E., Isaacs, K. R., Anderson, B. J., Alcantara, A. A., & Greenough, W. T. (1990). Learning causes synaptogenesis, whereas motor activity causes angiogenesis, in cerebellar cortex of adult rats. *Proceedings of the National Academy of Science, 87,* 5568–5572.

Bloom, B. S. (1985). Generalizations about talent development. In B. S. Bloom (Ed.), *Developing talent in young people* (pp. 507–549). New York: Ballantine Books.

Brown, W., & Thomson, G. H. (1921). *The essentials of mental measurement.* Cambridge, UK: Cambridge University Press.

Buonomano, D. V., & Merzenich, M. M. (1998). Cortical plasticity: From synapses to maps. *Annual Review of Neuroscience, 21,* 149–186.

Calderwood, R., Klein, G. A., & Crandall, B. W. (1988). Time pressure, skill and move quality in chess. *American Journal of Psychology, 101,* 481–493

Charness, N., Krampe, R. Th., & Mayr, U. (1996). The role of practice and coaching in entrepreneurial skill domains: An international comparison of life-span chess skill acquisition. In K. A. Ericsson (Ed.), *The road to excellence: The acquisition of expert performance in the arts and sciences, sports, and games* (pp. 51–80). Mahwah, NJ: Erlbaum.

Chase, W. G., & Ericsson, K. A. (1982). Skill and working memory. In G. H. Bower (Ed.), *The psychology of learning and motivation,* Vol. 16 (pp. 1–58). New York: Academic Press.

Cowley, M. (Ed.). (1959). *Writers at work: The Paris Review interviews*. New York: Viking Press.

Dawes, R. M. (1994). *House of cards: Psychology and psychotherapy built on myth*. New York: Free Press.

Deakin, J. M. (2001). What they do versus what they say they do: An assessment of practice in figure skating. In A. Papaioannou, M. Goudas, and Y. Theodorakis (Eds.), *In the dawn of the new millennium: Proceedings of the International Society of Sport Psychology 10th World Congress of Sport Psychology*, Vol. 3 (pp. 153–155). Tessaloniki, Greece: Christodoulidi Publications.

de Groot, A. (1978). *Thought and choice in chess*. The Hague: Mouton (original work published 1946).

Drake, C., & Palmer, C. (2000). Skill acquisition in music performance: Relations between planning and temporal control. *Cognition, 74*, 1–32.

Elbert, T., Pantev, C., Wienbruch, C., Rockstroh, B., & Taub, E. (1995). Increased cortical representation of the fingers of the left hand in string players. *Science, 270*, 305–307.

Ericsson, K. A. (1988). Analysis of memory performance in terms of memory skill. In R. J. Sternberg (Ed.), *Advances in the psychology of human intelligence*, Vol. 4 (pp. 137–179). Hillsdale, NJ: Erlbaum.

Ericsson, K. A. (1996). The acquisition of expert performance: An introduction to some of the issues. In K. A. Ericsson (Ed.), *The road to excellence: The acquisition of expert performance in the arts and sciences, sports, and games* (pp. 1–50). Mahwah, NJ: Erlbaum.

Ericsson, K. A. (1998). The scientific study of expert levels of performance: General implications for optimal learning and creativity. *High Ability Studies, 9*, 75–100.

Ericsson, K. A. (2001a). Attaining excellence through deliberate practice: Insights from the study of expert performance. In M. Ferrari (Ed.), *The pursuit of excellence in education* (pp. 21–55). Mahwah, N.J.: Erlbaum.

Ericsson, K. A. (2001b). The path to expert performance: Insights from the masters on how to improve performance by deliberate practice. In P. Thomas (Ed.), *Optimizing performance in golf* (pp. 1–57). Brisbane, Australia: Australian Academic Press.

Ericsson, K. A. (in press). The acquisition of expert performance as problem solving: Construction and modification of mediating mechanisms through deliberate practice. In J. E. Davidson and R. J. Sternberg (Eds.), *Problem solving*. New York: Cambridge University Press.

Ericsson, K. A., Chase, W., & Faloon, S. (1980). Acquisition of a memory skill. *Science, 208*, 1181–1182.

Ericsson, K. A., & Kintsch, W. (1995). Long-term working memory. *Psychological Review, 102*, 211–245.

Ericsson, K. A., Krampe, R. T., & Tesch-Römer, C. (1993). The role of deliberate practice in the acquisition of expert performance. *Psychological Review, 100*, 363–406.

Ericsson, K. A., & Lehmann, A. C. (1996). Expert and exceptional performance: Evidence on maximal adaptations on task constraints. *Annual Review of Psychology, 47*, 273–305.

Ericsson, K. A., Patel, V. L., & Kintsch, W. (2000). How experts' adaptations to representative task demands account for the expertise effect in memory recall: Comment on Vicente and Wang (1998). *Psychological Review, 107*, 578–592.

Ericsson, K. A., & Smith, J. (1991). Prospects and limits in the empirical study of expertise: An introduction. In K. A. Ericsson and J. Smith (Eds.), *Toward a general theory of expertise: Prospects and limits* (pp. 1–38). Cambridge, UK: Cambridge University Press.

Ericsson, K. A., & Staszewski, J. (1989). Skilled memory and expertise: Mechanisms of exceptional performance. In D. Klahr and K. Kotovsky (Eds.), *Complex information processing: The impact of Herbert A. Simon* (pp. 235–267). Hillsdale, NJ: Erlbaum.

Fitts, P., & Posner, M. I. (1967). *Human performance.* Belmont, CA: Brooks/Cole.

Galton, F., Sir (1869/1979). *Hereditary genius: An inquiry into its laws and consequences.* London: Julian Friedman Publishers.

Gibson, E. J. (1969). *Principles of perceptual learning and development.* Englewood Cliffs, NJ: Prentice-Hall.

Gobet, F., & Simon, H. A. (1996). The roles of recognition processes and look-ahead search in time-constrained expert problem solving: Evidence from grand-master-level chess. *Psychological Science, 7*, 52–55.

Greene, E. B. (1937). Practice effects on various types of standard tests. *American Journal of Psychology, 49*, 67–75.

Helsen, W. F., Starkes, J. L., & Hodges, N. J. (1998). Team sports and the theory of deliberate practice. *Journal of Sport and Exercise Psychology, 20*, 12–34.

Hodges, N. J., & Starkes, J. L. (1996). Wrestling with the nature of expertise: A sport specific test of Ericsson, Krampe and Tesch-Römer's (1993) theory of "Deliberate Practice," *International Journal of Sport Psychology, 27*, 400–424.

Howe, M. J. A., Davidson, J. W., & Sloboda, J. A. (1998). Innate talents: Reality or myth? *Behavioral and Brain Sciences, 21*, 399–442.

Karpov, A. (1995). Grandmaster musings. *Chess Life*, November, pp. 32–33.

Kintsch, W. (1998). *Comprehension: A paradigm for cognition.* Cambridge, UK: Cambridge University Press.

Kolb, B., & Whishaw, I. Q. (1998). Brain plasticity and behavior. *Annual Review of Psychology, 49*, 43–64.

Koltanowski, G. (1985). *In the dark.* Coraopolis, PA: Chess Enterprises.

Krampe, R. Th., & Ericsson, K. A. (1996). Maintaining excellence: Deliberate practice and elite performance in young and older pianists. *Journal of Experimental Psychology: General, 125*, 331–359.

Lehman, H. C. (1953). *Age and achievement.* Princeton, NJ: Princeton University Press.

Lehmann, A. C., & Ericsson, K. A. (1993). Sight-reading ability of expert pianists in the context of piano accompanying. *Psychomusicology, 12*(2), 182–195.

Lehmann, A. C., & Ericsson, K. A. (1995). *Expert pianists' mental representation of memorized music.* Poster presented at the 36th annual meeting of the Psychonomic Society, Los Angeles, CA, November 10–12.

Lehmann, A. C., & Ericsson, K. A. (1996). Music performance without preparation: Structure and acquisition of expert sight-reading. *Psychomusicology, 15*, 1–29.

Lehmann, A. C., & Ericsson K. A. (1997). Expert pianists' mental representations: Evidence from successful adaptation to unexpected performance demands. *Proceedings of the Third Triennial ESCOM Conference* (pp. 165–169). Uppsala, Sweden: SLU Service/Reproenheten.

Lehmann, A. C., & Ericsson K. A. (1998). The historical development of domains of expertise: Performance standards and innovations in music. In A. Steptoe (Ed.), *Genius and the mind* (pp. 67–94). Oxford, UK: Oxford University Press.

Miller, G. A. (1956). The magical number seven, plus or minus two: Some limits of our capacity for processing information. *Psychological Review, 63*, 81–97.

Mitchell, J. (1999). *Measurement in psychology: Critical history of a methodological concept.* Cambridge, UK: Cambridge University Press.

Miyake, A., & Shah, P. (Eds.). (1999). *Models of working memory: Mechanisms of active maintenance and executive control.* Cambridge, UK: Cambridge University Press.

Newell, A., & Simon, H. A. (1972). *Human problem solving.* Englewood Cliffs, NJ: Prentice-Hall.

Plimpton, G. (Ed.). (1977). *Writers at work: The Paris Review interviews.* New York: Penguin Books.

Saariluoma, P. (1991). Aspects of skilled imagery in blindfold chess. *Acta Psychologica, 77*, 65–89.

Salthouse, T. A. (1984). Effects of age and skill in typing. *Journal of Experimental Psychology: General, 113*, 345–371.

Schlaug, G., Janke, L., Huang, Y., Staiger, J. F., & Steinmetz, H. (1995). Increased corpus callosum size in musicians. *Neuropsychologica, 33*, 1047–1055.

Schulz, R., & Curnow, C. (1988). Peak performance and age among super-athletes: Track and field, swimming, baseball, tennis and golf. *Journal of Gerontology: Psychological Sciences, 43*, 113–120.

Simon, H. A., & Chase, W. G. (1973). Skill in chess. *American Scientist, 61*, 394–403.

Sloboda, J. A. (1984). Experimental studies in music reading: A review. *Music Perception, 22*, 222–236.

Sloboda, J. A. (1996). The acquisition of musical performance expertise: Deconstructing the "talent" account of individual differences in musical expressivity. In K. A. Ericsson (Ed.), *The road to excellence: The acquisition of expert performance in the arts and sciences, sports, and games* (pp. 107–126). Mahwah, NJ: Erlbaum.

Sloboda, J. A., Clarke, E. F., Parncutt, R., & Raekallio, M. (1998). Determinants of finger choice in piano sight-reading. *Journal of Experimental Psychology: Human Perception and Performance, 24*, 185–203.

Sloboda, J. A., Davidson, J. W., Howe, M. J. A., & Moore, D. G. (1996). The role of practice in the development of performing musicians. *British Journal of Psychology, 87*, 287–309.

Spearman, C. (1904). General intelligence objectively determined and measured. *American Journal of Psychology, 15*, 201–292.

Spearman, C. (1923). *The nature of 'intelligence and the principles of cognition.* London: Macmillan.

Spearman, C. (1937). *Psychology down the ages*, Vol. II. London: Macmillan.

Stael von Holstein, C.-A. S. (1972). Probabilistic forecasting: An experiment related to the stock market. *Organizational Behavior and Human Performance, 8*, 139–158.

Starkes, J. L., Deakin, J., Allard, F., Hodges, N. J., & Hayes, A. (1996). Deliberate practice in sports: What is it anyway? In K. A. Ericsson (Ed.), *The road to excellence: The acquisition of expert performance in the arts and sciences, sports, and games* (pp. 81–106). Mahwah, NJ: Erlbaum.

Williams, A. M., David, K., & Williams, J. G. (1999). *Visual perception and action in sport*. New York: Routledge.

Wissler, C. (1901). The correlation of mental physical tests. *Psychological Review Monographs, 3(6)*, 1–62 (Whole No. 16).

Woodworth, R. S., & Thorndike, E. L. (1901). The influence of improvement in one mental function upon the efficiency of other functions: III. Functions involving attention, observation and discrimination. *Psychological Review, 8*, 553–564.

Young, R. M. (1970). *Mind, brain and adaptation in the nineteenth century*. Oxford, UK; Clarendon Press.

5

On Abilities and Domains

Michael W. Connell, Kimberly Sheridan,
and Howard Gardner

INTRODUCTION

Questions concerning the relationships among an individual's innate abilities, learned competencies, and potential for success (for example, as measured by assessed level of expertise) in a given domain are important to theorists of human cognition and behavior; such questions are also germane to educators, policy makers, employers, and others who wish to make informed decisions that will both maximize human potential and make the most effective use of limited resources. In our view, a fundamental challenge inheres in any attempt to understand how an individual's unique profile of capabilities relates to possible future outcomes (for example, in terms of ultimate success within a domain). One must be able to parse the space of human biopsychological capacities (abilities), as well as the space of culturally valued knowledge and skills (competencies) that comprise domains, in such a way that the proposed link is predictive of success without being unnecessarily over-prescriptive. Most individuals could succeed in any of a number of domains, and many factors other than sheer ability determine this space of possibilities; any theorist seeking to link abilities to potential for expertise in one or more domains should seek to do so within these parameters. In particular, these considerations rule out the possibility of correlating individual ability profiles with suitable careers or jobs in anything approximating a one-to-one manner. At the other extreme, reducing individual variation to a single dimension (as is done with the IQ test for general intelligence, for instance) has proven to be problematic in that it fails to deal with important qualitative individual differences.

In this chapter, we seek to navigate a path between the two extremes just described. We propose an alternative approach for linking abilities to potential for expertise by identifying two qualitatively different kinds of human abilities (modular and integrative) that we believe correlate with corresponding categories of problems (modular *tasks* and integrative *situations*, respectively). We argue that different kinds of domains (and different roles within a single domain) are organized in terms of these categories in distinct ways, and that these different organizations impose different kinds of demands on individual abilities. In particular, *tasks* are targeted assignments that draw on specific abilities, like those confronted by mechanical engineers or political speech writers. *Situations*, in contrast, are inherently complex sets of problems that require an orchestration of capacities, such as those faced by CEOs or politicians. We argue, moreover, that individuals with highly developed specific capacities are more likely to be attracted to and excel in targeted task areas, whereas individuals with strong integrative capacities are more likely to be attracted to and excel in professions that require situational competencies.

In what follows, we attempt to formalize the widely held intuition that different kinds of individuals (for example, the individual with prodigious but narrow mathematical abilities versus the person who can efficiently identify a problem and coordinate an appropriate response) seem to "fit" best with distinct kinds of domains (for example, engineering or physics, as opposed to business or politics). We do this by examining how different types of roles identifiable across domains place correspondingly different kinds of demands on individual practitioners (that is, modular and integrative). This approach parses the world in a way that cuts across traditional domain boundaries as defined in terms of content; for example, a political speech writer and a circuit designer would be grouped together as task experts in our scheme, rather than the traditional grouping according to the domains of "politics" and "engineering," under which the speech writer and a senator would be grouped together as members of the politics domain.

One potential implication of our analysis for researchers of achievement and expertise is this: Individuals are likely to maximize their levels of performance and expertise in those (task-based or situation-based) domains that impose demands that fit well with their (modular or integrative) abilities. We end with a discussion of possible implications for tailoring assessment and teaching practices to the two dimensions of human ability and competence that we have identified.

Four Prototypical Experts

Alex is the CEO of a company that designs electronic devices. His role in the company is primarily to identify (by following current events, tracking economic indicators and forecasts, ordering and digesting market research, and so forth) and coordinate a response to high-level situations (for example, threats or opportunities) that may be significant for the company for better or worse. For example, by coordinating information and resources from management, marketing, engineering, accounting, and other departments, he has to make strategic decisions about company direction, high-level personnel, procurement and allocation of financial resources, potential partnerships and takeovers, and many other diverse matters.

Archie is an electrical engineer who works for Alex's company. In contrast to the broad and diverse demands of Alex's day-to-day job responding to various kinds of situations, Archie spends most of his time executing well-defined tasks using the standard tools of his trade. Typically, at the beginning of a new project, the lead engineer will hand Archie a detailed specification for a circuit that needs to be built to perform a particular function or calculation. Archie will spend several weeks or months designing the circuit and implementing a prototype using components like resistors and integrated circuits that are familiar elements in the tool kit of any electrical engineer.

Alex's job differs from Archie's in many ways. For our purposes, the key distinction is between the predominantly *integrative* nature of Alex's job, which requires him to orchestrate diverse capacities in order to address inherently complex situations in the world, compared to Archie's much more focused role, in which he dispatches targeted tasks or assignments that draw on specific (comparatively *modular*) abilities.

To see how the distinction we are proposing cuts across the typically content-based boundaries of diverse domains or disciplines, consider two other individuals chosen from the domain of politics. Regina is a senator, and Rita is her speech writer. Regina's responsibilities include defining policy, getting votes, negotiating with various other individuals and groups to garner support for her causes, providing political commentary on television programs like *Face the Nation*, appearing and speaking (often extemporaneously) at public events such as the funerals of public figures, and so forth. Rita, on the other hand, is usually given a fairly specific assignment such as "write a fifteen-minute speech summarizing our plan for education reform and highlighting the points that will appeal to the voters better than our opposition's proposal." The parameters (for example, length, topic, audience, intended effect) of Rita's assignments change from one assignment to the next, but the basic task (write a speech) does not. We do not mean to imply that tasks are necessarily less challenging than situations or vice versa. Writing an effective speech (think of Theodore's contribution, as speech writer, to John F. Kennedy's achievements) and designing an electrical circuit are both very challenging tasks that require years of special training and/or experience, just like running a company or representing a state in Congress. The point is that the *kind* (as opposed to the *level*) of complexity involved with a task is qualitatively different from the kind of complexity involved in identifying and responding to a situation, in that the former is quite modular and the latter quite integrative by comparison.

The senator and her speech writer are both involved with one content domain (politics), and the CEO and his engineer are both involved with another content domain (electronics); this is one (popular) way to parse the space of human activities into domains. However, our interest here is in linking individual abilities to domain expertise. It is unlikely that individuals have innate ability for politics or engineering content, and so this way of defining domains does not seem to cut nature at the proper joints for our purposes. Note that the senator's job is more similar to the CEO's than to the speech writer's in the specific sense that both require the ability to coordinate diverse types of information and resources to handle diverse and inherently multi-faceted situations. The circuit designer's job is more like the speech writer's than the CEO's in the sense that both demand the respective practitioners to carry out well-defined assignments using familiar sets of skills. We therefore propose to begin by separating out two dimensions of human ability: those that are relatively narrow and modular, and those that are comparatively broad and integrative.

THEORETICAL FRAMEWORK

Modular Cognitive Faculties: A Cross-Species Comparison

The species-typical cognitive armamentarium of most nonhuman species is dominated by vertical or modular faculties (Gallistel 1990); accordingly, a cross-species comparison is useful for introducing this concept of a modular faculty in a concrete way. Consider three creatures named Squeaky, Rover, and Sue. Squeaky is a bat. Like all bats, she can locate, identify, and track small moving objects by emitting high-pitched sound waves and interpreting their echoes (echolocation). Some bats of the same species have a slightly longer range than Squeaky, some have a shorter range, some have a little better resolution and some have a bit worse. As measured by scientists on the "echolocation battery," Squeaky is about average. Rover, on the other hand, is a bloodhound. He is particularly good at detecting even very low concentrations of scent-bearing molecules, making subtle distinctions between different scents, and following the gradient of a particular scent even when many other scents are present. Based on his superior scent discrimination "expertise" compared with other members of his cohort, he was selected by the police to help track missing persons and fugitives from the law. Finally, Sue is an adult human. She is fluent in her native tongue, highly literate, and very articulate.

Three important questions can be asked about any one of these individuals with regard to any of the mentioned functions (echolocation, tracking, or language use); these questions reflect the crucial distinctions between abilities, competence, and expertise as we conceive them:

- Does individual X (in principle) have the *potential ability* to perform function Y, regardless of whether she can actually do it or not at the present time?
- Has individual X *realized a competence* for doing Y, such that she is actually capable of demonstrating it at the present time?
- At what level of *exhibited expertise* in Y is individual X capable of performing at the present time (compared with members of another species, with other members of the same species, or with members of some other reference group)?

Table 5.1 summarizes the information for the individuals and capabilities described above with respect to these three questions. Note that for each function mentioned, exactly one of the species has the potential ability to perform that function. Furthermore, in each case the individual in question has a realized competence for the target function (that is, can actually execute it). Finally, as measured by some external set of criteria, the performance of each individual on the relevant capabilities can be measured, assessed, and ranked against the performance of his or her peers to give a sense of their level of "expertise" in that area. Note that if a species does not have a given ability, it is not meaningful to ask about an individual's realized competence or level of expertise.

TABLE 5.1. *Summary of data on abilities, competencies, and expertise for a bat, a bloodhound, and a human with respect to three tasks (echolocation, scent tracking, and language use)*

	Echolocation			Scent Tracking			Language Use		
	Abil	*Comp*	*Exp*	*Abil*	*Comp*	*Exp*	*Abil*	*Comp*	*Exp*
Squeaky	Y	Y	Avg	N	N/A	N/A	N	N/A	N/A
Rover	N	N/A	N/A	Y	Y	High	N	N/A	N/A
Sue	N	N/A	N/A	N	N/A	N/A	Y	Y	High

At first blush, these comparisons may seem uninteresting – after all, these creatures all look very different from one another, they inhabit different ecological niches, and they have been subject to different selective pressures, and so it is not surprising that they exhibit different behaviors. On the other hand, they also share many similarities. All these creatures are mammals and they all have brains that follow the basic mammalian blueprint (Tomasello 1999). All have eyes, ears, and noses, and all can emit sounds of one sort or another. The dramatic differences revealed in this table cannot be attributed simply to the creatures' different physical appearances or sensory arrays. Rather, the key differences arise from differences in underlying neural organization and function, which enable very different kinds of information processing to be carried out even on qualitatively similar kinds of raw inputs (for example, light waves, sound waves, or chemicals). Bats can echolocate and humans cannot because bat brains are organized in such a way that the sound-emitting function is linked to the sound-processing areas in ways that enable the bat to coordinate the two to extract useful information from its own carefully timed squeaks. Human brains do not have an analogous coordination between brain areas or functions, and therefore they do not have the potential ability to echolocate. Thus, no matter how hard they might try, humans cannot develop a competence for echolocation. This is why echolocation will never be an event in the Olympic games and there would be no point in setting up a panel of judges to determine which humans are most expert at it.

The differences shown in Table 5.1 serve to remind us of a fact that is easily overlooked when we focus exclusively on humans – that any given species-typical brain (including the human brain) evolved to carry out certain specific kinds of information processing tasks (Fodor 1983; Gallistel 1990; Tooby and Cosmides 1992), and therefore any species is only capable of developing some small subset of all possible competencies. In short, it seems fair to say that different species' brains are organized around different sets of modular processing capacities. In addition to its species-typical set of modular faculties, however, human cognition is further distinguished by its extensive complementary capacities for representational integration and abstraction (Fodor 2000; Karmiloff-Smith 1992; Tomasello 1999; Tomasello and Call 1997). The human capacity for integrating across modular faculties has supported the generation of a great diversity of human domains and skills, as we discuss in the next section.

Implications of Human Integrative Capacities and Human Culture

The cross-species comparison in terms of abilities, competence, and expertise is straightforward and fairly clear-cut. For most non-human species, there are a comparatively small number of species-typical competencies that each organism must acquire; these are strongly determined by either the genome or experience-dependent plasticity (there is little variation across populations in the abilities that will ever be widely realized as competencies under normal conditions); and there is a relatively narrow range of "expertise" exhibited by different individuals on most of these basic functions (cf. Gallistel 1990; Tomasello 1999; Tomasello and Call 1997). When we look more carefully within the human population, however, the picture is complicated by two features unique to humans: (1) the capacity for significantly greater representational abstraction and integration (and therefore greater cognitive flexibility) than in any other species (Karmiloff-Smith 1992) and (2) cultures that support both behavioral innovation and the permanent storage (and therefore the steady accumulation) of knowledge (Sperber 1996; Tomasello 1999; Tomasello and Call 1997).

The human brain, like all mammalian brains, is capable of performing a wide range of specialized and adaptive information processing tasks (Tooby and Cosmides 1992). However, structures and functions unique to the human brain enable the development of new kinds of abstract representations that (1) can recruit phylogenetically older and more specialized information processing functions and hierarchically integrate them to produce new kinds of information processing capacities (Luria 1966; Werner 1957), and (2) are more plastic than older brain structures and therefore less constrained in forms of self-organization in response to experience (Karmiloff-Smith 1992; Tomasello 1999). The implication is that the space of human potential abilities is effectively more continuous and much larger than in other species (although note that there are still many useful competencies, such as echolocation, that are beyond human ability absent external aids like sonar).

Furthermore, symbolic tools like spoken and written language have enabled the human race, in effect, to search the space of potential human abilities in ways simply not possible for other species, and to secure any gains made along the way in the form of recorded knowledge that serves as a road map guiding future generations to rapid rediscovery of a particular competence (Gardner 1991; Sperber 1996; Tomasello 1999; Tomasello and Call 1997). Much of this accumulated knowledge has been organized over the centuries and now serves as the basis for the various disciplines and other domains of human activity that make up contemporary human cultures.

For millennia people have been exploring the range of human capabilities, documenting their experiments and discoveries, and working to make the useful and appealing competencies easier for succeeding generations to acquire (Feldman 1994). As a result, humans are faced with the unprecedented situation wherein they have to make choices about what competencies they want to acquire, for there are far too many for any single person to master in a brief human lifetime. This is the reason people are so interested in making early assessments of abilities that can predict ultimate outcomes in terms of expertise – so that individuals can be guided toward domains where they will be most likely to flourish based on the fit between their cognitive strengths and the demands of the target domain.

The problem is that the same factors that create this situation in the first place (human cognitive flexibility and cultural accumulation of knowledge) make it challenging to conduct research on humans. For example, the cognitive flexibility that allows people to learn any number of different competencies also allows them to accomplish many observable behaviors using any number of distinct neural organizations. Where competence was fairly unproblematic in the case of other animals, it becomes problematic in the case of humans – because there is no longer even a rough one-to-one mapping between information processing functions in the brain and observable performances. For humans, there are many different ways to skin a cat, whereas for a dog there would probably be just one species-typical way (with minor variations). Whereas there probably is not that much qualitative difference between individual bats in the brain areas and information processing that underlie their echolocating behavior, there might be many qualitatively different neural organizations that support human problem solving of a particular kind. This can be seen, for example, in MRI scans that reveal different patterns of activation across groups of people on the exact same task (Changeux 1999), or in the case of Barbara McClintock who evidently approached science very differently from her colleagues (Keller 1983).

This versatility becomes a problem when one is trying to understand the relationship between ability and expertise, because there is a many-to-one relationship between the neural organizations that can support an observable behavior and the behavioral criteria that are used to assess expertise. To take a trivial example, it is possible for four students in an algebra class to get a perfect score on an exam using four completely different competencies: (1) memorizing all the answers from a stolen answer key, (2) graphing the mathematical equations and solving the problems by reasoning from the visual diagrams, (3) manipulating the mathematical formulas directly using the rules of algebra, and (4) copying the answers from one of the other three students. If no one gets caught cheating, then all four of these students will end up with the same assessment on the exam, although the underlying competencies being exhibited are qualitatively different.

Despite these complex factors, it is certainly useful to determine which humans are likely to flourish in which domains. But because of the flexibility and complexity of human cognition, and the enormous variety of potential target domains open to most individuals, precise predictions of this sort seem highly unlikely, at least given our current state of scientific knowledge. Decades of experience with the widespread application of instruments like the IQ test and the SATs in an attempt to match individuals with educational or occupational tracks based on their potential "abilities" suggest that this is an elusive goal indeed. Although these tests do predict something, it does not seem to be the ultimate levels of expertise we are interested in (cf. McClelland 1973). In the next sections we describe in more formal terms our proposed alternative approach for linking abilities to expertise and contrast it to other frameworks.

Traditional Approaches

Many researchers try to map abilities onto expertise in one of two ways. One group assumes that every human has the same set of abilities as every other human (that is, expertise is independent of ability, and mostly or only a function of practice); they would say that Alex and Archie could be equally successful circuit designers, CEOs, senators, or speech writers if each dedicated himself to it sufficiently (cf. Ericsson and Charness 1994). The other group assumes that there is a tight coupling between general abilities (for example, general intelligence) and attainable expertise in any domain; many of these theorists would claim that the ultimate levels of expertise achievable by Regina or Rita in any domain is a function of their general intellectual capacities (Herrnstein and Murray 1994).

Our approach derives from a third perspective, which holds that individuals have profiles of specific abilities (for example, for mathematics or music) that enable them to excel in particular domains (for example, in the field of mathematics or in musical composition, respectively). In this view, Alex is good in business and Archie is good at circuit design in large part *because* each has an ability profile that fits well with the demands of these different domains (Feldman 1994; Gardner 1983/1993, 1999a,b).

We begin with the observation that humans have both modular faculties like color vision and spoken language and integrative faculties that allow them to coordinate various modular faculties into more flexible and general representations and skills. Modular faculties develop automatically, have similar gross neurological organization across most normal individuals, and can be selectively disrupted in predictable ways (for example, with focal lesions). Recall that these are the predominant kinds of faculties that nonhuman animals have. Integrative faculties, on the other hand, are those that integrate across the modular faculties. They do not generally develop automatically, but usually require formal study; they may show more individual variation in their neurological organization across individuals, and they are difficult to disrupt predictably, because they are more diffuse and the brain can accommodate disruptions to them better than in the case of the more modular faculties.

Integrative faculties are far more significant in the case of humans than for any other species. This is one factor that makes it difficult to sort out the underlying causes of the observed differences between Alex and Rita, and to understand the connections among their innate abilities, learned competencies, and ultimate level of expertise as determined by the field. To make sense of these questions, we need a theoretical framework that captures the distinction between the modular and integrative faculties, while at the same time incorporating both the facts of human neurobiology and the values of human culture. In the next section we discuss such a framework, and define abilities, competence, and expertise in terms of it.

Intelligences as the Dimensions Underlying Abilities

Before we can define the space of human abilities, we must first introduce the fundamental dimensions of human information processing that underlie them. It is possible to parse the space of human cognitive capacities in many ways. For example, the classical paradigm of intelligence (cf. Eysenck 1967; Eysenck 1979; Jensen 1987) defined the key human information processing capacities in terms of a single dimension (g) that represents a summary index of a person's information processing capabilities across all domains and types of content compared to other individuals. In this view, intelligence is considered to be what Fodor (1983) calls a *horizontal faculty*, a single faculty like memory or perception that putatively works on all manner of content.

At the extreme opposite to this universal view of human cognition, neuroscientists have identified hundreds of different functional units in the brain, each responsible for a different kind of information processing, and there is variation across individuals in the relative sizes, processing speeds, and patterns of connectivity among these functional units (Changeux and Ricoeur 2000; Pinker 1997; Tooby and Cosmides 1992). Each of these functional units could be associated with a basic information processing function (for example, face processing, pitch processing, motor planning) that exhibits some variation across individuals. These functional units tend to be similar to what Fodor calls *vertical faculties*.

Although many different decompositions of the space of human information processing capacities are possible, we favor one that is intermediate between, on the one hand, the universal view of Jensen and, on the other hand, the highly differentiated picture emerging from neuroscience. In our view, humans as a species have certain gross biopsychological potentials, or fundamental capacities for processing different kinds of informational content, plus mechanisms that can coordinate these capacities into still more complex functional units. We find it useful to begin by defining a set of criteria that parses human cognitive functions vertically in ways that incorporate considerations from biology as well as cultural relevance, thereby providing a basis for representing culturally relevant individual differences without being too unwieldy.

Although our general analysis does not depend on our specific choice here (as long as it captures individual differences in some systematic way), Gardner's theory of multiple intelligences proves a useful organizing framework for our purposes. Gardner (1983; 1999a; 1999b) has distilled data from a number of sources including neuropsychology (for example, studies of brain damage that reveal something about the functional organization and processing capacities of the brain) and cultural relevance (that is, what kinds of information processing capacities are valued by different societies) to produce a list of eight biopsychological capacities (or intelligences). These intelligences represent an individual's potential for processing information of the following kinds: mathematical, verbal, spatial, musical, bodily kinesthetic, interpersonal, intrapersonal, and naturalistic (ability to make discriminations among natural objects based on subtle cues). An example of an intelligence profile is shown in Figure 5.1.

It is important to note that, in this view, the underlying intelligences represent raw information processing capacities of a fairly narrow kind. They are more vertical or modular than integrative in terms of Fodor's (1983) framework, although in general they are probably composites of even more tightly focused and modular faculties. This theoretical construct of multiple intelligences represents a framework that not only connects the biological constraints of human information processing to the world of culturally valued capabilities. In addition, it represents a particular compromise, balancing the need to deal with the richness and complexity of the underlying system against theoretical tractability, while still capturing the most important dimensions of the complex system.

Potential Abilities

Although intelligences have been defined in terms of macroscopic and rather narrow information processing capacities that are valued by societies and supported within cultures, they should not be confused with *abilities*. Note that although Gardner has identified only a handful of *intelligences*, there are a plethora of *potential abilities* (shortened to *abilities* here). It is clear that there can be no one-to-one mapping from intelligences to abilities in humans, especially because of the combinatoric explosion of possible ways to coordinate the modular faculties into more integrated capabilities. Therefore, human abilities are defined in terms of particular profiles or combinations of intelligences (capturing

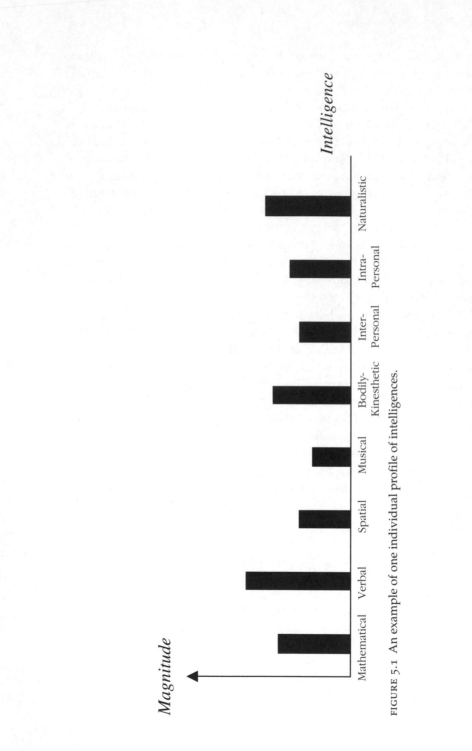

FIGURE 5.1 An example of one individual profile of intelligences.

the human capacity for developing a wide range of flexible integrative faculties). See Figure 5.2.

Abilities can be conceptualized in terms of *functionally integrated profiles* of intelligences. One way to represent this relationship graphically is to think of the individual intelligences as axes that define a space. A given point in this space represents a particular coordination of information processing modules (for example, intelligences) into an integrated information processing capacity. If we were able to measure an individual's various intelligences directly according to some meaningful summary metrics and plot these measures on each of the axes, they would mark off a volume of space that we can think of as the individual's space of potentially realizable information processing abilities. In other words, an ability can be thought of as a biopsychological potential for processing a certain kind of information that requires a particular combination or coordination of the information processing capacities represented by some combination of individual intelligences. For example, at one extreme, basic communication requires a combination of relatively low levels of linguistic and interpersonal intelligence (evidenced by the fact that even infants and non-human animals can communicate their basic desires and physical states to others). On the other hand, the kind of skilled oratory that can influence people's attitudes and beliefs requires high levels of both linguistic skill and interpersonal intelligence, and these must be *functionally integrated* in ways that support the target performance.

Here it becomes clear how our approach is different from many other approaches. On the one hand, those theorists who argue that any human is capable of developing any competence that any other human is capable of given appropriate experience (for example, Bruner 1960; Ericsson and Charness 1994) are assuming that the integrative human faculties are paramount, and able to override any differences between individuals in their less plastic modular faculties. Many counterexamples can be found by considering special populations. For example, there are probably severe limits on the ability of extremely dyslexic individuals to practice law at the present time due to their problems with language processing, given that the core competencies of a lawyer involve efficient processing of written linguistic input. Furthermore, many individuals with severe autism lack the basic verbal and interpersonal intelligence necessary to develop a competence for journalism, customer service, or door-to-door sales. No amount of practice in these cases can produce the target competencies.

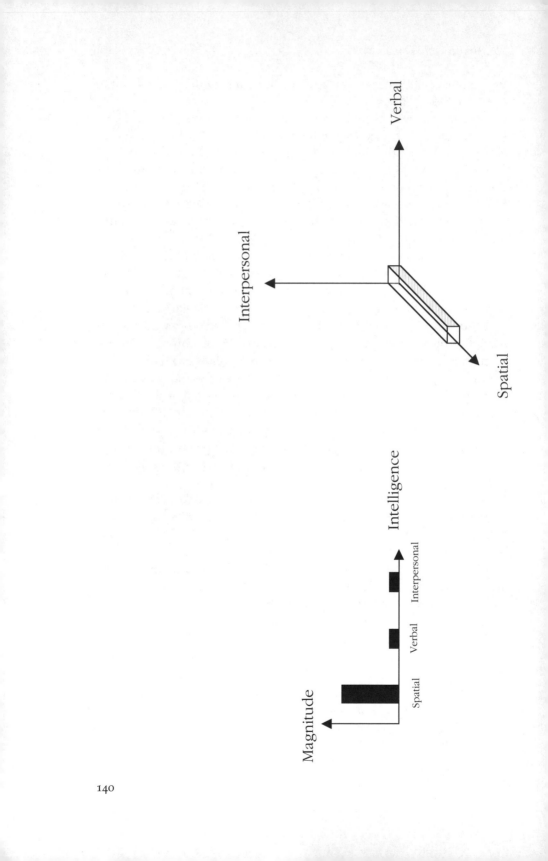

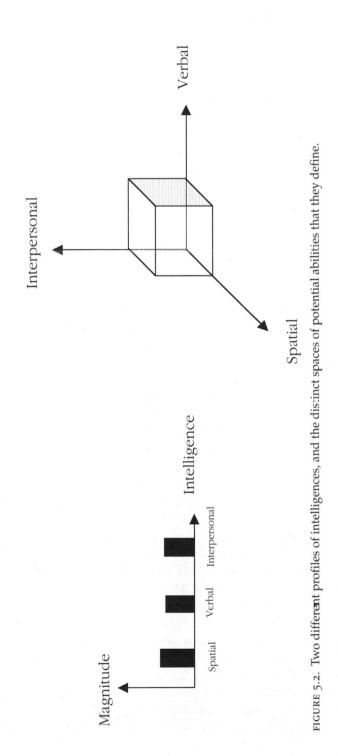

FIGURE 5.2. Two different profiles of intelligences, and the distinct spaces of potential abilities that they define.

On the other hand, theorists who posit a strong deterministic link between general ability and expertise are neglecting the significant plasticity inherent in the human cognitive system that allows them to augment, integrate, and compensate for many weaknesses in a particular modular faculty when they are coordinated into integrative faculties. For example, a person with deficits in face recognition (prosopagnosia) might develop strategies that recruit other discriminatory abilities and memory systems to develop a qualitatively different, but virtually indistinguishable compensatory skill for recognizing people by sight (for example, using context, gait, voice, hair style, or other secondary cues).

Figure 5.2 contrasts two different intelligence profiles (only a subset of three of the eight intelligences is shown), and shows the associated ability spaces that they define. The example on the top shows a very peaked profile with very high spatial intelligence and very low interpersonal and verbal intelligence (as is typical of autistic children, for example), which generates a long thin space of potential abilities. The example on the bottom shows a more balanced profile of intelligences and the more regular cube-shaped ability space it defines. This graphical representation is useful not only for comparing across groups with systematic differences in intelligence profiles (such as individuals with particular cognitive conditions such as autism or dyslexia), but also for highlighting individual differences among people within a single group (for example, musical prodigies versus the musically gifted versus those with little aptitude for music).

In short, abilities are innate profiles of biopsychological potentials representing coordinated profiles of individual intelligences. In our framework, these potential (or unrealized) abilities define a space of possible competencies (which are realized abilities). An individual only has one space of unrealized abilities, but many competencies can be realized within it. Note that intelligences and the space of potential abilities are completely internal to the individual. The interaction of the unrealized abilities of the individual with the constraints and content of a domain result in realized abilities (or competencies).

A key implication of our framework is that it reveals one possibility for identifying two qualitatively different sources of individual variation in human abilities. First, there is individual variation due to variation in raw intelligences (for example, some people may have more efficient or capacious information processing potentials for linguistic input due to the development of a larger language processing area relative to other people, or a larger capacity for distinguishing among and remembering people's faces due to a larger face-processing area in the brain). This kind of vertical variation in ability is analogous to the variation in proficiency exhibited by different bats at echolocation. The more tightly this source of variation is tied to vertical faculties, the more spontaneous and "innate" it will appear to be early in development, and the more we would expect it to be a factor in domains requiring competencies in which vertical faculties (including "pure" intelligences) play a central role (for example, theoretical mathematics, musical analysis).

Second, there is a different kind of variation due to the capacity for coordinating different vertical faculties into more integrated processing mechanisms. For example, developing models for economic forecasting requires mathematical intelligence, but integrated with an intuition for human psychology and behavior rather than in pure form. We propose that the vertical variation in mathematical intelligence that produces a great theoretical mathematician (for instance) is different from the horizontal (integrative) variation that produces a great economic adviser. The economist may, on the one hand, need less raw mathematical intelligence, but on the other hand, need to have reasonably high intelligence on a number of dimensions (mathematical and interpersonal, at least) plus the neurological organization necessary to coordinate them appropriately to produce the requisite competence(s) for her work in economics.

To summarize, we propose that there are two qualitatively different dimensions along which individual humans differ in their potential abilities: modular (comparatively more content-specific) and integrative. In contradistinction to other theoretical perspectives, we suggest that neither of these dimensions alone determines an individual's potential in any given domain. It should be obvious that domains differ in the demands they place on people in terms of modular faculties (for example, engineering is more math-centric, whereas politics requires more verbal skill). We are arguing, however, that this is not the only difference between domains. Perhaps less obvious is the fact that different domains require different levels of functional integration of these different modular faculties. We argue that these two qualitative dimensions of human ability are reflected in the structure of different kinds of domains; they correlate with qualitatively different kinds of competence and expertise. We believe that this novel conceptual distinction might provide some theoretical leverage in understanding how abilities can be linked to expertise.

Realized Competencies

We have argued that a potential ability is an abstract information processing capacity that is a function of an individual's innate profile of intelligences and capacity for functionally integrating them in various ways. In contrast, a *realized competence* (hereafter, *competence*) denotes some point in ability space that occurs as a result of learning and experience in a specific domain. A competence results from (and depends on) the interaction between individual potential abilities and actual experience in a domain. Whereas an individual has a single space of potential abilities, he or she can have any number of realized competencies within that space (although in a single lifetime it is impossible for any human being to realize all the recognized competencies within his or her space of potential abilities). Note that a competence, although it involves both the individual and the domain, is still a construct that refers to something (specific information processing capacities, but particularized to a certain set of problems or problem types) *internal* to the individual, but which depends on the interaction with a culturally constituted domain during learning.

Just as there are many possible ways to parse the information processing functions of the brain into meaningful units (that is, intelligences in our case), there are many ways to define the boundaries of a competence. For example, we might say of an employee who designs computer chips that he has a competence for engineering, for electrical engineering, for digital design, for symbolic logic, or for Boolean algebra. Although any or all of these attributions could be accurate, they use the same word (competence) to refer to realized abilities across a wide range of scales, from a very specific type of problem (Boolean algebra) to a sub-domain (electrical engineering) to a general domain (engineering). The ambiguities are only compounded when we apply the same terminology to a different kind of domain, such as politics. In that case, we might say our representative has a competence for keeping her constituents happy, for politicking, for foreign relations, for schmoozing, for oratory, for fund-raising, or for getting re-elected. In part, this problem arises from the attempt to apply a uniform ability-competence-expertise framework across all domains, as the traditional approach to expertise has tried to do. Such a general framework undoubtedly has its uses, but it masks important differences between qualitatively different kinds of domains.

To make matters worse, the word "competence" is often used in the literature indiscriminately to refer to either the observable performance (for example, the live bat actually navigating the environment) or the underlying neural functions that support the observable behavior (for example, the brain organization that makes it possible for the bat to navigate the environment). In the case of bat echolocation this is not much of a problem. "Echolocation" refers to a distinct and well-defined class of observable behavior, supported by an obvious and typical functional organization of bat brains that presumably does not vary much (at least qualitatively) across members of the species. In other words, there is a rough one-to-one mapping from the functionally defined class of echolocating behaviors to the functionally defined class of echolocation-supporting brain structures and functions across members of the species, which means that the distinction between the observable performance and the underlying competence is largely superfluous in this case.

In the case of human cognition, however, this distinction becomes important, because (as we discussed earlier) many qualitatively different organizations of neural structures and functions (realized competencies) can support most functionally defined classes of behavior (exhibited performances). For example, a trained elephant, a pre-school child, a paint-by-numbers hobbyist, a beginning art student, and Picasso can all exhibit performances that everyone could agree to call painting. If we are not careful to distinguish between the performance and the underlying realized competence that supports it, we would simply say (based on our definition of realized competence) that each of these individuals has a realized competence for painting.

Intuitively, however, this characterization is unsatisfying because it does not reflect what we really care about, which is the skill with which the painting is executed and the aesthetic merit of the work produced. The problem does not inhere in our definition of competence, but rather in the definition of "painting." As a set of functional criteria on behaviors that define a particular class of performance, "painting" is constructed in a way that picks out a particular competence – that is, "dip the brush in paint and spread it around the canvas." The problem: This competence is not the one people care about when they are judging skill and aesthetic merit. Rather, taking representational art as an example, one possible definition of painting behavior that better reflects the competence of interest would be "dip the brush in paint and spread it around the canvas in such a way that the resulting picture contains faithful or suggestive visual representations of the objects in the real-life scene." It would then be possible to determine that Picasso and the art student definitely have this competence, the elephant definitely does not, and the small child and the paint-by-numbers hobbyist might or might not (more specific criteria would be necessary to make these judgments). Theoretically, in order to determine conclusively whether a person has a *particular* competence, it would be necessary to specify functional criteria on the class of neural organizations that qualify for membership. Since it is not yet practical to do this (though it is becoming more feasible, for example by using sophisticated brain scanning technologies), in practice people generally try to define (either explicit or implicit) functional criteria on the behaviors that belong in a certain class of performance that, it is hoped, detect the presence or absence of the realized competence(s) of interest.

One way to deal with these complexities would be to investigate empirically the range of variation in underlying competencies that can support any given observable criterion behavior (for example, using behavioral assessment, interview data, brain scanning technologies, or other tools). This map of the qualitatively different realized competencies could then be used to refine the definitions of the assessments so that there is more of a one-to-one mapping between the functionally defined classes of observable behaviors and the qualitative categories of competence that support them. This approach is taken, for example, in assessing students to determine if they have learning disabilities. For example, even if a child has *a* competence for reading out loud (albeit very slowly and with poor comprehension), it may not be the *same* competence that other children have that produces what might appear to be superficially the same reading behavior. Such cognitive assessments attempt to distinguish among the different possible underlying competencies by identifying behavioral or other cues that give them away.

In the present analysis, however, we are more interested in general theoretical insights concerning the relationship between abilities and expertise rather than in the specific details of any particular domain or competence. Therefore, instead of attempting to provide a precise and general definition of the word "competence," we attempt to distinguish between two qualitatively different meanings of the word that reflect the differences between vertical faculties and horizontal faculties discussed in the section on abilities. *Task-competence* is a narrow competence for executing a specific kind of task within a domain (for instance, sight-reading music, solving a Boolean algebra problem, negotiating the terms of an agreement). *Situation-competence*, on the other hand, is a broad integrative competence for transforming some situation in the world from its current state into a more desired state by analyzing it into a set of appropriate tasks, delegating them if necessary to the people with the necessary task-competencies, and then integrating the results to produce key decisions or synthesize a plan of action for achieving the desired outcome (for example, organizing a theatrical production, running a computer design firm, or addressing constituent concerns about a state's environmental policies).

We propose that the distinction between task-competence and situation-competence is important because there are qualitatively different kinds of domains in the world (for example, designing a circuit is different from being a CEO of a technology firm), and different domains are structured in different ways in terms of these constructs (and therefore place different demands on individual practitioners). For example, electrical engineers are presented with situations specified in terms of the world ("I need to be able to multiply two integers") that translate in a straightforward way onto well-defined tasks that the domain of engineering provides strategies for executing directly ("design an electrical circuit that multiplies integers using off-the-shelf components and standard design practices"), as shown in Figure 5.3. Note, however, that the task could be accomplished in many different ways. A mechanical engineer could design a non-electronic calculator to do the job, or a mathematician could be hired to use pencil and paper. This is what

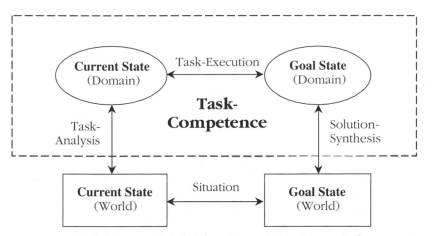

FIGURE 5.3. A *task* is a well-defined and targeted assignment (for example, "design a circuit that multiplies two integers," or "write a fifteen-minute speech describing the senator's education policy"). Whereas a domain-specific task derives from some situation in the world, the key task-competence involves applying the tools of a specific domain to solve some characteristic problem.

we mean when we say that situations are defined with reference to the world, whereas tasks are specified in terms of a specific domain. Sometimes, as in the case of the need for a calculator, the translation from situation to task and back is straightforward, so the focus falls on the task-competence in these cases. At other times, however, characterizing the problem, identifying the appropriate tasks to carry it out, and coordinating the task results to address the situation requires a separate set of capabilities altogether.

For example, as shown in Figure 5.4, situations in business ("our chief competitor is preparing for a hostile takeover") require an identification of the problem, an analysis of the situation into discrete tasks that are delegated to the appropriate departments or people having the necessary task-competencies, and an integration of the various results into a vision, strategy, or plan of action for the company (marketers are charged with identifying opportunities in the firm's area of expertise, engineers are charged with designing a specified component, sales people are

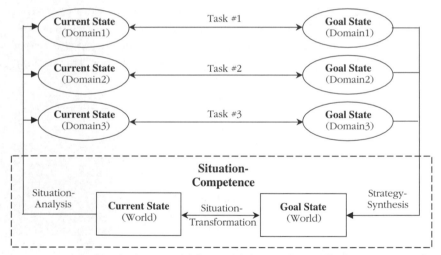

FIGURE 5.4. A *situation* is a state of the world that is relevant (for better or worse) to a domain practitioner and requires a response. For example, a situation for a CEO is the discovery that a competitor is preparing for a hostile takeover. The CEO does not execute all the tasks necessary to respond to the situation; rather, his job is to identify the situation as relevant, determine what tasks need to be carried out at the next level down, and then perhaps to integrate all the separate task results into a coordinated response to the situation. There are tasks implied by any situation, but the focus in this case is on the situation-competence that enables the CEO to deal with the situation in the world, whether he actually carries out any specific tasks or not.

mobilized to move the product, while the CEO determines what needs to be done and pulls all the pieces together to make it happen).

These distinctions seem useful for distinguishing among domains and competencies in ways that can be correlated with the differences between the content-focused and integrative dimensions of human ability. That is, people who are particularly strong along a single dimension of intelligence (for example, math) but without much integration among their various intelligences are probably more likely to do well in a domain organized around math-related task-competencies (such as engineering), and less well in a domain organized around functionally integrated situations (such as business). People who are reasonably strong along several dimensions of intelligence (for example, interpersonal, verbal, mathematical) and have the capacity for developing a high degree of functional integration among them are likely to do well in domains (like business) that are organized in terms of situations where they need to synthesize across different kinds of content (marketing data, financials, engineering plans) and interact with a variety of different people to produce outcomes, even though they may actually execute few of the tasks themselves.

The main examples of engineering, speech writing, business, and politics that we have used throughout the discussion are particularly good representatives of domains that are organized predominantly around tasks, on the one hand, or around situations, on the other. In general, however, these two categories are more aptly thought of as endpoints on a continuum along which different domains can be arrayed according to the ratio of tasks to situations that typically characterizes the demands placed on practitioners within the domain.

For example, consider the general domain of medicine, and three practitioners within it – a heart surgeon, a general practitioner, and the head of an HMO. In addition to a good deal of specific content knowledge, the surgeon will presumably need a high level of bodily kinesthetic intelligence (and perhaps spatial intelligence as well) to develop the repertoire of sensitivities and skills necessary for performing surgery on a patient's heart. The surgeon's competence is largely a task-competence, because the goal is usually well defined when the patient approaches the surgeon in the first place, and the strategies for achieving it are part of the surgeon's explicit training in the surgical sub-domain of medicine.

The general practitioner, on the other hand, is responsible for handling a combination of situations and tasks. A typical situation is defined by a patient who shows up with some unknown ailment and wants to get rid of it ("I have a sharp pain in my abdominal region"). During the diagnostic phase, the doctor may arrange for the patient to visit a number of departments and specialists to get specific tests performed (for example, blood work, X-rays, ultrasound). The doctor then has to synthesize all this information into a diagnosis, and formulate a plan of action. This is a clear example of a situation-competence; the doctor's role is mainly to analyze the situation, delegate tasks to other individuals with the appropriate task-competencies, and synthesize a strategy. If the diagnosis is something the doctor can deal with directly (for example, an ulcer), she can draw on one of her task-competencies to treat the patient herself (prescribe ulcer medication). If the diagnosis is something outside her area of competence (for example, a ruptured spleen), she may refer the patient to a specialist (a surgeon). The role of the general practitioner thus involves a more balanced blend of both situations and tasks than was the case for the surgeon. The head of an HMO, on the other hand, is like the CEO of a company, and therefore this role generally demands more situation-competence than task-competence.

Thus, considering medicine as a single general domain would place it somewhere between engineering and politics on the continuum ranging from domains that are organized completely around tasks to those that are organized completely around situations. Looking more closely at medicine in terms of the distinct sub-domains that comprise it, it is fair to say that the over-arching domain of medicine is really a loose collection of sub-domains that span the gamut from primarily task-organized (surgery) to mixed (general practice) to primarily situation-organized (HMO head).

The correlation between qualitatively different types of abilities (vertical and integrative), types of competencies (task-competencies and situation-competencies), and types of domains (organized predominantly around tasks or situations) leads naturally to the notion of "fit" between the abilities of an individual and the demands of a domain (in terms of the types of competencies they require). (See Figure 5.5.)

Assessed Expertise

Some researchers seem to treat expertise as something intrinsic to a person yet different from a competence, or as a special kind of competence that enables an individual to exhibit superior performance compared

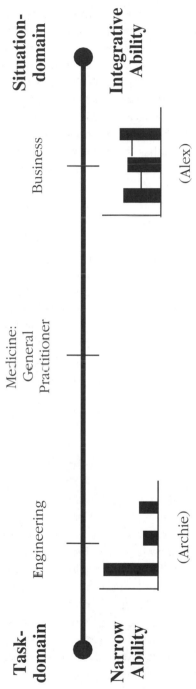

FIGURE 5.5. The dimension of "fit" between individuals and domains that we are exploring depends on the insight that humans have both narrow content-specific and broad integrative cognitive faculties, that domains can be described in terms of both narrowly defined tasks and diffuse situations, and that the qualitatively different kinds of ability profiles can be correlated with the qualitatively different kinds of domains systematically.

to her peers. In either sense, expertise is treated as something intrinsic to the individual. In our view, expertise is an extrinsic judgment assessed on an observable performance that depends on an intrinsic competence. In other words, from our perspective it does not make sense to say that someone "has an expertise." People have competencies (that is, coordinated skills and factual knowledge) that enable them to perform tasks, solve problems, create artifacts, or otherwise exhibit controlled and intentional behaviors. Other members of the society (designated by Csikszentmihalyi [1996] as the relevant field) may choose to specify a functionally defined class of behaviors (for example, creating a sculpture, running a marathon, designing a circuit, or running a company) that is valued in the culture for one reason or another. With respect to this class of behaviors the field can then construct a set of criteria for assessing the quality of a given performance of the target behavior (for example, the aesthetic merit of the sculpture, the runner's elapsed marathon time, the efficiency of the circuit, or the profit generated by a company). The individual who consistently meets the stated criteria or whose performance is assessed to be superior to those of his peers is judged *to be* an expert. To say that the person *has* an expertise unnecessarily conflates the extrinsic, socially constructed assessment of a behavior with the intrinsic, neurologically grounded competence that generates the behavior without respect to a particular cultural end.

Specifying a precise and general definition of "expertise" that would give insight into the criterion pertinent to any particular domain or individual is even more problematic than was the case for "competence." Fortunately, since expertise is by definition an assessment (albeit indirect) of a competence, the qualitative distinction between task-competence and situation-competence naturally implies a parallel distinction between task-expertise and situation-expertise. One hypothesis that stems from our analysis is that a better fit between individual and domain in the specific sense we have defined leads to higher expertise on average. There are too many variables and too many random influences on persons between the time they are young and the time they embark on a career to make it possible in most cases to predict ultimate outcomes (in terms of the domain they end up in and their level of expertise there) from early abilities with any degree of precision. But "fit" may be one theoretical construct that has robust predictive power across an individual lifetime, at least in a probabilistic sense.

CONCLUSIONS: IMPLICATIONS FOR EDUCATION

By and large, our educational system has been fashioned to develop specific kinds of competencies and to assess individuals in terms of their respective expertises. We know far more about how to train and assess engineers or writers than we do about the training and assessment of executives or politicians. Put in the terms of our analysis, education and assessment have long been skewed toward domain-specific abilities, competencies, and forms of expertise.

A skeptical observer might counter that our tests of general intelligence represent an effort to select out individuals who have situational rather than task expertise. The identification of future executives, politicians, or generalists may indeed be a goal of the architects of IQ or SAT tests. Yet on our analysis, such a program falls short: Most of the abilities tested are specific linguistic or logical-mathematical ones, rather than more general analytic, synthesizing, or planning ones. Nor is there evidence that such instruments select out the situation-experts; if anything, they are more likely to identify those who are experts with numbers or words: Professors of individual disciplines rather than effective principals, superintendents, or university presidents.

This bias is not restricted to testers, however. Our educational institutions in general are skewed toward individuals with vertical profiles. Individuals go into teaching with these profiles and they select "their own" in an effort to replicate themselves. Throughout history there have been educational institutions that seek to identify and develop broader capacities (for example, some of the institutes and military academies of continental Europe), but these are nearly always in the minority; and at a time of heightened interest in state and national testing, the inclination to go with standard disciplinary mastery is greater than ever.

In the final lines of this chapter, it is not possible to develop an alternative approach to education and assessment. As a prolegomenon to such an effort, we mention a few points to consider:

1. It should be possible to focus not on raw abilities per se but rather on the fit between an individual's profile and the available career options.
2. Both within and across domains, it would be useful to develop measures of task-competence, on the one hand, and situational-competence on the other.

3. For both cognitive and personality considerations, individuals may differ in their proclivities toward task- or situational-competence. Using our notion of an ability space, points close to an axis reflect a highly peaked ability profile and suggest an individual "at promise" for task-like pursuits. In contrast, individuals with points further from an axis, and a flatter profile of intelligences, may suggest more potential for situational mastery and integration of information across domains.

4. Greater efforts ought to be expended in modeling and training situational competence, synthesizing and integrating capacities and in documenting success in doing so. Computer-aided simulations are a promising means for accomplishing this end.

5. It might be useful to create a map charting the demands of different domains and sub-domains, in terms of both content demands and task-situation demands. On this map one could overlay a map of individual ability profiles known to be successful in those domains. In this way one might be able to develop assessments that have an early predictive ability using the formal measures of fit that we have defined.

References

Bruner, J. S. (1960). *The process of education*. Cambridge: Harvard University Press.

Changeux, J. P. (1999, October). Lectures on Mind, Brain, and Behavior. Harvard University, Cambridge, MA.

Changeux, J. P., & Ricoeur, P. (2000). *What makes us think?* Princeton, NJ: Princeton University Press.

Csikszentmihalyi, M. (1996). *Creativity*. New York: HarperCollins.

Ericsson, K. A., & Charness, N. (1994). Expert performance: Its structure and acquisition. *American Psychologist, 49*(8), 725–747.

Eysenck, H. J. (1967). Intelligence assessment: A theoretical and experimental approach. *British Journal of Educational Psychology, 37*, 81–98.

Eysenck, H. J. (1979). *The nature and measurement of intelligence*. New York: Springer-Verlag.

Feldman, D. (1994). *Beyond universals in cognitive development*. Norwood, NJ: Ablex.

Fodor, J. (1983). *The modularity of mind*. Cambridge, MA: MIT Press.

Fodor, J. A. (2000). *The mind doesn't work that way*. Cambridge, MA: MIT Press.

Gallistel, C. R. (1990). *The organization of learning*. Cambridge, MA: MIT Press.

Gardner, H. (1983/1993). *Frames of mind: The theory of multiple intelligences*. New York: Basic Books.

Gardner, H. (1991). *The unschooled mind*. New York: Basic Books.

Gardner, H. (1999a). *The disciplined mind*. New York: Simon and Schuster.

Gardner, H. (1999b). *Intelligence reframed: Multiple intelligences in the twenty-first century*. New York: Basic Books.

Herrnstein, R., & Murray, C. (1994). *The bell curve*. New York: Free Press.

Jensen, A. R. (1987). Individual differences in the Hick paradigm. In P. Vernon (Ed.), *Speed of information processing and intelligence*. Norwood, NJ: Ablex.

Karmiloff-Smith, A. (1992). *Beyond modularity: A developmental perspective on cognitive science*. Cambridge, MA: MIT Press.

Keller, E. F. (1983). *A feeling for the organism: The life and work of Barbara McClintock*. New York: W. H. Freeman and Company.

Luria, A. R. (1966). *The higher cortical functions in man*. New York: Basic Books.

McClelland, D. C. (1973). Testing for competence rather than for "intelligence." *American Psychologist, 28*(1), 1–14.

Pinker, S. (1997). *How the mind works*. New York: W. W. Norton and Company.

Sperber, D. (1996). *Explaining culture: A naturalistic approach*. Malden, MA: Blackwell Publishers Inc.

Tomasello, M. (1999). *The cultural origins of human cognition*. Cambridge, MA: Harvard University Press.

Tomasello, M. & Call, J. (1997). *Primate cognition*. New York: Oxford University Press.

Tooby, J., & Cosmides, L. (1992). The psychological foundations of culture. In J. H. Barkow, L. Cosmides, and J. Tooby (Eds.), *The adapted mind*. New York: Oxford University Press.

Werner, H. (1957). The concept of development from a comparative and organismic point of view. In D. Harris (Ed.), *The concept of development*. Minneapolis, MN: University of Minnesota Press.

6

Expertise and Mental Disabilities

Bridging the Unbridgeable?

Elena L. Grigorenko

Jean-Baptiste Grenouille, the main character of Patrick Süskind's *Perfume*, was an expert perfumer. His knowledge of aromas, his ability to differentiate, dissect, mix, and create various smells gave him a craft and made other people adore and hate him. And yet, from the very beginning of the book, it is clear that Grenouille was not a "typical" individual: His language development was delayed, his cognitive abilities were challenged, and his motor functioning appeared to be impaired. Yet he was a true expert of smell – he knew how to imitate the perfume of a blossom, the smell of a dog, various human odors, and even the aromas of those rare humans who inspire love. His skill was recognized and admired, and Grenouille kept developing and strengthening it.

The example of Grenouille poses an interesting question – can it really be that a person is simultaneously an expert in one domain and mentally handicapped in other domains? In broader terms, is it possible for mental disability and expert knowledge to coincide? To answer this question, I first cite and discuss various definitions of the word *expertise*. Second, I briefly review the literature on expertise. Third, I present a hypothesis suggesting the coexistence of expertise and disability, and support this model with a number of cases from the literature. Finally, I explore the application of this hypothesis to studies of the etiology of expertise.

DEFINITIONS OF EXPERTISE

Working Definition

Webster's *New Universal Unabridged Dictionary* (1996) offers the following definition of *expert*: "1. a person who has special skill or knowledge in some particular field; specialist. 2.... 3. possessing special skill or knowledge; trained by practice; skillful or skilled" (p. 681). There are three distinct features of these definitions: (1) they use the words *skill* and *knowledge* (that is, expertise is about knowing something or knowing how to do something); (2) they stress a specialization, at least relative, of skill and knowledge (that is, expertise is limited to a particular domain); and (3) they link expertise with practice. Yet another detail of these definitions relevant to the following discussion is that they do not make any reference to abilities, general or specific.

Here I assume a definition of expertise closely linked to those above, in that (1) it links expert performance to the relevant knowledge base; and (2) it presumes a remarkable amount of training needed for the construction of the knowledge base. Moreover, I extend the definitions by stating that the domain of expertise is defined through two limiting factors: (1) individual performance in the domain of expertise as compared to performance of the same individual in other domains, and (2) individual performance in the domain of expertise as compared to performance of other individuals from a comparable group in the same domain. According to this definition, domains of expertise are defined, first, within an individual and, second, between individuals. In the section below I try to establish connections between the proposed definitions of expertise with regard to some of the existing literature.

Selected Review of the Literature on Expertise

In line with the Webster definitions presented above, expertise has been thought of by psychologists in a number of different ways. Since the task of this chapter is not to provide a comprehensive review of the literature on expertise but to illustrate a number of points with regard to the working definition of expertise offered here, the literature summary is structured in the following way. First, I briefly summarize points of view with regard to the importance of the knowledge base for the development of expertise. Second, I delineate the spectrum of positions regarding the role of abilities in developing expertise. (For a more detailed review, see Sternberg, Grigorenko, and Ferrari, 2002.) Third, I briefly point out the importance of the concept of the adaptability of expert knowledge.

One conception is *knowledge-based*. The central idea of this conceptualization is that expertise is defined through domain-specific knowledge. However, theoreticians working within this approach to expertise stress that, although knowledge is a necessary condition, it is not a sufficient condition for becoming an expert. The knowledge-based theories of expertise originate from the work of de Groot (1946/1978) and Chase and Simon (1973). Their work was carried out in a specific domain of expertise – chess. Specifically, de Groot (1946/1978) used a think-aloud approach, asking chess players of differing levels of expertise (grand masters and chess experts who did not have the title) to share their thought processes while they contemplated their next moves. Whereas grand masters and experts without the title considered a similar number of moves and evaluated the moves similarly, the grand masters arrived at the best move earlier in their thought processes than did untitled experts. De Groot concluded that the grand masters relied on a more extensive knowledge base than did the more typical chess experts; specifically, they were able to conceptualize the position and find the match between the presented position as similar or identical to one they had seen before, which permitted them to select the optimal move more quickly. Thus, what distinguished the chess experts at different levels was knowledge from previous experience, not a particular type of information processing.

In addition, de Groot asked players at different levels of expertise to recall a middle-game position from a game they were not currently engaged in that was shown to them for just short amounts of time. The results showed that the level of recall of the grand masters was about 130 percent more accurate than that of untitled experts. In explaining this difference, de Groot again referred to differences in knowledge base: The grand masters were able to identify and recall a configuration as one they had seen before, integrating the position they were presented with into a holistic entity. Since, most likely, few untitled experts had seen a similar position before or had not seen it as often, it was more difficult for them to integrate it into a single whole or as easily to encode it so they could retrieve it quickly.

Clearly, de Groot's logic assumed the link between knowledge base and experience: He thought that better recall was directly linked to a more extensive knowledge base. This assumption was critically appraised by Chase and Simon (1973), who hypothesized that de Groot's results could be explained by the fact that the grand masters simply had better memories than did the more common experts. In other words, they suggested the hypothesis that the grand masters had exceptional generalized memory skills, which allowed them to build more extensive knowledge bases than those of common experts. To test this hypothesis, Chase and Simon devised a series of experiments in which they utilized both positions from real games (similar to de Groot's experimentation) and random configurations. If the group difference indeed was based on better memory for pieces among the grand masters than among the common experts, then their recall should have been better for all chess board configurations, regardless of whether they were real or not. The same logic can be applied to experts versus novices. Experts should remember both real and random configurations much better than novices. The results, however, did not support the hypothesis of better memory. Level of chess expertise did matter for the recall of real-game configurations and did not matter for the recall of random configurations. So de Groot was right: What distinguished the experts from the novices and the grand masters from the experts was not overall superior recall ability, but rather the extent and organization of their knowledge base. Although their initial hypothesis was not verified, Chase and Simon (1973) took the field beyond where it was before their experiment – they suggested an explanation of how chess players at various levels of expertise could produce their recall. They observed that the recall happened in single bursts, where a number of pieces were rapidly placed on the chess board followed by pauses – Chase and Simon referred to these bursts as "chunks," using Miller's (1956) terminology. Chunks are meaningful pieces of information whose size depends on degree of expertise – the chunk size of more expert players was larger than the chunk size of less expert players, including novices (Simon and Gilmartin, 1973).

It is important to note that the findings of Chase and Simon have been replicated in a number of other domains, such as the game of Go (Reitman, 1976), electronic circuit diagrams (Egan and Schwartz, 1979), and bridge (Charness, 1979; Engle and Bukstel, 1978). Thus, the importance of a vast and organized knowledge base and the problem schemas that come with it seems to be fundamental to many different kinds of expertise. Such schemas and the information contained within them are not rapidly acquired; the expert knowledge base is built up through vast amounts of deliberate practice.

The role practice plays in enhancing human performance has been central to the work of Ericsson and colleagues (for example, Ericsson and Smith, 1991). Although this position is an extreme one, it is important to discuss this point of view because it counterbalances other positions heavily stressing the importance of abilities in developing expertise (Chi, Glaser, and Farr, 1989). Throughout years of research, Ericsson and colleagues have demonstrated, both in laboratory conditions and through case-based investigations, that practice can change human performance dramatically on working memory tasks (Chase and Ericsson, 1982; Ericsson, 1988; Ericsson, Chase, and Faloon, 1980), long-term memory tasks (Ericsson and Kintsch, 1995; Ericsson and Lehmann, 1996), speed of performance (Ericsson, Krampe, and Tesch-Römer, 1993), physical fitness (Ericsson, 2001a, 2001b), chess (Ericsson and Staszewski, 1989), and music (Ericsson and Lehmann, 1996). A number of aspects of the work of Ericsson and colleagues are relevant to the present discussion. First, they argued for restricting the definition of expert to an individual with reliably superior performance characteristics (Ericsson and Smith, 1991). Second, Ericsson and colleagues identified characteristics of expert performance by the following components: (1) the ability to select superior actions; (2) the ability to generate rapid reactions; and (3) the ability to control movement/action production better than common performers. Third, neither in their work nor in the work of their colleagues in the field did they find any acceptable evidence that innate characteristics are required for healthy adults to attain an expert level of performance in any domain (Ericsson and Lehmann, 1996; Howe, Davidson, and Sloboda, 1998). Fourth, according to their interpretation of the field, they found no "innate requirements" that are crucial to expert performance and no expertise that cannot be acquired with extended practice (Ericsson, 1996; Ericsson and Lehmann, 1996). Fifth, they defined the type of practice that appears to be central to the development of an expert, referring to it as *deliberate* practice: specially designed training activities aimed at mastering increasingly complex and challenging sequences of actions, at increasing the expert's ability to monitor and control expertise-related cognitive processes, and at changing these processes, mediating mechanisms to avoid the premature automatization of their performance (Ericsson, 1996, 1998, 2001a, 2001b; Ericsson et al., 1993).

It is important to note that Ericsson and his colleagues are the only group of researchers in the field who take such an extreme position according to which developing expertise is much more a function of practice than a function of innate abilities. Most researchers in the field do not share such an opinion and either take the other extreme of the continuum, arguing that innate abilities are essential for the development of expertise (for example, Subotnik and Arnold, 1993), or take a middle-ground position, stating that both abilities and practice are extremely important for the development of expertise (Sternberg, 1998).

One more aspect of the literature on expertise is relevant to our discussion. Apparently, when the expert knowledge base is acquired, it can be costly, in that it may overpower the expert's ability to see novel aspects of experience and, thus, become entrenched in a point of view central to the existing knowledge base (for example, Adelson, 1984; Frensch and Sternberg, 1989; Hecht and Proffitt, 1995; Luchins, 1942; Sternberg and Lubart, 1995). This "captive danger" of the existing knowledge base has been demonstrated, for example, by Frensch and Sternberg (1989), who compared the performance of expert and novice bridge players when playing bridge against a computer. As expected, experts did better than novices when the game was played in the conventional way. The results changed, however, when the game was modified. First, the game was modified in such a way that only the names of the suits were changed and replaced by neologisms (the researchers referred to such a modification as a surface-structure modification); this modification hurt the performance of both novices and experts initially, but both groups recovered quickly. Second, the researchers changed the rules of the game (they referred to this modification as deep-structure modification), so that the player laying out the low card led off the next round of play rather than the player laying out the high card, as is typically done. This change disrupted fundamental strategies of game playing. It was expected that the experts would be hurt by this change more than the novices, who were less likely to have established effective strategies of playing the game. The results supported the expectations: Experts were actually disrupted more than novices in their playing, although only initially. They eventually recovered and outperformed the novices. True experts are adaptive in the usage of their knowledge base, being able to tailor their performance based on a critical consideration of the existing situation (Chi, Glaser, and Farr, 1989; Glaser, 1996; Gott, Hall, Pokorny, Dibble, and Glaser, 1993).

Thus, the definition suggested above overlaps closely with at least some other definitions of expertise in the literature in that it (1) links expertise with an extensive and flexible knowledge base (2) that can be acquired exclusively through large volumes of deliberate practice;

(3) assumes only relevant importance of innate abilities; (4) assumes relative stability (and, possibly, even rigidity of structures developed through deliberate practice); (5) stresses consistent superiority of the expert's performance as compared to common performance; and (6) suggests the relative superiority of performance in the domain of expertise to performance in other domains. Moreover, the literature stresses the importance of the flexible nature of expert knowledge – "true" experts are expected to be able to adapt their knowledge bases to novel demands. In the following sections of the chapter I attempt to apply this consensus definition of expertise to samples of individuals with cognitive handicaps.

HYPOTHESIS: THE CONCEPT AND THEORY OF EXPERTISE CAN BE USEFULLY APPLIED TO STUDIES OF MENTAL DISABILITIES

In the remaining parts of the chapter I illustrate the applicability of the concept of expertise to studies of disabilities. Here I argue that the concept of expertise can be applied to enhance our understanding of the functioning of individuals with otherwise challenged cognitive abilities. This application presupposes that (1) under an assumption of the modularity of cognitive functioning (Fodor, 1983), it is possible to suppose that, even in a situation of severe mental disabilities, certain cognitive modules can be preserved and (2) those modules can be developed under a substantial amount of practice (often obsessive) so that (3) an expert level of performance can be achieved by a handicapped individual in a specific (expert) domain when compared to the other domains of his or her own performance and when compared to the levels of performance of other handicapped individuals with similar conditions.

This point of view assumes an interactionist perspective. The presence of a preserved isolated function (for example, musical ability) and the meeting of the child's environment (for example, a musically enhanced family environment) and this maturing function might determine the specialization of the function. Subsequent training (trainer-guided in best-case scenarios and undirected but obsessively fixed in other scenarios) might determine the degree of superiority of the developing function. A visual analogy of this process is that of a plant growing under conditions with scarce lighting. In such conditions, the whole plant bends itself to get as much light as possible so some of its branches become grossly overdeveloped, whereas others wither and eventually die.

In the following section I try to show that both the development and the manifestation of superior isolated functions in individuals with mental handicaps map themselves well on the concept of developing expertise as defined by a process of capitalizing on strengths in the environment structured to support extensive practice and training of the preserved isolated function.

EXPERTISE AGAINST THE ODDS: CAN EXPERTISE BE ACQUIRED IN THE CONTEXT OF MENTAL HANDICAP?

Commonly, the term "idiot savant" is used to describe a person who, despite being challenged with a particular neuropsychiatric condition, possesses an outstanding ability in a specific domain such as art, music, or arithmetic.[1] The term "idiot savant" was used by Alfred Binet to describe those people who have great learning difficulties and cannot cope with life on their own, yet show an outstanding ability in a specific area.

In the classical meaning of this term, savants are rather rare. It is estimated that between 2 and 3 percent of the population suffer from some degree of mental handicap, but only 0.06 percent of these are estimated to possess an unusually high level of specific ability far above that of the average normal person. Savant talents manifest themselves primarily in the six following domains: calendar calculating, lightning calculating and mathematical ability, art (drawing and sculpting), music, mechanical abilities, and spatial skills. There are fewer than one hundred documented cases of idiot savants in the world literature. The condition was first named "idiot savant" in 1887 by Dr. J. Langdon Down. He chose that term because the word *idiot* was used at that time to describe severe mental retardation (IQ below 25) and the word *savant* means "knowledgeable person" (from the French verb *savoir*). The term currently most frequently used in reference to mentally handicapped savant individuals is *Savant Syndrome*. It is of interest that almost all the reported cases of Savant Syndrome describe individuals with IQs of 40 and above.

It has been reported that approximately 10 percent of persons with autism-spectrum disorder have some savant abilities. Savant abilities have also been observed in individuals with other developmental disabilities, but at a much lower rate (1:2,000). However, since other

---

[1] See http://members.authorsguild.net/treffert/ or http://www.wisconsinmedicalsociety. org/savant/default.cfm.

developmental disabilities appear at a much higher rate than autism-spectrum disabilities, approximately half the reported cases are those of individuals with autism whereas the other half are those of individuals with other developmental disabilities.

The literature on Savant Syndrome (SS) is rather scarce, due to the rarity of the condition. However, this literature contains some common themes that are relevant to the discussion in this chapter. Specifically, the emergence of savant skills and their manifestation can be viewed in terms of the model of developing expertise.

First, all literature-known cases of SS possess extensive knowledge bases in the area of the expertise. Consider the example of Christopher, 37, who, although never diagnosed formally with an autism-spectrum condition, meets the criteria for Asperger's Syndrome (Hermelin, 2001, pp. 63–76 [here, and throughout, used by permission]). Christopher can understand, speak, read, write, and translate Danish, Dutch, Finnish, French, German, Greek, Hindi, Italian, Norwegian, Polish, Portuguese, Russian, Spanish, Swedish, Turkish, and Welsh. He is apparently able to pick up foreign languages without any visible effort from all sources available to him – radio, people (both familiar and strangers), newspapers, TV. It is interesting to note that vocabulary and morphology are comparatively easier for him than phonology and grammar. Using his prodigious knowledge of foreign languages, Christopher prefers written to oral forms of communication – he would rather write notes than talk to people. Everything that has to do with foreign languages gives Christopher pleasure and preoccupation. Thus, he spends a remarkable amount of time acquiring and practicing foreign languages. However, there is a very interesting linguistic imbalance in his acquisition and usage of those languages: Christopher's linguistic strength is localized mainly in the speedy and correct acquisition of apparently unlimited vocabulary items, as well as morphemes of new languages. His phonological and semantic performance components are much weaker, however, and are linked to his English abilities; it is as if he applies English phonemic and semantic rules to the new languages he learns. Thus, Christopher's mastery of foreign languages is limited in that he can write the same word in a number of languages, but producing meaningful complex sentences is a challenge. Christopher's knowledge of languages reminds one of a multi-lingual word dictionary.

Second, individuals with SS acquire their unique skills through practice and, if trained continuously, can reach higher than the baseline levels of functioning. The majority of the known cases of SS report intense concentration, practice, compensatory drives, and reinforcement by family and teachers. Moreover, it was initially thought that "eliminating the defect" (for example, treating for autism) could result in a loss of special skills (destruction of the uniquely formed brain circuitry). On the contrary, it has been shown that training savant skills can both enhance the skill and help the person to compensate for weaknesses by developing increased socialization, language, and independence.

Third, there is no evidence of the importance of innate abilities for the manifestation of savant skills. Specifically, most of the theories of the development of savant skills assume the occurrence of some kind of left-brain damage (pre-, peri-, or post-natal) with migratory, right-brain compensation (Treffert, 1988). A part of the SS puzzle is that a number of individuals demonstrating savant skills after the trauma had not demonstrated such skills prior to the brain damage.

Fourth, individuals with SS are able to function at levels of performance superior to common performance. At the present time, there probably are fewer than twenty-five known living individuals with SS. Some of the names recognizable by the general public due to the popularization of their condition on TV or in popular science-oriented programs are Lesley Lemke (music), Alonzo Clements (sculpture), Richard Wawro (painting), Stephen Wiltshire (drawing), and Tony DeBlois (music). During his lifetime from 1849 to 1908, "Blind Tom" Bethune (Thomas Wiggins), a musical prodigy, was referred to as "the eighth wonder of the world." At age eleven, Tom played at the White House, and at age sixteen began a piano concert tour that took him around the world. Remarkably, his musical repertoire included over seven thousand pieces, one hundred of which were composed by him; in contrast, his vocabulary was barely over one hundred words.

Fifth, savant skills appear to develop in relative isolation in an individual.[2] Consider the example of Kate (Hermelin, 2001, pp. 49–62). Kate is an individual with Asperger's Syndrome. Kate does not make eye contact, exhibits repetitive speech, and experiences obsessive fixations on certain restricted topics. She also suffers from a relatively mild form of cerebral palsy, resulting in some loss of manual dexterity, clumsiness, and awkward gait. Kate received most of her education in a special school and, when transferred to a regular school, could not cope

[2] See http://www.twainquotes.com/archangels.html,
http://www.npr.org/programs/morning/features/2002/mar/blindtom/,
http://www.pbs.org/opb/life360/diversions/blindtom/page1.htm, or
http://www.wisconsinmedicalsociety.org/savant/blindtom.cfm.

with the social demands of interactions with teachers and peers or take part in lessons. When tested in her late forties, her scores on a test of social maturity and a test of daily living skills looked like those of an eight-year-old. Kate is not interested in other people's poetry and cannot memorize poetry but she writes poetry that, apparently, has depth and reflection:

> Here I give a finger: it's got no hand.
> I got a face: I never saw it.
> I touch a leg: didn't see the rest.
> Here I be: must have gone somewhere.
>   Gave a daisy: nothing else.
>   Got lost in clothes but not the body.
>   Sent my eyes into what I do.
>   Feet tip-a-toe: quick I was then not.
> I sat in heaven: the ground went.
> Sing come in: a sound got shouts.
> Screaming holes got not edges.
> I'm a something where fog lingers somewhere.
> No one comes where I go.
> I saw death when help came faster.
> The fish had not water.

> > > (as cited by Hermelin, 2001, pp. 52–3)

Or

> Words missing;
> directing links lost;
> every now and again
> a word pops up
> within my head
> that helps.
> Months go by;
> the connection
> just connects
> when I say it in right place,
> leading it to right person.
> She goes
> 'Ah, is that what you meant?'

> > > (as cited in Hermelin, 2001, pp. 54–5)

Hermelin and her colleagues analyzed about seventy poems by Kate. About half of them are concerned with self-analysis and reflection; about seventy percent are concerned with personal relationships; less frequent are descriptions of people and landscapes. The author voice predominantly used by Kate is one that talks to herself or to nobody; she is rarely concerned with addressing the audience or creating other characters.

> I was contradicting my own patterns
> very intelligently
> till society hit me.
> I knew my own patterns to create much
> leisure, pleasure, safety,
> till society whacked me.
> I knew how to start
> to control the input,
> slowly giving confidence,
> to my own upward surge powerfully
> till society heavily bounced on me.
>
> (as cited by Hermelin, 2001, pp. 58–9)

Hermelin and colleagues note interesting discrepancies in Kate's ability to handle words – Kate can use a word in her poetry (based on the analysis of her poems, her vocabulary is pretty large), but cannot define the word when asked to perform a vocabulary subtest of an intelligence test.

Sixth, there are some insights with regard to the importance of the expert-level knowledge base for the functioning of individuals with SS. For example, it appears that the extraordinary ability of calendar savants is closely linked to their skill of transforming single dates into a body of expert knowledge "mirroring the calendar structure" (Hermelin, 2001, p. 104) and engaging in the problem solving of a complex scaffold of relevant structural and functional information. Similarly, savant visual artists do not simply memorize hundreds of details characterizing a scene or an object, they construct an image from their own unique perspective combining the information available to them in such detail that they can reconstruct all its salient features almost exactly on their drawings (for example, art by Stephen Wiltshire and Richard Wawro).

In this section of the chapter, I have attempted to show that the acquisition and manifestation of remarkable savant skills in individuals with a severe mental handicap resemble the process of acquiring and manifesting expertise as presented in the literature on expertise. It is of interest that about half the population of people with a mental handicap, especially those with autism, obtain scores on at least one or more subtests of general intelligence that put them into the range of normal functioning (Hermelin, 2001). It is possible that these individuals, as children, have a potential to achieve superior (to the common level of performance of children with comparable handicaps) levels of performance if they develop in an enriched environment. It is possible for them to become experts in an isolated skill as compared to the common skills of children in comparable groups. If the model of expertise is applicable to various levels of expertness in the typically developing population (for example, from world-class chess masters to untitled expert chess players), then it can also be applied to various levels of expertise in the population of individuals with mental handicap. This assumption permits consideration of the potential implications of such an inclusive model of expertise in the context of examining the etiology of various mental functions across different populations.

IMPLICATIONS OF AN INCLUSIVE MODEL OF EXPERTISE FOR REVEALING THE GENETIC ETIOLOGY OF COMPLEX COGNITIVE FUNCTIONS

The objective of this section of the chapter is to demonstrate the methodological implications of the application of a broad theory of developing expertise for understanding the transmission of mental abilities and disabilities in the general population. To reveal these implications, I start by discussing a general issue of phenotype definition in the studies of the genetic etiology of complex cognitive functions.

The task of defining phenotypes transmitted in families at risk for the development of psychiatric conditions is now, inarguably, the central problem of the field of searching for the genetic etiology of complex behavioral traits (Pauls, 1993; Smoller and Tsuang, 1998; Tsuang, Faraone, and Lyons, 1993). In the field today, there are three general approaches for establishing phenotype statuses.

The first approach capitalizes on DSM criteria for specific disorders. In this approach, researchers usually start with the most conservative, strictly DSM-based, phenotype definition and end with the most inclusive phenotype definition (Crowe, Noyes, Pauls, and Slymen, 1983; Kendler, Neale, Kessler, Heath, and Eaves, 1993; Noyes et al., 1986; Weissman et al., 1993). In other words, the door to the affliction category is initially barely open because the criterion is very stringent (that is, the "affected" status requires that many symptoms last a significant period of time), but the door gradually opens wider and wider, and more and more people find their way into the affected category. In this approach, the essence of the phenotype is present regardless of subsequent modifications, but the severity varies. Consequently, genetic analyses are carried out on a set of phenotypes ranging from the most stringent to the most inclusive definitions.

The second approach to defining phenotypes involves considering the underlying theoretical components and defining multiple phenotypes based on these different components. The phenotype under study is split into its components, and then a diagnosis is made based on these components, rather than on the "essence" of the phenotype (Comuzzie et al., 1997; Grigorenko et al., 1997). The third and most recent approach defines phenotypes of interest across a complete ability spectrum (for example, Haseman and Elston, 1972; DeFries and Fulker, 1988; Risch and Zhang, 1996), spanning a phenotypic range from one extreme to another. The idea here is to include discordant pairs of relatives (that is, affected and unaffected individuals) in order to maximize the coverage of a trait.

Continuing the discussion of the applicability of the expertise model to individuals across the whole spectrum of ability, here I attempt to extend the third approach to establish the continuity of a phenotype of interest across different psychiatric diagnoses. The underlying logic here is to capitalize on the presence of a shared process across a number of diagnostic categories and then to investigate whether the observed comorbidity can be explained by symptom-specific genetic mechanisms. Studies in reading provide a case in point.

Argument

The general argument underlying the extension of the third approach to phenotype definitions states that:

If cognition is modular such that given cognitive functions can be observed at different levels of functioning,

and

If, when observed in different contexts, the function manifests integrity and similar features, then a phenotype value can be assigned based on this cognitive function, even though this value might cross "distinct" psychiatric diagnoses (or distinct populations, such as typically and atypically developing individuals) and be viewed and studied as variable manifestations of the same underlying genetic mechanism functioning in different behavioral contexts (Elena L. Grigorenko).

To illustrate, let us examine how this general argument can be discerned in research on reading. Phenomenologically, the process of acquiring expertise in reading and the mechanisms of this process have been described and studied across a wide spectrum of reading abilities. Research explores normal reading as well as specific reading disability (specific reading under-performance given the levels of other cognitive skills, that is, reading performance below that expected based on the level of general cognitive functioning) and reading precocity (specific reading over-performance given the levels of other cognitive skills, that is, reading performance above that expected based on the level of general cognitive functioning). One of the questions of interest in the field is whether normal reading, reading disability, and reading precocity can be accounted for by a single comprehensive model (which would represent the range of functioning of a single mechanism across a wide spectrum of abilities of the general population) – the inclusive expertise model (for example, Pennington, Johnson, and Welsh, 1987).

Researchers generally assume that reading involves two broadly defined sets of skills. The first set comprises those skills required for identifying printed words. The ability to move between oral and written language depends on the acquisition of these skills. Another important set of skills enables the reader to comprehend the meaning of the text. Evidence accumulated over years of research suggests that reading comprehension is somewhat separable from single-word decoding skills, both theoretically and in the performance of the extreme groups (Perfetti, 1985). Here I discuss single-word reading skills only, specifically, single-word reading in studies of typical reading (that is, when the level of single-word reading matches the level of general cognitive functioning), precocious reading[3] and hyperlexia[4] (that is, when the level of single-word reading is higher than that expected based on the level of

---

[3] Precocious reading ability is usually defined by comparing performance on single-word reading tests with what is expected on the basis of either age or IQ. By definition, precocious readers have had little or no exposure to standard reading instruction. The incidence of precocious reading ability has been estimated at 1 to 3.5 percent (Durkin, 1966; Durkin, 1970). The developmental course of precocious reading is not well studied.

[4] References to precocious ability in word recognition in developmentally disabled populations have been present in the literature for many years (Kanner, 1943; Parker, 1919; Phillips, 1930). Following Silberberg and Silberberg, the term *hyperlexia* is used to refer to an unusually well-developed ability to read single words in children with cognitive deficits and behavioral abnormalities (Silberberg and Silberberg, 1967). Currently, core features of hyperlexia are isolated, driven, compulsive, and indiscriminate reading abilities manifested as early as age two, but usually by age five. These abilities occur in the absence of specific reading instruction and exceed what would be expected or

general cognitive functioning), and dyslexia[5] (that is, when the level of single-word reading is below that expected based on the level of general cognitive functioning) – broadly speaking, three different levels of expertise in single-word reading. The remainder of this text discusses the two premises above and the plausibility of the argument's conclusion in this case.

Premise One: The Modularity of Single-Word Reading with Respect to Other Cognitive Abilities

The concept of modularity in cognition assumes the existence of functionally distinct modules (or units) that, to a certain degree, function separately (Fodor, 1983). The main characteristics of modularity are: (1) modules are relatively encapsulated informationally (that is, the flow of information between modules is restricted); (2) modules are domain-specific: they only operate on certain kinds of inputs (that is, they are specialized systems for specialized tasks); (3) once formed, modules tend to become automatized (that is, they facilitate the rapid processing of information); (4) modules offer rather rough and shallow information outputs that subsequently require further processing; (5) modularity assumes the independence of acquisition – that is, the possibility that a module A can develop despite a severe impairment of a module B (or vice versa); and (6) modules can be selectively impaired.

The modularity approach has attracted much attention and resulted in much controversy in the general field of cognitive psychology and in

predicted on the basis of intelligence. They also coexist with developmental disturbances that involve delays and deviances in language, deficits in procedural and patterned motor tasks, and interpersonal peculiarities (Cobrinik, 1982; Cobrinik, 1974; Cossu and Marshall, 1986; Cossu and Marshall, 1990; Goldberg and Rothermel, 1984; Mehegan and Dreifuss, 1972; Siegel, 1984). The frequency of hyperlexia, estimated in very few isolated studies, appears to be five to ten percent among PDD individuals (Burd, Kerbeshian, and Fisher, 1985).

[5] Dyslexia (specific reading disability) is a common, cognitively and behaviorally heterogeneous developmental condition, characterized primarily by severe difficulty in the mastery of reading. Dyslexia is considered to be undetectable in children of pre-reading age, even though many who will become dyslexic exhibit specific patterns of cognitive processing deficits that are thought to be a part of the dyslexia spectrum (Felton and Brown, 1990; Felton and Wood, 1992; Scarborough, 1984; Wood and Felton, 1994). Dyslexia is first reliably diagnosed in primary school ("Learning Disabilities Statistics Sheet," 1997); most dyslexic children exhibit deficient reading skills throughout youth and adolescence (Felton, 1998; Lyon, 1995), and most continue to manifest these difficulties throughout adulthood (Felton, Naylor, and Wood, 1990; Vogel and Adelman, 1992).

the narrow field of the psychology of reading (Carston, 1996; Garfield, 1994). With regard to single-word reading/decoding, the hypothesis of modularity assumes (1) the relative independence of single-word reading/decoding from other cognitive functions such as, for example, intelligence and language production; (2) the relative independence of single-word reading/decoding from comprehension of word meaning; (3) the rapid automatization of single-word reading/decoding when the function is formed; (4) the flexibility of information input (that is, the input of orthographical and phonological units) with the possibility of multiple interpretations in further processing; (5) an advance of single-word reading over other cognitive functions; and (6) a retardation of single-word reading/decoding compared to other cognitive functions. A significant amount of evidence in the literature on normal reading acquisition, dyslexia, and precocious reading acquisition supports the modularity of single-word reading/decoding and its independence from other cognitive abilities (Cossu and Marshall, 1986; Cossu and Marshall, 1990; Tønnessen, 1999; van Daal and van der Leij, 1999).

Specifically, in support of the modularity hypothesis, Seymour and Evans presented a longitudinal case study of literacy development in MP, a hyperlexic boy, who was followed over his first three school years (Seymour and Evans, 1992). Despite impaired language production and comprehension, MP developed an effective orthographic system indicated by normal reaction-time patterns, success in the reading and spelling of words and non-words, and adequate semantic processing of single-lexical items. The authors interpreted the results as supportive of the developmental modularity of the orthographic and semantic systems.

Whitehouse and Harris investigated the manifestation of hyperlexia in twenty boys diagnosed with infantile autism (Whitehouse and Harris, 1984). Researchers identified these boys early in life and then followed their development. The sample was extremely diverse in terms of the participants' levels of comprehension, and verbal IQ, performance IQ, and full IQ. Similarly, Burd and Kerbeshian presented a case in which a patient exhibited both hyperlexia and hypographia (Burd and Kerbeshian, 1985). The description of the patient's hypographia was rather brief, but it included references to poor spelling and limited syntax. Graziani, Brodsky, Mason, and Zager (1983) studied twenty-one hyperlexic children (eighteen boys and three girls) longitudinally. These children were initially identified at five years of age, based on the criteria of impaired language comprehension but advanced word recognition abilities (as compared with mental age). The researchers found that children with below-normal IQ scores beyond the age of eight years had a poor prognosis (namely, special education programs) irrespective of word-analytic abilities. Goldberg and Rothermel (1984) attempted to delineate the process employed in hyperlexic reading by administering a set of various reading tests to eight hyperlexics. The results revealed that hyperlexic children were able to comprehend, to a certain degree, single words and sentences but not paragraphs, suggesting, once again, the relative independence of single-word reading/decoding and comprehension modules.

Glosser, Friedman, and Roeltgen (1996) presented the case of a child, LA, diagnosed with a severe attentional disorder, hyperactivity, and mild-moderate mental retardation. The clinical presentation of this child matched that of hyperlexia (Full Scale IQ = 51, WRAT-R Single-Word Reading Score = 135). The researchers followed this child longitudinally and evaluated the developmental state and dynamics of his single-word reading and spelling skills. The team then demonstrated that LA's pseudoword reading and spelling followed a pattern, consisting of the selectively impaired decoding of pseudowords that have no lexical analogies. This finding (a failure to decode pseudowords that have no lexical orthographic analogies), in the authors' interpretation, could reflect deficiencies in the higher-order cognitive strategies necessary for forming the pronunciation of non-words that do not have analogous real words. This failure is consistent with a version of the connectionism model, according to which, under normal conditions, reading takes place exclusively through a single, automatic, lexically based, phonological processing system; when an unknown stimulus is encountered, however, the contribution of higher-level cognitive systems is critical (Plaut, McClelland, and Seidenberg, 1996).

Building on these results, Glosser, Grugan, and Friedman (1997) conducted two other experiments with LA. In the first experiment, LA, despite markedly impaired comprehension of word meaning, acquired and retained the orthographic patterns for new words with exceptional spellings. In the second experiment, which involved the repetition of words and pseudowords, LA demonstrated that the processing of complex lexical and phonological information could take place without relevant semantic knowledge. Thus, according to these researchers, both orthographic and phonological processing can be accomplished without input from the semantic system.

Additional support for the modularity of single-word reading and other reading-related processes also comes from studies of precocious readers with IQs in the normal or gifted range. Precocious readers tend to score high on the measure of verbal intelligence (Cassidy and Vukelich, 1980), but high verbal ability is neither necessary nor sufficient for reading precocity (Jackson, 1992). Thus, Jackson and colleagues (Jackson et al., 1988) presented a subgroup of kindergarteners who were precocious readers; they were extremely good at non-word reading but scored comparatively low on tests of verbal IQ, reading comprehension, and the reading of exception words.

Crain-Thoreson and Dale (1992) longitudinally studied a group of verbally precocious young children; although the children remained verbally precocious, researchers discerned a low incidence of precocious reading. Similarly, Patel and Patterson (1982) investigated twenty precocious readers and concluded that early reading acquisition is not necessarily linked to higher levels of general intelligence and precocious linguistic development.

Premise Two: Similarities in the Structure and Process of Single-Word Reading in Normal, Precocious, and Disabled Readers

The intensive efforts of numerous research groups over the last few years have unequivocally implicated phonological processing as the core processing that guides normal and challenged reading acquisition (Blachman, 1997; Snowling, 2000). Researchers have also learned, however, that individual variability in phonological processes does not fully predict individual variability in reading skills. Bus and van IJzendoorn (1999) conducted a meta-analysis of experimental intervention studies exploring the trainability of phonological awareness; the results showed that experimentally manipulated phonological awareness explains about 12 percent of the variance in reading skills. Thus, although phonological awareness is a substantial predictor of reading, it is not the only or the strongest predictor. For example, a meta-analysis of studies of parents' storybook reading to their preschoolers showed that early storybook reading explained about 8 percent of the variance in children's literacy skills (Bus, van IJzendoorn, and Pellegrini, 1995). Researchers are becoming more and more interested in other deficits that might play an important role in reading development (Wolf, 1997). Our discussion here, however, is limited to phonological processes (abilities).

Defined broadly, phonological abilities are one's sensitivity to and facility with the phonemes (basic sound elements) of an oral language (Wagner and Torgesen, 1987). There are a number of classifications of phonological abilities. For example, Wagner and Torgesen (1987) distinguished three major types of phonological abilities: phonological awareness (one's sensitivity to and access to the sound of phonemes in spoken words),[6] phonological coding in short-term memory (characteristics of one's temporary storage of verbal information, also referred to as verbal working memory); and retrieval of phonological codes from long-term memory (one's ability to access the pronunciations of letters, digits, and words, also referred to as rapid naming). It has been noted that these abilities substantially correlate with each other (Wagner, Torgesen, Laughon, Simmons, and Rashotte, 1993; Wagner, Torgesen, and Rashotte, 1994). However, there is a substantial amount of evidence suggesting that different abilities make differential contributions to reading achievement at various developmental stages (Bowers, Sunseth, and Golden, 1999; Jong and van der Leij, 1999; Torgesen, Wagner, Rashotte, Burgess, and Hecht, 1997), and that the relationships between phonological abilities and reading acquisition are of a complex, reciprocal nature (that is, some phonological abilities might precede reading acquisition, whereas others might be consequential to learning to read [Perfetti and McCutchen, 1987]).

Phonological abilities have been shown to be causally related to early reading acquisition, meaning that progress in learning to read can be predicted from the development of phonological abilities, and that training in phonological abilities prior to the beginning of reading instruction has substantial effects on early reading acquisition (Olson, Wise, Conners, Rack, and Fulker, 1989; Yopp, 1988). Moreover, phonological deficits are considered to be one of the core deficits in the development and manifestation of reading disability (Olson, Wise, Conners, Rack, and Fulker, 1989; Stanovich and Siegel, 1994).

Similarly, some studies (though fewer in number) have addressed the componential structure of precocious reading. Several early studies indicated that a number of reading-spectrum cognitive processes that have been reported as correlates of both reading ability and reading disability (real- and non-word decoding, auditory short-term memory

---

[6] This ability can be further differentiated into phonological synthesis (one's ability to blend a sequence of phonemes into a word) and phonological analysis (one's ability to break spoken words into their constituent phonemes).

span, naming speed, and text-reading accuracy) also correlate with precocious reading ability (Jackson, Donaldson, and Cleland, 1988; Jackson and Myers, 1982; Roedell, Jackson, and Robinson, 1980).

Backman (1983) found that kindergarten-age precocious readers performed substantially better than age-matched nonreaders on a phoneme deletion task (that is, say *cat* without *c*). In addition, within this sample of twenty-four precocious readers, performance on the sound deletion tasks moderately correlated with individual differences in pseudoword reading accuracy and spelling, but not with other aspects of reading skills. Backman found, however, that specific isolated phonological measures correlated with isolated reading skills. Because there is significant variance in specific skills among precocious readers, this evidence does not support the hypothesis that precocious performance on phonological tasks is a prerequisite for precocity in reading.

As if in support of Backman's cautious note, Pennington, Johnson, and Welsh (1987) described the case of a preschool boy of superior intelligence who read very early and at a level well beyond what his verbal, performance, and full IQ would have predicted. The boy was assessed by a number of phonological tasks, but the results were somewhat unexpected: his reading precocity for single words exceeded by far his performance on phoneme segmentation, auditory verbal short-memory, and lexical retrieval tasks. The boy's level of reading comprehension, writing, and spelling matched his level of oral comprehension and his verbal IQ.

Researchers have also investigated indicators of the naming process (for example, naming letters) as concurrent and predictive correlates of reading among precocious readers (Jackson, Donaldson, and Cleland, 1988; Jackson and Myers, 1982; Jackson and Biemiller, 1985). It was found that extremely precocious readers named letters faster than moderately precocious readers did; however, the group as a whole was substantially slower at naming letters than reading-level-matched older children were. It has been shown, however, that performance on letter-naming tasks is strongly influenced by chronological age; therefore, it is possible that the observed difference might be attributed to the relative youth of the precocious readers, compared to their reading-level matched controls (Stanovich, Nathan, and Zolman, 1988).

Researchers have found that the greatest strength of precocious readers is text-reading speed (both oral and silent) (Jackson and Biemiller, 1985; Jackson and Donaldson, 1989; Mills and Jackson, 1990; Tobin and

Pikulski, 1988). The superiority of this skill is obvious, when compared to both the precocious readers' own single-word reading speed and to the text-reading speed of reading-matched older children. In addition, the precocious readers' reading of isolated words is characterized by the accuracy rather than the speed of their pronunciation (Jackson and Donaldson, 1989).

Taken together, this evidence supports the two premises of the argument. First, the process of single-word reading/decoding appears to be modular; we can thus assert its relatively independent development/maturation and its relatively independent impairment. Second, the processes of single-word reading and decoding manifest the same structure (at least with respect to reading-related phonological processes). Therefore, it is conceivable that we can extend the phenotype-extremes approach to phenotype definition by bridging heterogeneous psychiatric conditions and assuming a shared genetic basis underlying the modular system of interest. There are some dispersed pieces of evidence that suggest the clustering of disabled reading among relatives of hyperlexia probands (Healy, Aram, Horwitz, and Kessler, 1982). In addition, there is strong evidence indicating a broad variation in reading skills (including exceptional reading performance) among relatives of dyslexia probands (Felton, Naylor, and Wood, 1990). To conclude, studies of phenotypes characteristic of a specific modular cognitive system (for example, single-word reading) by means of a complete coverage of its extremes should enhance our understanding of the genetic bases underlying the functioning of this system.

CONCLUSION

In this chapter I have attempted to apply the definition and current understanding of expertise to research on cognitive disabilities. This application is helpful in the following ways. First, it allows us to encompass in one broad theoretical framework the development of abilities and disabilities. Using the example of hyperlexia, the model explains the development and manifestation of a super-skill (with regard to the level of other cognitive skills) largely as an outcome of committed practice targeted at isolated modular function (Nation, 1999).

Second, the model of expertise is instrumental in terms of understanding such a striking phenomenon as Savant Syndrome. The isolated expertise of savants appears to be explainable in the same terms as that of socially recognized experts in other domains. Jean-Baptiste

Grenouille, for example, is a colorful illustration of the applicability of the expertise model to an individual with an uneven profile of cognitive abilities (that is, one that spans the spectrum from very high to very low).

Finally, the application of the expertise model to the study of the etiology of complex traits suggests the possibility of introducing a methodological innovation in that, for example, single-word reading expertise can be studied across various neuropsychiatric conditions (for example, in families of children with autism, dyslexia, and normal reading). This methodological application could be instrumental in detecting the genes that might operate all the way through the continuum of reading ability (even though different alleles of these genes might predispose one to disabled or precocious reading).

References

Adelson, B. (1984). When novices surpass experts: The difficulty of a task may increase with expertise. *Journal of Experimental Psychology, 10*, 483–495.

Aram, D. M., Ekelman, B. L., & Healy, J. M. (1984, June). *Reading profiles of hyperlexic children*. Paper presented at the meeting of the International Neuropsychology Society, Aachen, West Germany.

Aram, D. M., & Healy, J. M. (1988). Hyperlexia: A review of extraordinary word recognition. In L. Obler & D. Fein (Eds.), *Neuropsychology of talent* (pp. 70–102). New York: Guilford.

Aram, D. M., Rose, D. F., & Horwitz, S. J. (1984). Hyperlexia: Developmental reading without meaning. In R. M. Joshi & H. A. Whitaker (Eds.), *Dyslexia: A global issue* (pp. 518–533). The Hague, Netherlands: Martinus Nijhoff.

Backman, J. (1983). Psycholinguistic skills and reading acquisition: A look at early readers. *Reading Research Quarterly, 18*, 466–79.

Blachman, B. A. (1997). *Foundations of reading acquisition and dyslexia: Implications for early intervention*. Mahwah, NJ: Lawrence Erlbaum Associates.

Bowers, P. G., Sunseth, K., & Golden, J. (1999). The route between rapid naming and reading progress. *Scientific Studies of Reading, 3*, 31–53.

Burd, L., & Kerbeshian, J. (1985). Hyperlexia and a variant of hypergraphia. *Perceptual and Motor Skills, 60*, 940–42.

Burd, L., Kerbeshian, J., & Fisher, W. (1985). Inquiry into the incidence of hyperlexia in a statewide population of children with pervasive developmental disorder. *Psychological Reports, 57*, 236–38.

Bus, A. G., & van IJzendoorn, M. H. (1999). Phonological awareness and early reading: A meta-analysis of experimental training studies. *Journal of Educational Psychology, 91*, 403–14.

Bus, A. G., van IJzendoorn, M. H., & Pellegrini, A. D. (1995). Joint book reading makes for success in learning to read. A meta-analysis on intergenerational transmission of literacy. *Review of Educational Research, 65*, 1–21.

Cain, A. C. (1969). Special "isolated" abilities in severely psychotic young children. *Psychiatry, 32,* 137–149.

Carston, R. (1996). The architecture of mind: Modularity and modularization. In D. Green et al. (Eds.), *Cognitive science: An introduction,* (pp. 53–83). Cambridge, MA: Blackwell.

Cassidy, J., & Vukelich, C. (1980). Do the gifted read early? *The Reading Teacher, 33,* 578–82.

Charness, N. (1979). Components of skill in bridge. *Canadian Journal of Psychology, 33,* 1–16.

Chase, W. G., & Simon, H. A. (1973). The mind's eye in chess. In W. G. Chase (Ed.), *Visual information processing* (pp. 215–281). New York: Academic Press.

Chase, W. G., & Ericsson, K. A. (1982). Skill and working memory. In G. H. Bower (Ed.), *The psychology of learning and motivation* (Vol. 16, pp. 1–58). New York: Academic Press.

Chi, M. T. H., Glaser, R., & Farr, M. (Eds.). (1989). The nature of expertise. Hillsdale, NJ: Erlbaum.

Cobrinik, L. (1974). Unusual reading ability in severely disturbed children. *Journal of Autism and Childhood Schizophrenia, 4,* 163–75.

Cobrinik, L. (1982). The performance of hyperlexic children on an "incomplete words" task. *Neuropsychologia, 20,* 569–78.

Cohen, M. J., Campbell, R. C., & Gelado, M. (1987). Hyperlexia: A variant of aphasia or dyslexia. *Pediatric Neurology, 3,* 22–28.

Cohen, M. J., Hall, J., & Riccio, C. A. (1997). Neuropsychological profiles of children diagnosed as specific language impaired with and without hyperlexia. *Archives of Clinical Neuropsychology, 12,* 223–229.

Comuzzie, A. G., Hixson, J. E., Almasy, L., Mitchell, B. D., Mahaney, M. C., Dyer, T. D., Stern, M. P., MacCluer, J. W., & Blangero, J. (1997). A major quantitative trait locus determining serum leptin levels and fat mass is located on human chromosome 2. *Nature Genetics, 15,* 273–76.

Cossu, G., & Marshall, J. C. (1986). Theoretical implications of the hyperlexic syndrome: Two new Italian cases. *Cortex, 22,* 579–89.

Cossu, G., & Marshall, J. C. (1990). Are cognitive skills a prerequisite for learning to read and write? *Cognitive Neuropsychology, 7,* 21–40.

Crain-Thoreson, C., & Dale, P. S. (1992). Do early talkers become early readers? Linguistic precocity, preschool language, and emergent literacy. *Developmental Psychology, 28,* 421–29.

Crowe, R. R., Noyes, R., Pauls, D. L., & Slymen, D. (1983). A family study of panic disorder. *Archives of General Psychiatry, 40,* 1065–69.

DeFries, J. C., & Fulker, D. W. (1988). Multiple regression analysis of twin data: Etiology of deviant scores versus individual differences. *Acta Geneticae Medicae et Gemellologiae: Twin Research, 37,* 205–216.

de Groot, A. (1978). Thought and choice in chess. The Hague, Netherlands: Mouton. (Original work published 1946.)

De Hirsch, K. (1971). Are hyperlexics dyslexics? *The Journal of Special Education, 5,* 243–246.

Durkin, D. (1966). *Children who read early.* New York: Teachers College Press.

Durkin, D. (1970). A language-arts program for pre-first grade children: Two-year achievement report. *Reading Research Quarterly, 5*, 9–61.

Egan, D. E., & Schwartz, B. J. (1979). Chunking in recall of symbolic drawings. *Memory and Cognition, 7*, 149–158.

Elliott, D. E., & Needleman, R. M. (1976). The syndrome of hyperlexia. *Brain and Language, 3*, 339–349.

Engle, R. W., & Bukstel, L. (1978). Memory processes among bridge players of differing expertise. *American Journal of Psychology, 91*, 673–679.

Ericsson, K. A. (1988). Analysis of memory performance in terms of memory skill. In R. J. Sternberg (Ed.), *Advances in the psychology of human intelligence*, Vol. 4 (pp. 137–179). Hillsdale, NJ: Erlbaum.

Ericsson, K. A. (1996). The acquisition of expert performance: An introduction to some of the issues. In K. A. Ericsson (Ed.), *The road to excellence: The acquisition of expert performance in the arts and sciences, sports, and games* (pp. 1–50). Mahwah, NJ: Erlbaum.

Ericsson, K. A. (1998). The scientific study of expert levels of performance: General implications for optimal learning and creativity. *High Ability Studies, 9*, 75–100.

Ericsson, K. A. (2001a). Attaining excellence through deliberate practice: Insights from the study of expert performance. In M. Ferrari (Ed.), *The pursuit of excellence in education* (pp. 21–55). Mahwah, NJ: Erlbaum.

Ericsson, K. A. (2001b). The path to expert performance: Insights from the masters on how to improve performance by deliberate practice. In P. Thomas (Ed.), *Optimizing performance in golf* (pp. 1–57). Brisbane, Australia: Australian Academic Press.

Ericsson, K. A., Chase, W., & Faloon, S. (1980). Acquisition of a memory skill. *Science, 208*, 1181–1182.

Ericsson, K. A., & Kintsch, W. (1995). Long-term working memory. *Psychological Review, 102*, 211–245.

Ericsson, K. A., Krampe, R. T., & Tesch-Römer, C. (1993). The role of deliberate practice in the acquisition of expert performance. *Psychological Review, 100*, 363–406.

Ericsson, K. A., & Lehmann, A. C. (1996). Expert and exceptional performance: Evidence on maximal adaptations on task constraints. *Annual Review of Psychology, 47*, 273–305.

Ericsson, K. A., Patel, V. L., & Kintsch, W. (2000). How experts' adaptations to representative task demands account for the expertise effect in memory recall: Comment on Vicente and Wang (1998). *Psychological Review, 107*, 578–592.

Ericsson, K. A., & Smith, J. (1991). Prospects and limits in the empirical study of expertise: An introduction. In K. A. Ericsson and J. Smith (Eds.), *Toward a general theory of expertise: Prospects and limits* (pp. 1–38). Cambridge, UK: Cambridge University Press.

Ericsson, K. A., & Staszewski, J. (1989). Skilled memory and expertise: Mechanisms of exceptional performance. In D. Klahr and K. Kotovsky (Eds.), *Complex information processing: The impact of Herbert A. Simon* (pp. 235–267). Hillsdale, NJ: Erlbaum.

Felton, R. H. (1998). The development of reading skills in poor readers: Educational implications. In C. Hulme & R. M. Joshi (Eds.). *Reading and spelling: Development and disorders*, (pp. 219–233). Mahwah, NJ: Erlbaum.

Felton, R. H., & Brown, I. S. (1990). Phonological processes as predictors of specific reading skills in children at risk for reading failure. *Reading and Writing*, 2, 39–59.

Felton, R. H., Naylor, C. E., & Wood, F. B. (1990). Neuropsychological profile of adult dyslexics. *Brain and Language*, 39, 485–497.

Felton, R. H., & Wood, F. B. (1992). A reading level match study of non-word reading skills in poor readers with varying IQ. *Journal of Learning Disabilities*, 25, 318–326.

Fodor, J. A. (1983). *The modularity of mind*. Cambridge, MA: MIT Press.

Fontenelle, S., & Alarcon, M. (1982). Hyperlexia: Precocious word recognition in developmentally delayed children. *Perceptual and Motor Skills*, 55, 247–252.

Frensch, P. A., & Sternberg, R. J. (1989). Expertise and intelligent thinking: When is it worse to know better? In R. J. Sternberg (Ed.), *Advances in the psychology of human intelligence*, Vol. 5 (pp. 157–188). Hillsdale, NJ: Erlbaum.

Garfield, J. (1994). Modularity. In S. Guttenplan (Ed.), *A companion to the philosophy of mind*, (pp. 441–448). Cambridge, MA: Blackwell.

Glaser, R. (1996). Changing the agency for learning: Acquiring expert performance. In K. A. Ericsson (Ed.), *The road to excellence: The acquisition of expert performance in the arts and sciences, sports, and games*, (pp. 303–311). Hillsdale, NJ: Erlbaum.

Glosser, G., Friedman, R. B., & Roeltgen, D. P. (1996). Clues to cognitive organization of reading and writing from developmental hyperlexia. *Neuropsychology*, 10, 168–75.

Glosser, G., Grugan, P., & Friedman, R. B. (1997). Semantic memory impairment does not impact on phonological and orthographic processing in a case of developmental hyperlexia. *Brain and Language*, 56, 234–47.

Goldberg, T. E., & Rothermel, R. D. (1984). Hyperlexic children reading. *Brain*, 107, 759–85.

Goodman, J. (1972). A case study of an "autistic savant": Mental function in the psychotic child with markedly discrepant abilities. *Journal of Child Psychology and Psychiatry*, 13, 267–278.

Gott, S. P., Hall, E. P., Pokorny, R. A., Dibble, E., & Glaser, R. (1993). A naturalistic study of transfer: Adaptive expertise in technical domains. In D. K. Detterman & R. J. Sternberg (Eds.), *Transfer on trial: Intelligence, cognition, and instruction* (pp. 258–288). Stamford, CT: Ablex Publishing Corp.

Graziani, L. J., Brodsky, K., Mason, J. C., & Zager, R. P. (1983). Variability in IQ scores and prognoses in children with hyperlexia. *Journal of the American Academy of Child Psychiatry*, 22, 441–43.

Grigorenko, E. L., Wood, F. B., Meyer, M. S., Hart, L. A., Speed, W. C., Shuster, A., & Pauls D. L. (1997). Susceptibility loci for distinct components of developmental dyslexia on chromosomes 6 and 15. *American Journal of Human Genetics*, 60, 27–39.

Haseman, J. K., & Elston, R. C. (1972). The investigation of linkage between a quantitative trait and a marker locus. *Behavior Genetics*, 2, 3–19.

Healy, J. M. (1982). The enigma of hyperlexia. *Reading Research Quarterly, 17,* 319–338.

Healy, J. M., & Aram, D. M. (1986). Hyperlexia and dyslexia: A family study. *Annals of Dyslexia, 36,* 226–253.

Healy, J. M., Aram, D. M., Horwitz, S. J., & Kessler, J. W. (1982). A study of hyperlexia. *Brain and Language, 9,* 1–23.

Hecht, H., & Proffitt, D. R. (1995). The price of expertise: Effects of experience on the water-level task. *Psychological Science, 6*(2), 90–95.

Hermelin, B. (2001). *Bright splinters of the mind: A personal story of research with autistic savants.* London, England: Jessica Kingsley Publishers.

Howe, M. J. A., Davidson, J. W., & Sloboda, J. A. (1998). Innate talents: Reality or myth? *Behavioral and Brain Sciences, 21,* 399–442.

Huttenlocher, P. R., & Huttenlocher, J. A. (1973). A study of children with hyperlexia. *Neurology, 23,* 1107–1116.

Jackson, N. E. (1988). Precocious reading ability: What does it mean? *Gifted Child Quarterly, 32,* 200–204.

Jackson, N. E. (1992). Precocious reading of English: Origins, structure, and predictive significance. In P. S. Klein, & A. J. Tannenbaum (Eds.), *To be young and gifted* (pp. 171–203). Norwood, NJ: Ablex Publishing.

Jackson, N. E., & Biemiller, A. J. (1985). Letter, word, and text reading times of precocious and average readers. *Child Development, 56,* 196–206.

Jackson, N. E., & Donaldson, G. W. (1989). Precocious and second-grade readers' use of context in word identification. *Learning and Individual Differences, 1,* 255–81.

Jackson, N. E., Donaldson, G. W., & Cleland, L. N. (1988). The structure of precocious reading ability. *Journal of Educational Psychology, 80,* 234–43.

Jackson, N. E., & Myers, M. G. (1982). Letter naming time, digit span, and precocious reading achievement. *Intelligence, 6,* 311–29.

Jong, P. F., & van der Leij, A. (1999). Specific contributions of phonological abilities to early reading acquisition: Results from a Dutch latent variable longitudinal study. *Journal of Educational Psychology, 91,* 450–76.

Kanner, I. (1943). Autistic disturbances of affective contact. *Nervous Child, 2,* 217–50.

Kendler, K. S., Neale, M. C., Kessler, R. C., Heath, A. C., & Eaves, L. J. (1993). Panic disorder in women: A population based twin study. *Psychological Medicine, 23,* 397–406.

Learning Disabilities Statistics Sheet. (1997). The Orton Dyslexia Society.

Luchins, A. S. (1942). Mechanization in problem solving. *Psychological Monographs, 54* (6, # 248).

Lyon, R. G. (1995). Toward a definition of dyslexia. *Annals of Dyslexia, 35,* 3–27.

Mehegan, C. C., & Dreifuss, F. E. (1972). Hyperlexia: Exceptional reading ability in brain-damaged children. *Neurology, 22,* 1105–11.

Miller, G. A. (1956). The magical number seven, plus or minus two. *Psychological Review, 63,* 81–97.

Mills, J. R., & Jackson, N. E. (1990). Predictive significance of early giftedness: The case of precocious reading. *Journal of Educational Psychology, 82,* 410–19.

Nation, K. (1999). Reading skills in hyperlexia: A developmental perspective. *Psychological Bulletin, 125*, 338–355.

Noyes, R., Jr., Crowe, R. R., Harris, E. L., Hampa, B. J., McChesney, C. M., & Chaudry, D. R. (1986). Relationships between panic disorder and agoraphobia: A family study. *Archives of General Psychiatry, 43*, 227–32.

Olson, R., Wise, B., Conners, F., Rack, J., & Fulker, D. (1989). Specific deficits in component reading and language skills: Genetic and environmental influences. *Journal of Learning Disabilities, 22*, 339–48.

Parker, S. W. (1919). Pseudo-latent for words. *Psychological Clinics, 11*, 1–7.

Patel, P. G., & Patterson, P. (1982). Precocious reading acquisition: Psycholinguistic development, IQ, and home background. *First Language, 13*, 139–53.

Pauls, D. (1993). Behavioural disorders: Lessons in linkage. *Nature Genetics, 3*, 4–5.

Pennington, B. F., Johnson, C., & Welsh, M. C. (1987). Unexpected reading precocity in a normal preschooler: Implications for hyperlexia. *Brain and Language, 30*, 165–80.

Perfetti, C. A. (1985). *Reading ability.* New York: Oxford University Press.

Perfetti, C. A., & McCutchen, D. (1987). Schooled language competence: Linguistic abilities in reading and writing. In S. Rosenberg (Ed.), *Advances in applied psycholinguistics* (pp. 105–41). New York: Cambridge University Press.

Phillips, A. (1930). Talented imbeciles. *Psychological Clinics, 18*, 246–265.

Plaut, D. C., McClelland, J. L., & Seidenberg, M. S. (1996). Reading exception words and pseudowords: Are the two routes really necessary? In J. P. Levy, B. Bairaktaris, J. Bullinaria, & P. Cairns (Eds.), *Proceedings of the Second Neural Computation and Psychology Workshop* (pp. 145–59). London: University College London Press.

Reitman, J. (1976). Skilled perception in GO: Deducing memory structures from interresponse times. *Cognitive Psychology, 8*, 336–356.

Richman, L. C., & Kitchell, M. M. (1981). Hyperlexia as a variant of developmental language disorder. *Brain and Language, 12*, 203–212.

Risch, N. J., & Zhang, H. (1996). Mapping quantitative trait loci with extreme discordant sib pairs: Sampling considerations. *American Journal of Human Genetics, 58*, 836–43.

Rispens, J., & Van Berckelaer, I. A. (1991). Hyperlexia: Definition and criterion. In R. M. Joshi (Ed.), *Written language disorders* (pp. 143–163). The Netherlands: Kluwer Academic Publishers.

Roedell, W. C., Jackson, N. E., & Robinson, H. B. (1980). *Gifted young children.* New York: Teachers College Press.

Scarborough, H. S. (1984). Continuity between childhood dyslexia and adult reading. *British Journal of Psychology, 75*, 329–48.

Seymour, P. H. K., & Evans, H. M. (1992). Beginning reading without semantics: A cognitive study of hyperlexia. *Cognitive Neuropsychology, 9*, 89–122.

Siegel, L. S. (1984). A longitudinal study of a hyperlexic child: Hyperlexia as a language disorder. *Neuropsychologia, 22*, 577–85.

Silberberg, N. E., & Silberberg, M. C. (1967). Hyperlexia: Specific word recognition skills in young children. *Exceptional Children, 34*, 41–42.

Silberberg, N. E., & Silberberg, M. C. (1968). Case histories in hyperlexia. *Journal of School Psychology, 7*, 3–7.

Silberberg, N. E., & Silberberg, M. C. (1971). Hyperlexia: The other end of the continuum. *Journal of Special Education, 3*, 233–242.

Simon, H. A., & Gilmartin, K. (1973). A simulation of memory for chess positions. *Cognitive Psychology, 8*, 165–190.

Smoller, J. W., & Tsuang, M. T. (1998). Panic and phobic anxiety: Defining phenotypes for genetic studies. *American Journal of Psychiatry, 155*, 1152–62.

Snowling, M. J. (2000). *Dyslexia* (2d ed.). Malden, MA: Blackwell.

Snowling, M. J., & Frith, U. (1986). Comprehension in hyperlexic readers. *Journal of Experimental Child Psychology, 42*, 392–415.

Stanovich, K. E., Nathan, R. G., & Zolman, J. E. (1988). The developmental lag hypothesis in reading: Longitudinal and matched reading-level comparisons. *Child Development, 59*, 71–86.

Stanovich, K. E., & Siegel, L. S. (1994). Phenotype performance profile of children with reading disabilities: A regression-based test of the phonological-core variable-difference model. *Journal of Educational Psychology, 86*, 24–53.

Sternberg, R. J. (1998). Abilities are forms of developing expertise. *Educational Researcher, 27*, 11–20.

Sternberg, R. J., & Lubart, T. I. (1995). *Defying the crowd: Cultivating creativity in a culture of conformity*. New York: Free Press.

Sternberg, R. J., Grigorenko, E. L., & Ferrari, M. (2002). Fostering intellectual excellence through developing expertise. In M. Ferrari (Ed.), *The pursuit of excellence through education* (pp. 57–84). Mahwah, NJ: Erlbaum.

Subotnik, R. F., & Arnold, K. D. (1993). Longitudinal studies of giftedness: Investigating the fulfillment of promise. In K. A. Heller & F. J. Moenks (Eds.), *International handbook of research and development of giftedness and talent* (pp. 149–160). Elmsford, NY: Pergamon Press, Inc.

Tobin, A. W., & Pikulski, J. J. (1988). A longitudinal study of the reading achievement of early and non-early readers through sixth grade. In J. Readance & R. S. Baldwin (Eds.), *Dialogues in literacy research. Thirty-seventh yearbook of the National Reading Conference* (pp. 49–58). Chicago, IL: National Reading Conference.

Tønnessen, F. E. (1999). Options and limitations of the cognitive psychological approach to the treatment of dyslexia. *Journal of Learning Disabilities, 32*, 386–393.

Torgesen, J. K., Wagner, R. K., Rashotte, C. A., Burgess, S., & Hecht, S. (1997). Contributions of phonological awareness and rapid automatic naming ability to the growth of word-reading skills in second- to fifth-grade children. *Scientific Studies of Reading, 1*, 161–85.

Treffert, D. A. (1988). The idiot savant: A review of the syndrome. *American Journal of Psychiatry, 145*, 563–572.

Tsuang, M. T., Faraone, S. V., & Lyons, M. J. (1993). Identification of the phenotype in psychiatric genetics. *European Archives of Psychiatry and Clinical Neuroscience, 243*, 131–42.

van Daal, V., & van der Leij, A. (1999). Developmental dyslexia: Related to specific or general deficits? *Annals of Dyslexia, 49*, 71–104.

Vogel, S. A., & Adelman, P. B. (1992). The success of college students with learning disabilities: Factors related to educational attainment. *Journal of Learning Disabilities, 25*, 430–441.

Wagner, R. K., & Torgesen, J. K. (1987). The nature of phonological processing and its causal role in the acquisition of reading skills. *Psychological Bulletin, 101*, 192–212.

Wagner, R. K., Torgesen, J. K., Laughon, P., Simmons, K., & Rashotte, C. A. (1993). Development of young readers' phonological processing abilities. *Journal of Educational Psychology, 85*, 83–103.

Wagner, R. K., Torgesen, J. K., & Rashotte, C. A. (1994). Development of reading-related phonological processing abilities: New evidence of bi-directional causality from a latent variable longitudinal study. *Developmental Psychology, 30*, 73–87.

Weissman, M. M., Wickramaratne, P., Adams, P. B., Lish, J. D., Horwath, E., Charney, D., Woods, S. W., Leeman, F., & Frosch, E. (1993). The relationship between panic disorder and major depression: A new family study. *Archives of General Psychiatry, 50*, 767–80.

Whitehouse, D., & Harris, J. (1984). Hyperlexia in autism. *Journal of Autism and Developmental Disorders, 14*, 281–89.

Wolf, M. (1997). A provisional, integrative account of phonological and naming speed deficits in dyslexia: Implications for diagnosis and intervention. In B. Blachman (Ed.), *Cognitive and linguistic foundations of reading acquisition: Implications for intervention research* (pp. 177–210). Hillsdale, NJ: Erlbaum.

Wood, F. B., & Felton, R. H. (1994). Separate linguistic and attentional factors in the development of reading. *Topics in Language Disorders, 14*, 42–57.

Yopp, H. K. (1988). The validity and reliability of phonemic awareness tests. *Reading Research Quarterly, 23*, 159–177.

7

The Early Progress of Able Young Musicians

Michael J. A. Howe and Jane W. Davidson

DESCRIPTIVE AND THEORETICAL APPROACHES

Many people have strong opinions concerning the possible reasons for particular individuals becoming exceptionally skilled in one or other sphere of excellence, but only rarely are views about this matter accompanied by detailed knowledge of the actual circumstances in which unusual capabilities are gained. When we set out to investigate the early progress of successful young musical instrumentalists in the late 1980s, we began with a firm conviction that it would not be possible to decide between rival theories until a fuller body of descriptive knowledge could be made available. Largely for that reason, our own research has been essentially descriptive. Naturally, we had ideas of our own about the possible roles of various influences, and we were somewhat skeptical about the common belief, firmly held by many musicians, that innate gifts and talents are vital ingredients of excellence at music. In our investigations, however, we have attempted to concentrate on extending descriptive knowledge rather than arguing the merits of alternative theoretical positions. Theorizing, we think, should be preceded by descriptive studies aimed at expanding our knowledge of the phenomena that – eventually – need to be explained. And we are not convinced that a clear distinction can be made between expertise, as revealed by the competence reflected in measures of performance, and broader abilities that take the form of qualities that lie beneath a person's expertise. Our preference is for describing what can be observed before making strong inferences or developing theories about underlying processes that may enable experts' capabilities to be acquired. The success of scientists such as Darwin demonstrates that, in some circumstances at least, research that is essentially descriptive can go a long way toward providing explanations (Howe, 1999).

Approaches to human capabilities and expertise that have a strong theoretical component purport to identify specific causes of high performance levels and help explain why some people become more capable than others. Researchers who favor theoretical approaches often have firm views concerning essential prerequisites of special expertise. For instance, they may assume that the highest levels of performance within certain fields of ability are restricted to a minority of individuals who are born possessing certain biological dispositions in the form of specific gifts or talents (Winner, 1996). Or they may believe that underlying a person's specific particular skills are broader and more fundamental abilities that constrain individual achievements. Other investigators take the view that the reasons for individuals varying in their capabilities reside at least partly in the extent to which people are born possessing particular intelligences (Gardner, 1984), or innate general intelligence (Jensen, 1988).

Alternative approaches are largely or entirely descriptive rather than theoretical. Here there is an attempt by researchers to restrict themselves to statements of fact. Descriptive approaches to human expertise are likely to involve the collection of data concerning a person's observed actions and capabilities. There may be extended observations of events and activities that take place during the period when expertise is being acquired and extended. Researchers who favor descriptive approaches tend to be reticent about making statements that purport to explain why a particular individual has made a given amount of progress, or why one person has been more successful than another. Of course, even those investigators whose research methods are most exclusively descriptive will often have strong hunches about the reasons why people differ in their accomplishments, and they may express definite views about the relative potency of various biologically based or experience-based possible sources of individual variability (see, for instance, Ericsson, 1996). Nonetheless, those investigators who take care to avoid starting off with preconceptions or unproven assumptions concerning the causes of the phenomena they are observing reap an important benefit: they avoid the mistakes and the false starts that erroneous preconceptions inevitably create.

Our own strong preference for a mainly descriptive exploration of the circumstances in which young people gain expertise in music is partly rooted in an awareness that investigators can easily be blinkered or impeded, by their unproven assumptions, if these turn out to be faulty. Theories can create obstacles even when no conscious decision is made to adopt a particular theoretical position. Take, for example, the case of a researcher who, wishing to understand how and why some individuals become experts in a particular field of accomplishment, accepts the widespread assumption that the individuals being studied can be designated as gifted or innately talented individuals. On the surface, at least, there is nothing objectionable about those labels; they seem to be nothing more than commonplace everyday descriptions. However, it only takes a moment's reflection to see that when we call someone a gifted or innately talented individual we are doing more than just describing the person: we are offering an (implied if not explicit) explanation for their superior ability. What we mean by saying that certain people are gifted (or innately talented) is not merely that they are especially able, but that they are able *because they possess a gift (or innate talent)*. In other words, the presence of a gift or talent is regarded as a reason why someone is especially capable. So, merely by calling a person gifted or innately talented one is actually introducing a theory, one that purports to identify the reason for an observed capability.

There is nothing wrong with having theories. But if a theory is to be taken seriously as an element of a broadly scientific enterprise, it is vital to have convincing grounds for believing that theory to be correct. In particular, there needs to be supporting evidence. In connection with gifts and talents such evidence is rarely, if ever, supplied, however. In our experience, when someone who states that an individual is unusually accomplished in a field of skill such as music because they possess an innate gift for music, is pressed to provide evidence to support his or her belief in innate gifts, the person is likely to respond in one of three ways. First, they may simply say that "everybody knows" that innate gifts are part of the explanation of unusual expertise. Second, they may say that innate gifts are commonsense or self-evident facts of life. Or third, someone may assert that innate gifts *must* be the explanation of high capabilities because the person cannot think of a better explanation of the phenomena that such gifts are supposed to explain.

In reality, none of these three responses provides any genuine support at all for the innate gift theory. Even the third, which might appear to be more compelling than the others, is sadly unconvincing. It is analogous to arguing that my theory that the presents that appeared in my fireplace on Christmas Day must have been delivered there by Father Christmas has to be true because I cannot think of a better explanation for their arrival. In the absence of better reasons for believing in the innate talent account, we regard it as a theory that is rarely questioned but that lacks the support of convincing evidence (Howe, Davidson, and Sloboda, 1988). Our own preference is for the pragmatic and largely atheoretical kind of approach to exploring the determinants of expertise associated with researchers such as Anders Ericsson (see, for example, Ericsson and Charness, 1994).

By and large, we are also unconvinced by theoretical approaches to the study of human capacities that attribute differences between people in their capabilities to the presence or absence of inherent attributes taking the form of abilities (such as "musical ability") or underlying aptitudes. We are dubious about the possibility of there being an ability construct that is genuinely explanatory (Howe, 1996). In the sphere of music, one reason why we are not convinced that the concept of musical ability has much explanatory value is that there appears to be no satisfactory way of drawing boundaries that delineate where musical abilities begin and end. As Sloboda (1985) has pointed out, a competent musician draws on a substantial number of different skills and different kinds of knowledge, each of which is likely to be present or absent to varying degrees in different individuals. Deciding on the precise combination of these different capacities to include in a definition of "musical ability" seems to be an impossible task.

A further difficulty is that there are, in our judgment, no firm grounds for believing that any one indicator of "musical ability" or "musical aptitude" identifies qualities that are more stable or more fundamental than the specific varieties of knowledge and skill that are present in expert performers. Consequently, the proposal that someone is a good musician *because* he or she possesses abundant musical ability, or a high degree of aptitude, with the implication that these concepts help identify the underlying reasons, is not very persuasive. In our view, the statement that a person has fine musical abilities can never mean more than that the person possesses some of the capacities that a musician draws on. That statement describes an existing state of affairs, but it cannot also explain it.

OUR OWN APPROACH

Our decision to study musical skills rather than alternative forms of expertise was influenced by the fact that one member of our initial research team, John Sloboda, is an expert musician, as is Jane Davidson, who became involved in the research at the outset of its second stage. Sloboda has a longstanding interest in musical development (see, for example, Sloboda, 1985; 1991). Fortunately for us, instrumental music, in comparison with some other fields of expertise, provides some definite practical advantages for researchers investigating the acquisition of skills. These advantages are partly a consequence of musical education being relatively uniform and somewhat structured, and regulated to a considerable extent by conventions that most teachers keep to, and partly an outcome of the fact that there is a grade system for assessing young performers' degree of expertise. For example, in Britain, where our research was conducted, there is a series of examinations involving eight successive grade levels. That makes the process of ascertaining the degree to which a performer has progressed a fairly straightforward one. As a result, it is not too difficult to compare the relative levels of expertise achieved by different young instrumentalists, even when they live in different regions.

In planning our own empirical research we decided on an approach that traced the early musical progress of successful young instrumentalists. We were interested in a number of aspects. For instance, we wished to examine various elements of young people's family backgrounds that might be significant for musical development. We were especially interested in knowing about the extent to which the parents involved themselves in their child's music training, and we enquired into the ways in which families supported their child's musical activities. We also looked at the contributions of young people's music teachers. We obtained information about activities that directly contribute to a learner's expertise, such as lessons and practicing. We hoped to build up a picture of the varied influences, events, and activities that enable certain young people to grow into capable instrumentalists. Musical expertise is a unique kind of capability, and it is inevitable that the outcome of our efforts to delineate the contributions of individuals' experiences to their growing skills will have only limited applicability to other fields of expertise. On the other hand, the fact that one particular component of expertise, practicing, is such a powerful influence on performance in this area of skill makes music-based investigations especially valuable for addressing questions relating to the links between practice and performance.

One important influence on our approach was an investigation undertaken by Lauren Sosniak (1985; 1990), who studied the musical development of twenty-two young American concert pianists. These individuals were all exceptional musicians; each of them had been a finalist in at least one of six major international piano competitions. To achieve that degree of success, and make a living as a concert pianist in the highly competitive world of musical performance, it is necessary to be quite extraordinarily competent. The individuals studied by Sosniak were thus some of the very best performers of their generation. Sosniak interviewed them at some length, and in most cases she also talked to their parents.

It might have been expected that virtually all of Sosniak's exceptionally able musicians would have had parents who were either musicians themselves or held strong musical interests. Sosniak discovered, however, that the parents of half her participants had at most a passive interest in music, restricted to listening. Yet even those parents who did not have musical interests of their own were strongly and actively supportive of their child's early efforts. They gave plenty of help and encouragement, they stayed in close contact with the music teacher (often sitting in on music lessons), and, especially in the early years, they did much to help to make their child's learning and practicing activities more enjoyable.

It might have been anticipated that Sosniak's pianists, all of whom eventually became exceptionally accomplished, first began to display signs of special promise or talent at an early age, when they first began playing the instrument. By and large, however, that did not happen (Sosniak, 1990). Sosniak discovered that even at the time they were thirteen or fourteen, and had already been studying the piano for seven years, those individuals in her sample who took part in competitive events failed as often as they succeeded. In most cases, no very early signs of exceptional ability had been evident. In two instances the parents of Sosniak's musicians remarked that another sibling had demonstrated more obvious signs of early talent. In these cases it was tenacity rather than manifest early promise that marked out the child who did eventually excel.

Sosniak also enquired into the instrumentalists' music teachers. She discovered that the first piano teachers were especially influential, although not because of their musicianship or instructional skills: these were often rated as being no more than average. When it came to motivating the young players, however, the first teachers were uniformly effective. The participants described their initial piano teachers as "warm," "friendly," "gentle," and "encouraging." What these music teachers had in common was a capacity to motivate their students and encourage them to enjoy playing the piano and regard that activity as a rewarding one. As a consequence, the young pianists looked forward to their lessons and enjoyed them. They were encouraged to feel special, to see themselves as being capable of achieving things that other children could not do. Objectively, there was nothing very unusual about these musicians' capabilities in the earliest years, but being made to *feel* special seems to have been important for the young performers, encouraging them to persist at the training and practice activities that their future progress depended on.

As the young instrumentalists became older and more skilled, there were a number of changes. Increasing amounts of time were devoted to practicing, and because a firm habit of practicing had been formed, it was no longer necessary for the parents to provide company and encouragement. By the time they had been learning for five years, most of the participants had switched to a different teacher, who was typically someone who had established a good reputation as an instructor for more advanced pianists.

When we came to design our own initial investigation (Sloboda and Howe, 1991) we chose to adopt a number of the features of Sosniak's investigation. In particular, we placed some emphasis on attempting to trace each participant's musical development, beginning with the earliest years. It was clear to us that talking to the participants and their parents would be the best way to acquire the information we required. Right from the beginning we included questions that were designed to elicit quantitative data, but we were also aware of the likelihood of our participants being aware of influential events that we had not even thought to enquire into. Accordingly, in the earlier phase of our research we made sure that a number of the questions we asked were relatively open-ended. Also, we encouraged the participants to talk about any early experiences that they perceived as having been influential but that had not been raised in our questioning.

Our investigation followed broadly the same lines of Lauren Sosniak's study, but we extended and expanded on her approach in a number of ways. First, we examined the progress of musicians who possessed a wider range of abilities than Sosniak's sample did. Sosniak only studied extraordinarily successful instrumentalists. Our main sample was made up of young musicians who were markedly competent, to the extent that most of them could realistically contemplate musical careers, but (in most cases) not so exceptional as the individuals studied by Sosniak. Our comparison groups contained some individuals who were only moderately competent. Because Sosniak's study included no participants who were *not* exceptionally successful, it was not possible to identify, which, if any aspects of her musicians' training activities or experiences were exclusive to unusually successful individuals rather than being shared with other performers. Most of the individuals who formed our comparison groups had been less successful than the young people in our main target group. Since one of our goals was to identify some of the factors that make some learners especially competent, we needed to be able to compare their learning activities with those of other learners, who had shared some of their learning experiences but without achieving a comparable degree of success.

Second, in order to ensure that our samples were reasonably representative, we examined a considerably larger number of young musicians than Sosniak did. Whereas Sosniak's participants numbered just twenty-two, ours were in excess of two hundred.

Third, unlike Sosniak, whose musicians were exclusively pianists, we included individuals who were learning a variety of different instruments. This gave our findings greater generality and made certain additional comparisons possible. In contrast with Sosniak's musicians, most of whom played only the piano, the majority of the young people we studied were learning more than one instrument.

Fourth, we wanted to examine a wider range of possible influences than Sosniak's relatively small-scale study could take account of. We therefore included a number of items designed to gather detailed information about various aspects of our participants' backgrounds and early experiences.

Fifth, we thought it desirable to place more emphasis than Sosniak was able to on obtaining data that was precise and quantified. Toward this end, in the second phase of our research, we included a large number of questions designed to allow all permissible responses to be encoded.

And sixth, because our participants were considerably younger than the musicians who participated in Sosniak's study, the amount of time that had elapsed between the time of the events our participants reported and the date at which the interviews took place was substantially less. As a result, it is likely that the information we acquired was more accurate.

There were two main stages of our research. In the first stage we conducted an investigation that in certain respects might be regarded as a preliminary study. There were a relatively small number of participants, all of whom were competent young musicians, and there were no control or comparison groups. The aim of this phase of the research was partly to elicit quantifiable data concerning background influences and early progress, but partly to add to our own knowledge of the potential influences that would merit closer examination in future research.

The investigation forming the second stage of the research consisted of a study in which each of over two hundred participants was asked to provide a substantial amount of detailed information. Participants were asked about their family backgrounds, the contributions of their parents and their music teachers, the form and duration of learning activities such as music lessons and practicing activities during successive one-year periods. They were also asked about a number of other events and activities considered likely to influence progress. To make it possible to distinguish between those elements that are common to most young performers' experiences of learning to play an instrument, and the ones that are specific to those learners who make especially good progress, the investigation incorporated a number of control or comparison groups. These consisted of young people who were broadly comparable to the target group, except in their actual musical progress.

The First Stage

In the first phase of our research we conducted an investigation that examined a number of potentially important aspects of the backgrounds of promising young musicians. The participants were forty-two pupils (twenty-one male and twenty-one female) attending a selective specialist music school for children between the ages of eight and eighteen (Chethams School, Manchester, England). The participating pupils were rated by their teachers as being "average" or "exceptional" by the (somewhat high) standards of the school. Entry is by competitive audition. About a third of each pupil's scheduled time is devoted to music. Each child was interviewed by one of the researchers in a face-to-face situation, and we also talked to the parents of half the pupils, usually by telephone. The interviews followed a semi-structured format designed to probe significant elements of a child's first years as an instrumental pupil. Twenty specific questions were asked (see below), but respondents were also encouraged to talk freely and discursively.

The interviews, most of which were completed within forty-five minutes, were transcribed and coded. In order to provide an indication of reliability, eight of the interviews were independently coded by two researchers. The mean level of agreement was a satisfactory 93 percent. In the few cases in which a child's account and the parent's account disagreed, we chose to accept the parent's account when the disagreements were about facts such as dates or ages. We accepted the child's account when there were disagreements about subjectively rated variables such as the warmth of the teacher or the child's motivation for practicing.

The sample of forty-two pupils consisted of roughly equal numbers of students whose current main instruments were the piano, violin, cello, a woodwind instrument, or a brass instrument.

Findings
The quantitative findings are most conveniently reported by presenting the respondents' answers to each of the twenty main questions. Because in a few instances a respondent did not answer every question, the total number of responses is not always forty-two. In addition to the responses reported here, this stage of the investigation also yielded valuable information in the form of insights by children and their parents that could not be readily quantified but which informed the second stage of our research (Howe and Sloboda, 1991a; 1991b; 1991c; 1992; Sloboda and Howe, 1992).

1. *To what extent are/were your parents involved in music?* Of twelve of the forty-two pupils at least one parent was a regular amateur performer or a professional music teacher or performer. The parents of another fifteen pupils had had some instrumental playing experience at one time, typically in the form of childhood music lessons. With fifteen pupils the parents had no involvement in music that extended beyond listening. Surprisingly, the students described by their teachers as being exceptional had parents who were, on average, less musically active than the parents of the other pupils.

2. *What was your earliest spontaneous involvement of any sort with music?* Half of the participants were unable to recall anything. Six could remember singing activities in toddlerhood, and fifteen had memories of trying to play tunes on an instrument. There were no differences between the average and exceptional pupils. These responses provided no apparent support for the view that precocious early development is a necessary precursor of high achievement in music.

3. *From what age was there an instrument present in the house?* Two-thirds of the children believed that there had been an instrument in the house from the earliest time they could remember. It is interesting that,

of the six students who reported that there had not been an instrument in their house until they were six or older, all were rated as being exceptional.

4. *What (if any) organized musical activity did you take part in prior to starting formal lessons?* Half of the participants had some involvement in musical activities at school.

5. *At what age did you begin formal instrumental lessons?* Almost all the children began between the ages of four and eight, with the mean and median ages both being six. However, two children began lessons when they were only three, and four did not start until they were nine or older. There was no difference between the average and exceptional pupils in the age at which lessons had begun.

6. *Why did formal instrumental lessons begin?* In half the children, the reasons for beginning lessons had nothing to do with the children's own interests or adults' impressions of their abilities. For ten children, lessons started as an aspect of the school's routine practice for all pupils. Another fourteen began lessons as a consequence of the parents believing that all children should learn to play an instrument. For the other half of the participants, lessons were initiated as a response to the child's expression of interest. In twelve individuals the child's own interest was said to be the main reason. In another six cases the first lessons were initiated as a result of the parents or the school perceiving the child as having a special interest or ability.

7. *On how many instruments did you have individual lessons prior to entering your present school?* Only a small minority of children (three) had only studied one instrument. Twenty-five studied two, eleven studied three, and three pupils studied as many as four different musical instruments. There was no difference between exceptional and average players in the number of instruments studied. (To some extent, the finding that most of the pupils in our sample had learned more than one instrument may have been a reflection of their teacher's or parents' awareness that candidates for the pupils' present school were normally expected to play more than one instrument.)

For sixteen of the children, the piano had been the first instrument on which the child had received instruction (although for only nine of them was the piano still their main instrument at the time of the investigation). Ten children had started with the violin and the recorder had been the first instrument for another nine. Among the pupils whose first instrument was not the piano, almost 90 percent chose it as one of their subsequent instruments.

8. How involved were your parents with your teacher and your instrumental lessons? Half of the parents regularly spoke with the teacher, receiving feedback on their child's progress, and ten parents sat in on their child's music lessons over a significant period of time.

9. How involved were your parents with your instrumental practice at home? Only in three cases was it reported that the parent had no involvement at all. With another thirteen children, parental involvement was restricted to making sure that the child kept practicing for an agreed daily period. The parents of the other half of the children took a more active role. In fourteen cases the parents actively supervised practicing on a moment-to-moment basis. They usually stayed with the child throughout the practice sessions and actively directed the child's work. The parents of another eleven children were less directive, but they did give considerable support and encouragement. There was no difference between the two ability groups in the amount of parental supervision or support they were given while practicing.

10. How motivated were you to do daily instrumental practice? All but six of the participants reported that at some stage they had depended to some extent on parental encouragement, or pressure, to keep practicing. Five of the pupils said quite candidly that they would probably not have practiced at all had there not been strong pressure from their parents. Another seventeen participants reported that they had needed considerable parental encouragement in order to maintain a regular practicing schedule. Clearly, the children who did not depend on their parents in respect to this essential learning activity were a small minority.

11. What influence did older children have on your motivation prior to coming to your present school? Fourteen children said that the fact that an older sibling was involved in music had helped to motivate them to begin playing an instrument themselves. Four participants said an older child outside their own family had influenced them. In the majority of cases (twenty-four), however, no special influence from other child players was mentioned.

12. What influence, if any, did professional performances have on your motivation prior to attending your present school? Half the participants could not recall any specific influence of this kind. It is interesting that, among the six children who could not and who also reported no influences of older children such as siblings, five were from the group of pupils rated as being exceptional. Among the participants who did report being inspired by a musical performance, half referred to performances that were live.

13. What kind of musical involvement did you have with musical activities and events outside individual lessons? There were no respondents at all who restricted their out-of-home musical activity solely to lessons and examinations. Thirty-six of the participants had been involved in at least two of the following activities: orchestras, groups, competitions, festivals, school concerts, concerts organized by a music teacher.

14. How many different teachers did you have? In common with the musicians studied by Sosniak, the majority of our respondents had at least two teachers per instrument prior to being admitted to their current school. On some occasions the reasons were nonmusical ones, for instance, the family or the teacher moving house. In many cases, however, the change was directed toward providing a different or superior kind of teaching.

15. What was the quality of your teacher? This question was asked in conjunction with each instrument and each teacher. Three-quarters of the most recent teachers were rated as being of "national" or "good local" standard. In contrast, the quality of half of the first teachers was rated as being "poor" or "local average." The improvement in the quality of teacher when a change took place was most marked for the first instrument.

16. What was your teacher like as a teacher/person? This was designed to be a fairly open-ended question, but it proved possible to isolate two dimensions on which most respondents rated their teachers. The first was warmth, signaled by positive terms such as friendly, fun, loving, encouraging, and nice, and negatively by words such as cold, distant, unfriendly, serious, indifferent, fearsome. Among the eighty-three teachers who were commented on, seventy-three were rated positively. It also proved possible to rate the extent to which a teacher was perceived as stretching or challenging the learner. Of the sixty-three teachers for whom information in this regard was available, forty-one were seen as stretching.

17. What grade standard did you reach prior to coming to your current school? One of the reasons for posing this question was to gain information about the rate at which the students progressed. Predictably, progress through the grades had been faster in those young instrumentalists rated by their teachers as being exceptional. Two-thirds of the participants had progressed at a rate of more than one grade per year.

18. How many hours of lessons did you have? The majority of children had received less than forty hours of lessons per year. It is surprising that the young people rated as being exceptional had, on average, attended fewer lessons per year than the other students.

19. *How many hours of practice did you do?* Prior to attending their present school, most of the young instrumentalists had done substantial, although not heroically large, amounts of practice. Only 10 percent had practiced for more than ninety minutes per day. Two-thirds had practiced for less than an hour, on average. However, most of these learners had practiced for at least forty minutes.

20. *How many hours playing in total did you do?* Participants were asked to give separate estimates for each of the instruments they had studied. The amounts of time ranged between two hundred and six hundred hours per year, and there was no significant difference between the ability groups. However, there was a strong tendency for those individuals rated by their teachers as being exceptional to distribute their time more evenly across the different instruments they were learning.

Discussion of the Stage One Findings

Despite the inevitable limitations of a small-scale interview study, the first phase of our research produced findings that were informative in a number of respects. They helped us to decide on the content and form of a subsequent investigation, which was more extensive and finer-toothed. The responses to the questions about family backgrounds and parental involvement with various aspects of the training process provided firm support for Sosniak's conclusion that the support and encouragement that parents provide is of crucial importance for the progress of a young musician. The lack of evidence concerning very early signs of excellence suggested that the importance of these may have been overestimated in the past, but it was clear to us that only further research could clarify this question. The information that emerged concerning the importance of practicing indicated that this was one aspect of the learning process that demanded closer examination.

Our findings indicated that Sosniak's portrayal of young musicians' progress is not entirely applicable to students from a wider band of competence levels than the extraordinarily successful young instrumentalists she studied. For instance, although Sosniak's findings give the impression that most young instrumentalists stay with the instrument they begin with, the picture that emerged from our findings was more complicated. Not only was it uncommon for a young participant in our study to play as many as three instruments, but in many cases a young player's eventual main instrument was not the one he or she began on.

The investigation forming the second stage of our research was intended to be larger in scale than the earlier study, and more definitive. It differed from the initial study in two particular ways. First, it was designed to provide more detailed information. For instance, in seeking information about early signs of musical talent, researchers asked parents a number of questions concerning a number of possible specific indicators. Second, whereas the initial phase lacked any kind of control or comparison group, a number of comparison groups were included in the second stage. The necessity for some kind of comparison group comprising individuals who, unlike the main target group, had *not* succeeded in becoming unusually capable young musicians, is obvious enough. In the absence of any basis for comparison there is no way of knowing whether, and to what extent, any observations made about the backgrounds and training of successful young musicians are identifying factors exclusive to the population being studied.

Perceiving the need for some kind of comparison group was not the end of the matter, however. It remained to be decided how such a group should be formed. There was no obvious correct choice. One possibility was to have a comparison group made up of young people who, unlike the target group, had never learned to play a musical instrument at all. For making certain kinds of comparisons, it definitely would be valuable to have such a group. For instance, it would permit a comparison between the target group and young people with no musical training. It would not, however, help us to identify background influences that distinguish between the relatively large numbers of young people who begin learning to play a musical instrument and the considerably smaller numbers who are especially successful.

In the context of this research there is no one kind of comparison group suitable for all purposes. To make all the comparisons we might wish to make, there need to be a number of different comparison groups. It would be prohibitively expensive, however, to include, for every comparison it would be desirable to draw, a separate comparison group comprising the same number of participants as the target group. A compromise solution, and the one we adopted, was to have a number of comparison groups, numbering *in total* approximately the same as the target participants. Consequently, in those instances where it was appropriate to compare the target group with a varied sample of individuals, we were able to do that. When it was necessary to compare the target group with individuals who differed from them in a specific way, that too was possible, although the relatively small number of individuals forming each of the particular comparison groups placed some restrictions on what can be achieved.

The Second Stage

The second stage of our investigation involved a total of 257 young people aged between eight and eighteen years (Davidson, Howe, Moore, and Sloboda, 1996; Davidson, Moore, Sloboda, and Howe, 1998; Howe, Davidson, Moore, and Sloboda, 1995; Sloboda, Davidson, Howe, and Moore, 1996). All the participants had received tuition on at least one musical instrument. There were five separate groups. As well as the main target group there were four comparison groups of young people, containing individuals with differing levels of musical competence. The groups were similar to one another in the proportions of male and female participants and in the kinds of instruments they played.

The target group (Group 1) contained 119 pupils studying at the same selective specialist music school (Chethams) that provided the participants in the first stage of our investigation. (None of the participants in the first stage took part in the second stage.) Forty percent of the pupils were sixteen to eighteen years of age (the age ranges of the comparison groups were similar).

Groups 2, 3, and 4 consisted of young people who had continued learning a musical instrument over a period of years, and had gained a degree of competence, but differed from Group I in their level of achievement. Group 2 contained thirty individuals who had applied for, but failed to be admitted to, the specialist music school. Group 3 consisted of twenty-three young music pupils who had at some stage been sufficiently serious about a musical career to have considered applying to the specialist music school, but who had not made a formal application. Group 4 was made up of young people who had learned an instrument over a period of years but who had never taken steps toward getting the kind of training that can lead to a professional musical career.

Group 5 consisted of fifty-eight children who had begun to play an instrument, but had been relatively unsuccessful. In most respects they were comparable to the participants in Group 4, except that they had ceased learning to play a musical instrument at least one year prior to the present study.

Objective ratings of the participants' levels of achievement on their musical instruments, and the rate of their past progress, were made available in the form of their grade examination results. This information confirmed that mean grade levels differed significantly in their achievement levels, with Groups 1 and 3 having the highest average grade levels and the other groups intermediate levels. At each age Group 1 was the most accomplished and Group 5 the least accomplished, on average.

Each participant was interviewed alone by one of the researchers. In most cases (75 percent) they were face-to-face interviews, but the telephone was used in 25 percent of the cases. Interviews were recorded, enabling the reliability of the codings assigned by each interviewer to be checked. On a 10 percent random sample of interviews, the inter-rater concordance between any two interviewers averaged 95 percent. A parent of each child was also interviewed. On questions where the same information was sought from both parent and child, there was only one case where parent and child disagreed on the answer.

On a typical question, a participant chose a response from between three and six response categories. For purposes of analysis, these categories were treated as points on an ordinal scale. Assessment of changes in activities over time was made possible by obtaining data for successive three-year periods that spanned the period from when a child was three years old to when he or she was seventeen. In most cases the interviewer asked interviewees to choose from a number of responses, typically in the form of concrete examples of the activities or behaviors that the question asked about. Here, for instance, is the wording of material accompanying a question concerning parental involvement in lessons. (This particular question was given to both child and parent.)

I would like to ask you about parental involvement in lessons. We're looking at the period from the very first music lesson until now. Therefore, there may have been changes over time. So, at the first lessons:

(a) did you attend the lessons together, with parent sitting in on the lesson; (b) did the parent wait outside the lesson, but speak to the teacher as soon as the lesson was over; (c) did parents provide transportation to and from the lessons, without engaging in discussion with the teacher; (d) did parents have no involvement in the lessons (because, for example, the lessons happened at school)? Did this involvement change over time? If so when and how?

Participants selected the one of the above four responses that most closely matched their experience.

In addition to the main study, which was based on interviews, there was a diary study, involving forty-five children from the target group and a control group consisting of forty-nine other young people. The diary study was designed to provide up-to-date information on current training and practicing activities, and involvement in other musical activities.

Findings 1: Parental Influences on Musical Progress

Up to the age of eleven, there was more parental involvement in lessons in Group 1 than in the two lowest-achieving groups. However, from the age of twelve, there were no inter-group differences in the amount of parental involvement in this aspect of children's musical training (a finding that reflects the young learners' growing independence). Unsurprisingly, the parents of those children who began learning an instrument at an especially early age had a greater degree of active involvement in their children's first lessons. There were no significant differences between the groups in the extent to which the parents were involved in practicing activities. However, on a composite measure of involvement in both lessons and practicing, the parents of the more able groups of young musicians were more involved than the parents of the children who had achieved less. Groups 1 and 2 were characterized by high levels of parental involvement, whereas Groups 3 and 4 showed intermediate levels of involvement, and Group 5 displayed consistently low levels (Davidson, Howe, Moore, and Sloboda, 1996; Davidson, Howe, and Sloboda, 1997).

The groups differed significantly in the degree to which one or more parents were involved in playing or listening to music themselves. However, even with Group 1, the involvement of a typical parent was restricted to listening at home. In Groups 1 and 2, but not Groups 4 and 5, a substantial number of parents reported having become more involved in music since their child began having lessons.

Broadly speaking, these findings confirm the results of the previous stage of the investigation in showing that children who successfully acquire musical skills experience high levels of parental support in music, an involvement maintained throughout the earlier years of music training.

Findings 2: Practicing

The average amount of daily practicing varied between a minimum of ten minutes at age four and a maximum of three hours at age sixteen.

At each age from eight upward, Groups 1 and 5 differed significantly in the amount of practice done, and from the age of nine onward, Group 1 also differed significantly from Groups 2 and 4 (Sloboda, Davidson, Howe, and Moore, 1996).

By the age of twelve, there were substantial differences between the groups in the amounts of time devoted to practicing. Group 1 averaged around two hours per day, Groups 2 and 3 around one hour per day, Group 4 around thirty minutes, and Group 5 around fifteen minutes per day. In other words, between the lowest and highest achieving groups there was, by the age of twelve, a substantial difference in the amount of regular practicing that was being done. In consequence, by the age of thirteen the mean cumulative hours of practicing differed greatly between the groups. By that time the total amounts of practice since beginning to play their first instrument averaged 2,572 hours for Group 1, compared with 1,434 hours, 1,438 hours, 807 hours, and 439 hours for Groups 2 to 5 respectively. (On average, it takes around 3,300 hours of practicing for a young performer to reach Grade Eight.)

The cumulative amount of practice for Group 1 up to the age of thirteen is in line with the estimates obtained for the most successful violinists and pianists in other investigations (Ericsson, Krampe, and Tesch-Römer, 1993). Conceivably, the inter-group differences in cumulative practicing times could have been partly due to the fact that students in Group 1 were more likely than the others to play more than one instrument and to have begun learning an instrument unusually early. The findings indicated, however, that the differences largely reflected greater amounts of time being spent practicing the main instrument, especially in the period following the initial two years of instruction.

As well as practicing more, the children in Group 1 tended to spend more time having lessons than the less successful players. For instance, Group 1 averaged fifty minutes of lessons per week, from the age of six, compared with thirty minutes in Group 5. However, whereas practicing time increased by a factor of three between the ages of ten and sixteen in Group 1, there was only a slight increase in the amount of time devoted to lessons.

The rate of progress, as assessed by the age at which successive grade examinations were successfully attempted, differed appreciably between the groups. For instance, on their main instrument most Group 1 participants progressed to Grade 3 or Grade 4 by their fourth year of instruction, whereas few of the other participants exceeded

Grade 2. However, although the Group 1 students undoubtedly made more progress in a given amount of chronological time, there was no evidence that they made more progress with an equivalent amount of practice, for their faster progress was paralleled by larger amounts of time spent practicing. There was no evidence at all to suggest that the most successful young instrumentalists would have progressed faster if they had not practiced more.

Indeed, the Group 1 students did not differ significantly from the other youngsters on a measure of the ratio of progress to effort. That was obtained by dividing the amount of progress by the time devoted to practicing (making allowances for the fact that with successive grades it requires increasing amounts of training to proceed from one to the next). It therefore is likely that the faster progress of the more competent young musicians was largely a consequence of their greater commitment to training and practicing activities.

Since the retrospective nature of the data obtained from the interviews places limits on their accuracy and reliability, it is useful to compare the findings obtained from interviews with the results that emerged from a diary study, in which reports of current practicing activities were recorded over a forty-two-week period. Reassuringly, there was a large positive correlation ($r = .75$) between the most recent retrospective estimates of formal practice and the diary evidence. The diary responses confirmed the interview finding that, at various ages, the groups differed significantly in the amount of time that students devoted to practicing. Group 1 not only practiced more than the others, but spent a larger proportion of the total practicing time on formal practice activities such as scales and technical exercises. The diary findings also revealed that Group 1 students, in comparison with the others, were more likely to practice scales in the mornings rather than later in the day. Group 1 participants also displayed more stable patterns of practicing. For example, they displayed less week-to-week variation than the other groups in the amount of time spent practicing scales. Unsurprisingly, all groups practiced less during holiday periods than during the school terms.

Findings 3: Early Signs of Musical Ability
Anecdotes abound of celebrated musicians having displayed clear signs of special musical talent at very early ages. Although the findings of the first stage of our own research revealed virtually no evidence of clear,

early signs of future excellence, it seemed appropriate to explore this matter more fully. Parents were asked to report on the earliest indications of a number of activities that could have been indicative of unusual musicality. For example, there were a number of questions that asked the parents to state the age at which they first noticed their child engaging in various activities, such as singing, making rhythmic or dance movements in time with music, displaying a liking for musical sounds, and showing a high degree of attentiveness to music. In most cases the parents' responses to these questions were based on their memories for events that had taken place a substantial time earlier. To make sure that parents were as well prepared as possible for these questions, and had time to locate any documentary evidence (such as diary reports) that might help them to give accurate answers, they were informed in advance about the kinds of issues that would be raised. The parents were discouraged from making guesses when they were not sure of the answer to a question.

With only one of five questions that concerned possible early indicators of talent in a child did the responses yield any evidence of a difference between the groups. Children in Group 1 were reported to have first sung at a significantly earlier age than the other children (Howe, Davidson, Moore, and Sloboda, 1995). The majority of the parents reported, however, that they themselves sung to their children in the first year, well before any singing was observed in the children. It therefore seems likely that any singing activities in the young people were preceded by repeated experiences of being sung to, rather than being totally unprepared behaviors. Singing apart, no evidence of very early signs of special abilities became apparent in either stage of our research, suggesting that such early indicators are not a common characteristic of competent young musicians.

A number of other questions asked about children's earliest parent-initiated musical experiences. On the whole, there were few differences between the groups in the ages at which they first experienced events such as being sung to sleep, being sung to at other times, being introduced to musical toys, or being encouraged to move to music, to listen to music, or engage in musical play. There was a small but significant relationship between the age at which children first sang and the age at which parent-initiated musical activities first started. A greater proportion of those children who first sang relatively early had previously experienced four or more parent-initiated musical behaviors than the other children.

Findings 4: Teacher Influences

As in the earlier stage of our investigation, the majority of music teachers were favorably rated for their personal qualities, but the specific musical skills of first teachers were often regarded as having been no better than average. Unusually in our findings, a gender difference was evident here, with the most recent teachers of the boys being rated as significantly more demanding than the girls' most recent teachers. There were main group effects in respect to ratings of teachers' friendliness, the degree to which they were relaxed, to which they were considered to be chatty, and to which they were seen as being encouraging. In all cases, Group 5 respondents gave the least positive ratings. However, no differences between the groups were noted in the professional skills of the first teachers. With the first teachers, although Group 5 teachers were rated less favorably than the others, the teachers of the other groups received similar ratings, a finding also largely true of the most recent teachers.

Comparisons between first teachers and most recent teachers revealed significant differences in a number of their characteristics. Most recent teachers were regarded as more friendly, more relaxed, more chatty, more encouraging, and also more demanding than the first teachers were. The most recent teachers were also rated as being better teachers in general and better players than the first teachers. Compared with the less successful children, the more successful participants rated their most recent teachers as possessing higher levels of professional expertise.

On the first instrument they learned to play, the better players (Group 1 and Group 2) had been taught by a larger number of teachers than the students in Groups 3, 4, and 5. That difference remains significant even when an adjustment is made for the fact that the better players had been learning the instrument for a longer period of time. The same finding was observed in respect to the instrument that players nominated as their main instrument.

A minority of learners had received some group instruction on their first instrument or their main instrument. This was more common in the least successful students (Group 5) than in the other groups.

GENERAL DISCUSSION AND CONCLUSIONS

Broadly speaking, the findings obtained in the second stage of our investigation confirmed the earlier results. They add weight by showing

that a number of the background features and the experiences characteristic of successful young instrumentalists are less commonly observed
in players who are not so successful. The findings add detail by identifying additional features that play significant roles in the early lives of
successful young musicians. For instance, those children who eventually grow into capable players are more likely than other youngsters to
have first instrumental teachers who are perceived as being warm and
encouraging. They are more likely to have been taught by subsequent
music teachers who possess these same qualities and are also very good
musicians. They are more likely to have received plenty of parental support, especially during the earlier years of music lessons. Typically, these
parents take a strong interest in their child's progress, keeping in close
contact with the teacher and not only giving their child plenty of encouragement, but also providing regular support whenever it is needed. In
particular, these parents support their children's practicing activities,
thus ensuring that a fair amount of practicing is done and that real
progress is made. One consequence is that it becomes relatively easy for
children to get into the habit of doing the regular practicing essential if
they are to gain genuine expertise.

It is noteworthy that even parents who themselves have little or no
expertise at music are nevertheless able to provide considerable support. The pattern of findings suggests that the degree to which the parents support their children's efforts is more important than the extent
to which the parents have musical interests or skills of their own. As a
consequence of receiving high levels of help and encouragement from
teachers and parents, the more successful children regularly and enthu-
siastically engage in the kinds of activities that promote high levels of
expertise. For instance, compared with less successful young players,
they practice more regularly and for longer periods of time.

By no means do all those young beginners at an instrument who experience high levels of support and encouragement thrive as learners.
Nevertheless, our findings suggest that the chances of success are considerably higher when teachers and parents provide these advantages.
Among the three hundred or so young people who participated in one
or another stage of our investigation, instances of individuals who managed to thrive as young musicians in the absence of considerable adult
support appear to be rare, if they exist at all.

Although it seems reasonable to suggest that the high levels of support received by the successful youngsters was an underlying cause of
their success, it is important to be wary about drawing straightforward

causal inferences from the descriptive findings that emerge from re-search of this kind. For instance, on discovering that especially success-ful young players tend to have especially warm and encouraging first teachers, one is tempted to identify teachers' varying degrees of warmth and support as factors that help account for differences between chil-dren in their early progress. It is possible, however, that the extent to which teachers display these qualities toward particular children de-pends on their own perceptions of the children. A teacher may react more warmly to a child whom she regards as being especially keen to learn, or especially responsive. Hence it is possible that when young learners are asked to assess factors such as warmth in a teacher, what they are actually rating are not stable characteristics of the teacher but the specific behaviors of the teacher in relation to a particular learner. Other children might have elicited different patterns of response in the identi-cal teacher, and, in consequence, might have rated the same teacher less favorably.

Our research findings are definitely consistent with the view that differences between children in their experiences of musical training can go a long way toward accounting for the fact that children vary in their musical abilities. However, many people, including numerous music teachers, would argue that although a learner's experiences are important, the really crucial determinants of very high levels of musical expertise are ones that cannot be acquired, and take the form of innate gifts and talents which, it is assumed, are genetically transmitted. As we noted earlier, our own stance toward this position has been somewhat skeptical, and although our own findings cannot either confirm or refute it, some of the results are far from being consistent with the innate talent account.

For instance, if the innate talent account is correct, and a young per-son's musical accomplishments largely depend on the presence of innate processes, it would seem likely that the presence of innate gifts or talents would be apparent at an early age. We would expect to find early signs of special capabilities in those individuals who (largely as a result of their inborn gifts, according to this account) eventually achieve unusu-ally high levels of expertise. But our findings revealed no evidence at all that those young people who eventually became the most able dis-played special signs of talent at very early ages. Such evidence as does exist is largely anecdotal (Howe, Davidson, and Sloboda, 1998; Sloboda and Howe, 1991). In our investigation there was no evidence at all that the most able young musicians in our investigation had shown any early indications of special musical capabilities that were not preceded by special learning experiences.

We decided to make a broader survey of the various kinds of evidence that appears to have some bearing on the question of whether or not the talent account is essentially correct (Howe, Davidson, and Sloboda, 1998; Sloboda, Davidson, and Howe, 1994). Our final conclusion was that although biologically based sources of variability between people have influences that can affect musical capabilities, the scientific evidence does not support the view that there exist specific innate talents that form a necessary underlying condition for high levels of musical ability.

There is no denying that there exist biological differences between individuals that can influence a person's career, that determine a person's physical attributes such as weight, strength, height, or vocal qualities, or psychological ones such as personality, temperament, or general intelligence. We do not think, however, that the actual ways in which variability that has biological origins contribute to differences between children in the ways in which they develop are anything so selective as suggested by the notion of a gift for a specific kind of capability, be it musical or mathematical, literary or scientific. Although we do not claim to have conclusively disproved the innate talent account, which many scientists and numerous musicians continue to believe in, we do think that innate gifts and talents are mythical rather than factual.

Our own approach has clear limitations. It concentrates on the lifestyles and some of the activities (such as practicing) that contribute to high levels of expertise, but apart from identifying the important roles of the support and encouragement provided by teachers and parents it adds little to our understanding of why certain young people, but not others, adopt the regular working habits that steady progress depends on. (That issue is addressed by Csikszentmihalyi, Rathunde, and Whalen, 1993.) Our approach is also somewhat broad-toothed. To fully understand how and why certain people gain expertise, it will be necessary to follow the progress of individuals more closely, and over lengthy periods of time. Also, the components of learning activities such as practicing need to be observed in more detail than was possible in our research (see Krampe, 1994, for ways in which that can be achieved).

References

Csikszentmihalyi, M., Rathunde, K., & Whalen, S. (1993). *Talented teenagers: The roots of success and failure*. New York: Cambridge University Press.

Davidson, J. W., Howe, M. J. A., Moore, D. G., & Sloboda, J. A. (1996). The role of family influences in the development of musical ability. *British Journal of Developmental Psychology, 14,* 399–412.

Davidson, J. W., Howe, M. J. A., & Sloboda, J. A. (1997). Environmental factors in the development of musical performance skill over the life span. In D. J. Hargreaves and A. C. North (Eds.), *The social psychology of music.* Oxford, UK: Oxford University Press.

Davidson, J. W., Moore, D. G., Sloboda, J. A., & Howe, M. J .A. (1998). Characteristics of music teachers and the progress of young instrumentalists. *Journal of Research in Music Education, 46,* 141–160.

Ericsson, K. A. (1996). The acquisition of expert performance: An introduction to some of the issues. In K. A. Ericsson (Ed.), *The road to excellence: The acquisition of expert performance in the arts and sciences, sports, and games.* Mahwah, NJ: Erlbaum.

Ericsson, K. A., & Charness, N. (1994). Expert performance. *American Psychologist, 49,* 725–747.

Ericsson, K. A., Krampe, R. Th., & Tesch-Römer, C. (1993). The role of deliberate practice in the acquisition of expert performance. *Psychological Review, 100,* 363–406.

Gardner, H. (1984). *Frames of mind.* London: Heinemann.

Howe, M. J. A. (1996). Concepts of ability. In I. Dennis & P. Tapsfield (Eds.), *Human abilities: Their nature and measurement.* Mahwah, NJ: Erlbaum.

Howe, M. J. A. (1999). *Genius explained.* Cambridge, UK: Cambridge University Press.

Howe, M. J. A., Davidson, J. W., & Sloboda, J. A. (1998). Innate gifts and talents: Reality or myth? *Brain and Behavioral Sciences, 21,* 399–442.

Howe, M. J. A., Davidson, J. W., Moore, D. G., & Sloboda, J. A. (1995). Are there early childhood signs of musical ability? *Psychology of Music, 23,* 162–176.

Howe, M. J. A., & Sloboda, J. A. (1991a). Young musicians' accounts of significant influences in their early lives: 1. The family and the musical background. *British Journal of Music Education, 8,* 39–52.

Howe, M. J. A., & Sloboda, J. A. (1991b). Young musicians' accounts of significant influences in their early lives: 2. Teachers, practising and performing. *British Journal of Music Education, 8,* 53–63.

Howe, M. J. A., & Sloboda, J. A. (1991c). Early signs of talents and special interests in the lives of young musicians. *European Journal of High Ability, 2,* 102–111.

Howe, M. J. A., & Sloboda, J. A. (1992). Problems experienced by talented young musicians as a result of the failure of other children to value musical accomplishments. *Gifted Education International, 8,* No. 1, 16–18.

Jensen, A. R. (1988). *The g factor: The science of mental ability.* Westport, CT: Praeger.

Krampe, R. Th. (1994). *Maintaining excellence: Cognitive-motor performance in pianists differing in age and skill level.* Berlin: Max-Planck-Institute für Bildungsforschung.

Sloboda, J. A. (1985). *The musical mind.* Oxford, UK: Clarendon Press.

Sloboda, J. A. (1991). Musical expertise. In K. A. Ericsson & J. Smith (Eds.), *Toward a general theory of expertise.* New York: Cambridge University Press.

Sloboda, J. A., Davidson, J. W., & Howe, M. J. A. (1994). Is everyone musical? *The Psychologist, 7*, 349–354.

Sloboda, J. A., Davidson, J. W., Howe, M. J. A., & Moore, D. G. The role of practice in the development of performing musicians. *British Journal of Psychology, 87*, 287–309.

Sloboda, J. A., & Howe, M. J. A. (1991). Biographical precursors of musical excellence: An interview study. *Psychology of Music, 19*, 3–21.

Sloboda, J. A., & Howe, M. J. A. (1992). Transitions in the early musical careers of able young musicians: Choosing instruments and teachers. *American Journal of Research in Musical Education, 40*, 283–294.

Sosniak, L. A. (1985). Learning to be a concert pianist. In B. S. Bloom (Ed.), *Developing talent in young people*, pp. 19–67. New York: Ballantine.

Sosniak, L. A. (1990). The tortoise, the hare, and the development of talent. In M. J. A. Howe (Ed.), *Encouraging the development of exceptional abilities and talents*, pp. 149–64. London: British Psychological Society.

Winner, E. (1996). *Gifted children: Myths and realities*. New York: Basic Books.

8

Expertise, Competence, and Creative Ability

The Perplexing Complexities

Dean Keith Simonton

Albert Einstein is often considered one of the greatest creators of the 20th century. Indeed, he is frequently viewed as a prototypical example of creative genius. Yet what was the psychological basis of his creativity? In particular, consider the following three issues:

1. Samuel Johnson (1781, p. 5), the author of the first English dictionary, claimed that "the true Genius is a mind of large general powers, accidentally determined to some particular direction." In other words, creativity may consist of a generalized information processing capacity that may be channeled to almost any endeavor. Does this statement hold for Einstein? Could he have become a Picasso or a Stravinsky had his childhood experiences only directed him toward art or music rather than toward science? Or did Einstein possess a more specialized ability that would not have served him well had he ventured outside of theoretical physics?

2. Whether Einstein's creative powers were general or specific, where did his capacity originate? Was Einstein's creativity an innate ability, as expressed by John Dryden's (1693/1885, p. 60) famous remark that "genius must be born, and never can be taught"? Or was the capacity slowly and arduously acquired through education, practice, and training? Was Einstein merely the most expert and competent theoretical physicist of his day?

3. In response to the last question, there is no doubt that Einstein made major contributions to our understanding of physical phenomena – from space and time to gravitation, from Brownian motion to the photoelectric effect, and from blackbody radiation to cosmology. Even so, Einstein was by no means the most skilled and informed theoretical

physicist of his time, whether in physics as a whole or in any particular specialty area. Einstein was able to pass his university examinations only with the help of a college classmate, Marcel Grossmann, and his academic performance was insufficient to enable him to secure a regular academic position. One of Einstein's former teachers said that his later fame "came as a tremendous surprise ... for in his student days Einstein had been a lazy dog. He never bothered about mathematics at all" (Seelig, 1958, p. 28). Einstein subsequently had to take on Grossmann as a mathematical collaborator to fill a major gap in his expertise. Even worse, he was not fully proficient or fluent in those areas of physics wherein he should have been the world's greatest expert. In a debate with Niels Bohr over quantum theory, Einstein saw one of his well-crafted arguments destroyed when Bohr simply indicated that Einstein had failed to take into consideration his own relativity theory! Worse still, Einstein wasted a good part of his later career developing the Unified Field Theory, an effort almost universally rejected as theoretically and empirically impossible. How can these episodes in his life be rendered consistent with the notion that Einstein's extraordinary creative genius was a straightforward consequence of his superior mastery of a chosen domain?

The life and career of Einstein thus raise some very profound questions about the status of creativity as a psychological capacity. My goal in this chapter is to address these and related questions. I do so because I believe that the phenomenon of creativity highlights some critical issues about the nature of abilities, expertise, and competencies. At the close of this chapter I discuss whether other human capacities operate in a manner similar to creativity.

WHAT IS CREATIVITY?

Before I can examine where creativity stands as an ability, expertise, or competency, I must first define creativity itself. The definition adopted here is standard in the field: creativity entails the capacity to generate ideas that are simultaneously original and adaptive. Originality signifies low frequency of occurrence. The most original ideas might emerge only once (such as Einstein's relativity theory or Planck's quantum theory). Adaptiveness means that the idea satisfies the criteria appropriate to the creative domain. For example, artistic creations must satisfy certain aesthetic and semantic requirements, whereas scientific creations must meet certain standards of logic and fact. Because both originality and adaptiveness can vary along some implicit scale, the degree of creativity may vary as well. Furthermore, the capacity to generate creative ideas constitutes an individual-difference variable that can range from everyday forms of creativity – like planning a surprise birthday party – to the kinds of creativity evinced by Albert Einstein. I have decided to concentrate discussion here on the highest levels of creativity. This focus reflects my belief that it is precisely at the level of creative genius that the complexities and ambiguities become most conspicuous.

Given the above definition of creativity, does the capacity to create entail an ability, an expertise, or a competency?

Is Creativity an Ability?

An ability is defined as the cognitive capacity to perform some mental or behavioral task. The better the performance of that task, the higher is the presumed level of ability. Most abilities are assumed to have nontrivial heritability coefficients – say, between .30 and .70 – and thus be in a certain sense innate. However, the genetic potential only becomes realized when the individual develops in an environment that offers opportunities for appropriate stimulation; for example, an individual with an inherited capacity for above-average intelligence will only manifest that ability if his or her infancy, childhood, and adolescence take place in supportive familial and educational settings. Finally, abilities are presumed to vary in specificity. At one end of the continuum would be abilities like general intelligence, whereas at the other end might be the ability to taste certain flavors. Highly specialized innate abilities can be called talents (Simonton, 1999b).

Perhaps the best approach to deciding whether creativity can be considered an ability is to compare it with some other human attribute whose status as an ability is well established. The most obvious exemplar is general intelligence, as roughly gauged by so-called intelligence tests. Such comparisons suggest some fundamental difficulties regarding creativity's place in the list of well-accepted abilities. Ponder the following three questions: Can creativity be measured? How is it distributed in the population? Is it inherited?

Can Creativity Be Measured?
Corresponding to most abilities are psychometric instruments designed to assess individual differences in those abilities. Thus, intelligence can be assessed using the Stanford-Binet, the Wechsler, or a host of other

measures. For the most part, these measures also meet high psychometric standards with respect to reliability and validity. Creativity clearly departs from this pattern. In the first place, although researchers have proposed several measures that purport to assess individual differences in creativity, it is probably safe to say that there exist no "creativity tests" in the same sense that tests of intelligence abound (Simonton, in press). Most of the more widely used instruments assess individual differences in thought processes believed to be essential to the generation of creative ideas, such as remote association (Mednick, 1962) or divergent thinking (Guilford, 1967). Furthermore, none of these suggested measures can be said to have passed all the psychometric hurdles required of established ability tests. For instance, scores on separate creativity tests often correlate too highly with general intelligence (that is, low divergent validity), correlate very weakly among each other (that is, low convergent validity), and correlate very weakly with objective indicators of overt creative behaviors (that is, low predictive validity; McNemar, 1964).

Several solutions have been proposed to improve the assessment of individual differences in creativity (Hocevar and Bachelor, 1989). Three of the more important proposals are as follows:

1. Perhaps creativity tests must be domain-specific (Baer, 1993, 1994). Rather than a generalized ability, like "Spearman's g" (Spearman, 1927), creativity may be more comparable to a special aptitude. For instance, rather than assess the capacity for divergent thinking in some global fashion, it may be better to tap divergent thought with respect to the concepts of the specific field in which creativity is to be displayed. Although domain-specific tests often exhibit greater predictive validity than do global measures, the validity coefficients remain too low to affirm with confidence that the measurement problem has been solved.

2. Another approach is to assume that creativity is not just a cognitive capacity, but rather a dispositional one (Cattell and Butcher, 1968; Sternberg and Lubart, 1995). That is, creative individuals can be characterized by a set of traits, interests, motives, and values. Some investigators have even suggested that personality is far more crucial than intellect in the making of a creative individual (Dellas and Gaier, 1970). Instruments predicated on this conception have been devised and have been found to have some degree of predictive success (for example, Cattell and Butcher, 1968; Gough, 1979). Even so, the very existence of such dispositional measures greatly complicates any attempt to conceive of creativity as some kind of ability. After all, the concept of ability would then have to be defined far more loosely for it to

encompass non-cognitive factors underlying creative behavior. The term would probably become so inclusive as to become scientifically useless.

3. A final solution is to assess creativity in terms of behaviors that can be considered indicative of creativity. This assessment can be carried out in a number of ways. One approach is to give research participants problems that require creative solutions, and then have their responses evaluated by judges (Amabile, 1982, 1996). One drawback to this approach is that it obliges all individuals to have their creativity assessed by the same means, when a particular participant's creative ability may lie elsewhere. For example, a creative musician may not necessarily prove creative when asked to construct an artistic collage or an effective poem. A method that circumvents this problem is to have respondents list accomplishments that can be deemed representative of creative behavior (Amelang, Herboth, and Oefner, 1991; Richards et al., 1988). Artistic creators can then provide an inventory of their art work, literary creators of their compositions, and so forth, yielding an index sensitive to the domain-specific nature of creativity. Needless to say, such self-report measures have their own distinctive set of methodological problems, including distortions produced by the social desirability of creativity. A closely related variation on this method accordingly gauges creativity in terms of publicly available products, such as exhibited artwork, published poems, performed compositions, or successful patent applications (for example, Dennis, 1955; Huber, 2000; Simonton, 1997a). The main limitation of this measurement strategy is that it is only applicable to those individuals whose creativity enables them to contribute overtly to a given creative domain. Such measures leave out the Sunday afternoon painters and the poets who only write for their own personal consumption.

Unfortunately, these last behavioral measures of creativity have not really solved the problem of how to measure creative ability. Rather than assess creativity directly, such instruments gauge the consequences of creativity. If the capacity to produce original and adaptive ideas eventually results in products that can be called creative, then it clearly follows that those products can be taken as indicative of underlying ability. Yet the ability is not being assessed directly, nor do the behavioral measures provide any information about the psychological processes involved, unlike what holds for, say, tests of divergent thinking ability. Hence, these instruments are not really comparable to a psychometric measure of intelligence that tries to ground itself in basic cognitive processes (short- and long-term memory, reaction time, discrimination, induction and deduction, analogical reasoning, and so forth). In a way, behavioral measures beg the question about whether creative ability can be measured. As a consequence, the ability becomes a mere latent construct that is inferred rather than assessed.

How is Creativity Distributed in the Population?

Francis Galton (1869) first established that human abilities tend to be distributed in the population according to the "normal" or "bell-shaped" curve. His demonstration was based partly on data – the fit of the normal curve to performance on examinations – and partly on analogy to the distribution of physical traits, such as height and weight. Since Galton, the normal distribution has become almost an article of dogma, firmly ingrained in the statistics psychologists use and in their conception of individual differences, including intelligence (Burt, 1963). Moreover, it is clear that this faith is not unfounded, for the bell curve provides a reasonable approximation to most empirically observed distributions. Not surprisingly, creativity has often been perceived after the same fashion (Nicholls, 1972). Presumably, most human beings exhibit average levels of the capacity, the frequencies tapering off in either direction, with creative genius being about as rare as those who are virtually incapable of producing a creative idea.

This received tradition notwithstanding, many human abilities are not normally distributed, and skewed distributions are especially characteristic of exceptional performance (Walberg, Strykowski, Rovai, and Hung, 1984). Furthermore, creativity belongs in this latter category. If creative ability is gauged by the generation of creative products, then the distribution is extremely skewed. A small percentage of the creators account for the lion's share of the total output (Lotka, 1926). Typically, the top 10 percent of the most prolific producers in any field can be credited with half or more of the products, placing them a great many standard deviations above the mean (Dennis, 1954a, 1954b, 1955). To put this disparity in concrete terms, if intelligence and height were distributed the same way as creative output, people with IQs exceeding 300 would be commonplace, and basketball players would all be at least fifteen feet tall (Simonton, 1997b).

The blatantly non-normal distribution of creative productivity suggests that creativity does not function in the same manner as the more standard or everyday abilities. Hence, creative ability may be a more complex phenomenon.

Is Creativity Genetically Inherited?

It is curious that Galton (1869) believed that the normal distribution of ability showed that individual differences were inherited. If height was genetically inherited and normally distributed, then perhaps the normal distribution of ability was also indicative of a genetic foundation. Although this argument is obviously unsound, it does have a grain of truth. Very few inheritable human traits are the function of a single gene. On the contrary, most genetically influenced characteristics, such as human abilities, are the consequence of a large number of genes, each making its own separate contribution to the overall trait. Hence, general intelligence is not an upshot of a single gene, but rather the composite effect of still uncounted genes. One repercussion of such *polygenic* inheritance is that the composite trait will likely be normally distributed in the population. Most persons will receive an average amount of relevant genes, whereas those who either receive very few or a large number will be much rarer.

Galton (1869) did not base his argument about the heritability of ability solely on the cross-sectional distribution. He also introduced the family pedigree method to draw the same conclusion. Of special relevance here are his results for individuals who attained eminence in domains of creative achievement. Galton showed that creative genius tended to run in family lines, at least at a rate appreciably higher than what would be expected by chance. This finding was replicated by others (for example, Bramwell, 1948). Nevertheless, not everyone drew the same conclusion that Galton did. Rather than attributing these distinguished creative pedigrees to genetic determinism, many claimed that environmental factors were responsible (for example, Candolle, 1873; Kroeber, 1944). In addition, close scrutiny of the record reveals that not all great creators come from notable pedigrees (Simonton, 1994). The exceptions include such illustrious geniuses as Michelangelo, Beethoven, and Newton! Creativity may not be inherited after all. Yet this latter conclusion seems rather implausible. Given that creativity displays positive correlations with characteristics that boast substantial heritability coefficients, such as general intelligence, it seems unlikely that its own heritability would be nil.

Happily, modern behavior genetics provides a solution to this problem, and at the same time resolves the issue of the highly skewed distribution of creative output. The resolution comes from a form of genetic inheritance known as emergenesis (Lykken, 1982). Emergenic inheritance occurs for polygenic traits that are combined in a multiplicative rather than additive fashion. This means that there exist certain essential component traits that must be inherited if the characteristic can be inherited at all. If one requisite component is missing, the composite trait will not appear no matter how well represented are the other traits. It is interesting that behavorial geneticists have already reported evidence that creativity may constitute just such an emergenic ability (Waller et al., 1993). If creative ability indeed emerges from emergenesis, the following four implications result:

1. Creativity must consist of several essential components, that is, it must be a multidimensional rather than unidimensional capacity. Some of these components may be cognitive, including general intelligence, whereas others might very well include dispositional traits (Martindale, 1989). For instance, Galton (1869) himself claimed that creative genius required a mix of intellect, energy, and determination, the last two representing motivational rather than cognitive attributes. The full list of requirement components is probably much longer still.

2. In contrast to naive conceptions of genetic inheritance, emergenesis implies that creative genius will not necessarily exhibit family pedigrees (Lykken, 1982; Simonton, 1999b). Because the individual must inherit just the right configuration of traits, it becomes extremely unlikely that a creative genius would have highly creative offspring. For emergenic characteristics, only monozygotic (identical) twins will display any familial resemblance, whereas dizygotic (fraternal) twins will be no more similar than unrelated individuals. Accordingly, the family pedigrees identified by Galton (1869) may be best interpreted in terms of nurture rather than nature. That is, to the extent that creative ability must be cultivated in appropriate environments, the distinguished lineages merely reflect continuity in those environmental influences.

3. One special asset of multidimensional and multiplicative inheritance is its implication for cross-sectional distributions of the traits so produced. Even if the component traits are normally distributed in the population, the composite characteristic will not be, but rather it will display a highly skewed distribution (Simonton, 1999b; see also Burt, 1943; Shockley, 1957). Most of the population will cluster near the bottom of the distribution, whereas the elite few will be placed far out on the upper right-hand tail. Consequently, the highly skewed distribution of creative productivity can be explicated as a necessary repercussion of emergenic endowment. This sets creativity apart from many other polygenic abilities, such as general intelligence, that are more likely to result from simple, additive inheritance.

4. The preceding three consequences imply that the prediction of creativity should be rather difficult (Simonton, 1999b). First, if creativity is multidimensional, a large number of variables must be assessed to maximize the predictive validity of any composite. Second, parental characteristics will not provide very good predictors, owing to the emergenic pattern of inheritance. Third, the highly skewed distribution means that most of the cross-sectional variance will reside in a few individuals, whereas the vast majority of persons will have pretty similar levels of creative ability. In addition, prediction will only be maximized by using complex equations instead of the linear and additive equations most often used in differential psychology.

It should be made clear that according to an emergenic model, the first consequence has repercussions for the final three (Simonton, 1999b). The greater the underlying dimensionality of creative ability, the lower the degree of familial inheritance, the more conspicuous the skew in the cross-sectional distribution, and the lower the expected validity coefficients obtained when attempting to predict creativity from the component traits and other factors.

Does Creativity Require Expertise?

In the previous section I discussed the possibility that creative ability might consist of a rich cluster of traits, some cognitive and others dispositional. Furthermore, to some extent this cluster of component traits is subject to genetic inheritance. This last assertion is not equivalent to saying that genius is entirely born. The heritability coefficients for the participating traits suggest otherwise (Waller et al., 1993). Even general intelligence, which boasts perhaps the highest heritability for any major psychological component of creative ability, owes a considerable part of its cross-sectional variance to environmental factors (Plomin and Petrill, 1997). Such non-genetic factors tend to play an even bigger role for those personality traits that most likely contribute to creative development (Bouchard, 1994). Many psychologists would argue that even this highly qualified position still places far too much stress on nature, and far too little on nurture (Howe, 1999). Some psychologists view creativity exclusively in terms of an acquired expertise, with no genetic contribution whatsoever (Ericsson, 1996a). Before I address this alternative viewpoint, I must define the terms of discussion.

Here an expertise consists of acquired skills and knowledge in a specific domain. Presumably, the domain is sufficiently rich that considerable training and practice are required before it can be fully mastered. An expertise is necessarily acquired rather than innate. More specifically, the amount and quantity of deliberate practice has the primary role in determining the amount of expertise a particular individual can claim (Ericsson and Charness, 1994; Ericsson, Krampe, and Tesch-Römer, 1993). At the highest level is the master who has acquired virtually all the skill and knowledge that defines a particular specialty. Colleagues recognize the bona fide master as having world-class expertise in the area. At the lowest level, in contrast, is the novice, who has only acquired the most basic skills and knowledge. Not only do domain experts easily recognize a novice as such, but also novice status is usually recognizable by individuals with no skills or knowledge in the domain. A "beginner" in a musical instrument or in a particular sport can be discerned by casual observers, not just virtuosos or champion athletes.

If creativity is merely an expertise, then it is inherently domain-specific. Mastery of chess will have no utility to the novice in physics or painting. Only expertise acquisition in closely related domains would have any usefulness, such as mathematical training as preparation for a career in theoretical physics. In addition, to the extent that creativity can be reduced to an acquired expertise, the role of innate abilities is necessarily minimized. At best, the rate of expertise acquisition might vary according to individual differences in relevant abilities, such as general intelligence. Yet once domain mastery is acquired, those abilities recede into the background, the accumulated repertoire of knowledge and skills assuming the major role in the production of creative products.

The empirical research on expertise has not concentrated on creative domains, but rather on those domains in which skill and knowledge acquisition is paramount, such as exceptional performances in music, sports, and games (Ericsson, 1996b; Howe, Davidson, and Sloboda, 1998). This research has consistently demonstrated that nobody attains world-class performance levels without first undergoing a long, arduous period of deliberate practice and training. This period of intense preparation often takes a full decade, a finding that is often generalized as the "ten-year rule" (Ericsson, 1996a; Hayes, 1989; compare Gardner, 1993). Moreover, some evidence exists that the same ten-year rule applies to creativity as well. In particular, after scrutinizing the careers of 76 classical composers, Hayes (1989) noted that the first notable compositions typically do not appear until at least a decade after the composer has begun the extensive study of music. There were only three relatively minor exceptions – Satie, Shostakovich, and Paganini – who managed to produce masterworks after only eight or nine years of preparation.

These findings fit so nicely with what has been found for chess, sports, and instrumental performance, that it would seem that creativity is indeed a type of acquired expertise. Even so, the Hayes (1989) study has problems that render it far less convincing on closer examination. The investigation was not published in a refereed journal, but was reported briefly in a book intended for popular consumption. As a consequence, many crucial methodological details are omitted. Furthermore, Hayes did not systematically examine individual differences in the rates at which domain mastery is acquired. As we shortly demonstrate, such cross-sectional variation may betray the operation of innate contrasts in musical talent. Finally, there are signs that Hayes may have made some inadvertent errors in data collection. Take, for instance, the assertion that "Albeniz's first masterwork was written in the 72nd year of his career" (p. 296). This is plain wrong. This Spanish composer's last major work – the one universally acclaimed as his greatest composition – was *Iberia,* which appeared between 1906 and 1909 when Albéniz was 46 to 49 years old. Worse still, Albéniz died in 1909, at age 49, and so he could not have lived to the 72nd year of his *life,* let alone the "72nd year of his career." There is no knowing for how many other composers there are comparable mistakes.

I examine below some empirical findings that do not seem very compatible with the theory that the capacity for creativity is a simple function of domain mastery. These complicating results fall into three areas: biographical antecedents, personal characteristics, and career development.

Biographical Antecedents
A vast literature has emerged that attempts to tease out the early developmental experiences that contribute to creative potential (Simonton, 1987a, 1999a). These findings often contradict what would be predicted according to the expertise-acquisition hypothesis (Simonton, 2000). For instance, the relation between formal training and creative achievement often runs counter to expectation. Specifically, exceptional creativity can sometimes be a curvilinear, inverted-U function of education or training (Simonton, 1983). In addition, exceptional academic performance, as gauged by grade-point average and scholastic honors, is not highly predictive of later creative behavior (Goertzel, Goertzel, and Goertzel, 1978;

Hudson, 1958; MacKinnon, 1978; McClelland, 1973). Sometimes, too, the most innovative individuals are those whose training is marginal rather than central to the field of major achievement (Hudson and Jacot, 1986; Kuhn, 1970; Simonton, 1984b). If the expertise hypothesis were correct, it would seem that the most outstanding creators would receive the highest levels of training and exhibit the most exceptional levels of achievement in the specialty in which they eventually attain eminence. Yet that is not necessarily the case.

Perhaps the most striking result concerns the biographical influence that Hayes (1989) investigated: the decade-long preparation period. A far more extensive and detailed inquiry revealed that the ten-year rule does not operate in the anticipated manner (Simonton, 1991b). Like that of Hayes (1989), the sample consisted of classical composers, with the sample size extended to 120. Because just 100 composers account for nearly all the works heard most regularly in the classical repertoire (Moles, 1958/1968), these 120 subjects exclude no composer of any importance. Furthermore, these composers were assessed on a much greater number of variables. For instance, musical preparation prior to the first important work was gauged two distinct ways: years accumulated since first formal music lessons and years accumulated since first attempted compositions. Each composer's first important work was determined by two different criteria, one objective (performance frequencies) and the other subjective (expert ratings). The ultimate impact of the composer was evaluated various ways, including eminence in the classical repertoire, total number of works contributed to the repertoire, and the age at which the composer stopped making contributions to that repertoire.

In one respect, the Hayes (1989) results were replicated: Composers rarely launch their careers right off with the production of masterpieces (Simonton, 1991b). On the contrary, a considerable amount of preparation is almost invariably required. Although the first truly great work usually appeared when the composer was between twenty-six and thirty-one years old, the average age for beginning music lessons was around nine, and that for the first compositional efforts around seventeen. This means that the first notable products were created seventeen to twenty-two years after the first lessons, and ten to fourteen years after the first compositions. If anything, the ten-year rule seems a bit too brief. Yet these averages cannot tell the whole story, for the dispersion around the mean was considerable. Some composers required only a few years before they began to make lasting contributions to the repertoire, whereas others had to wait decades for their first enduring accomplishment. These individual differences show that some creators take less time to attain domain mastery than do others. This variation in the rate of expertise acquisition implies that the composers might vary in initial levels of musical ability or talent. In line with this inference are some telling facts. Those composers with accelerated preparation periods tend also to be those who (a) have the largest lifetime output of distinguished works, (b) are the oldest when making the last notable contribution, and (c) display the highest posthumous reputation in the world of classical music.

Significantly, comparable results have been found for other creative domains (Cox, 1926; Raskin, 1936), such as scientific creativity (for example, Roe, 1953; Simonton, 1991a, 1992; Zuckerman, 1977). Therefore, these findings are not restricted to classical composers, but rather likely apply to all forms of creative endeavor. The greatest creators – those that reach the heights of genuine genius – achieve more with less. That is, they have *more* accomplishments to their credit even though they spent *less* time in the rigors of expertise acquisition. What can this mean? For now, let us consider two possibilities:

1. Outstanding creators might possess exceptional abilities that enable them to master the domain in less time. These inordinate capacities also help the creator produce an impressive lifetime output over a long career, and thereby achieve the highest degrees of eminence. And these abilities may have a genetic basis, at least in part. If this interpretation is correct, expertise acquisition may simply constitute a necessary but not sufficient factor in creative development.

2. Exceptional creators exhibit shorter preparation periods not because of accelerated acquisition, but rather because they have actually opted out of the learning process before attaining complete domain mastery. That is, some individuals decide to become creators rather than experts within a given domain. Unlike experts who strive to master everything known so far, creators wish to venture into the unknown, to ask new questions rather than learn old answers (compare Getzels and Jackson, 1962; Getzels and Csikszentmihalyi, 1976; McClelland, 1973). The choice of whether to become a domain creator rather than a domain expert may be deeply rooted in a person's character structure.

Personal Characteristics
Apropos of the second conjecture, numerous individual-difference variables appear to separate those who merely master domain-specific skills

and knowledge from those who actually make creative contributions (Feist, 1998; Simonton, 1999a). For example, psychometric studies have indicated that those who are considered notable creators in a domain have identifiably different character traits than do mere domain experts (that is, persons who are otherwise comparable in training, experience, and professional standing; see, for example, Barron, 1969; Helson and Crutchfield, 1970; MacKinnon, 1978; Rostan, 1994). Among the distinguishing attributes are the creator's greater inclination toward nonconformity, unconventionality, independence, openness to experience, ego-strength, aggressiveness, risk-taking, and introversion. Curiously, exceptional creators may also have a certain inclination toward psychopathology (Barron, 1969; Ludwig, 1995; Eysenck, 1995), suggesting that genius-grade creativity may entail some degree of *disability*, not just ability (Simonton, 1999a).

Of special interest to the issues addressed in this volume is the tendency for highly creative individuals to have broader interests and greater versatility than their less creative colleagues (Gough, 1979; Manis, 1951; Raskin, 1936; R. J. Simon, 1974; Simonton, 1976; Sulloway, 1996; White, 1931). This empirical finding raises two profound questions about the doctrine that creativity can be reduced to an acquired expertise:

1. Because the amount of time available for creative development is more or less constant, individuals who devote more time to varied interests and to the acquisition of multiple skills are necessarily allotting less time to the acquisition of a single specialized domain. So again, it seems that highly creative persons can acquire the required domain knowledge and expertise in an accelerated fashion. After all, each minute spent on developing outside interests and capacities must take away from time spent on the mastery of any specific domain of achievement. To a certain extent, information and skill acquisition should be a zero-sum game, so that the choice should be between being an expert or being a dilettante.

2. Better yet, the breadth and versatility of outstanding creators may actually make a direct contribution to their creative accomplishments. If exceptional creativity tends to be associated with the acquisition of mastery in more than one domain, there may be gains from "cross-training" in creative domains that may not have equivalents in chess, sports, or music performance. It is conceivable that persons who spend excessive amounts of time specializing in a single domain may fall victim to "overtraining" – with adverse consequences for the development of

creative potential (see also Frensch and Sternberg, 1989). This possibility receives some empirical endorsement in the next section.

Career Development

The expertise-acquisition hypothesis presumes that once an individual has reached world-class knowledge and skill in a selected domain, then he or she should be able to maintain consistently high levels of performance. That is, mastery provides a necessary and sufficient basis for the onset of achievement within the domain. Furthermore, continued practice and training should suffice for continued accomplishment. Yet the actual characteristics of creative careers in adulthood seem to be inconsistent with this view (Simonton, 1988, 2000). To start with, if the expertise-acquisition account were correct, creativity should increase over the career course as the creator acquires more experience writing creative products, yielding a positive monotonic "learning curve" (see, for example, Ohlsson, 1992). Yet creative productivity typically increases only at the beginning of the career, output tending to decline after the creator attains the career peak (for example, Dennis, 1966; Diamond, 1986; Lehman, 1953, 1962; Simonton, 1984a, 1989). Detailed scrutiny reveals that such decrements cannot be ascribed simply to the obsolescence of domain-relevant knowledge and skills (for example, McDowell, 1982), nor can such declines be completely attributed to the cognitive and physiological repercussions of aging (Simonton, 1988, 1997a). In this critical respect creative output departs from what clearly holds for such achievement domains as chess and sports where age decrements also occur (Elo, 1965; Schulz and Curnow, 1988; compare Krampe and Ericsson, 1996).

The foregoing findings need not signify that expertise is totally irrelevant to creativity. But these empirical results do suggest that the role of expertise acquisition is probably far more complex than usually envisioned for such achievement domains as sports and instrumental performance (Simonton, 2000). A pro golfer, for instance, can practice at the driving range hour after hour until distance and accuracy are maximized. A musician can play particularly difficult passages over and over until they sound just right, both with respect to correctness and interpretation. Yet creativity operates in a rather contrary manner. If someone were to offer the same creative idea time after time, he or she would not be considered creative at all. Because an essential component of creativity is originality, a person who adopts a "formulaic" approach to generating products is considered a mere "hack" (if repeating his or her own works) or a simple "imitator" (if repeating someone else's). Hence, whereas a pianist can replicate a perfect interpretation of Beethoven's "Moonlight" Sonata in concert after concert and still be counted a virtuoso, Beethoven could not compose one "Moonlight" Sonata after another and still be considered a compositional genius. As a consequence, "practice makes perfect" in the first case, but not the second. Overuse of the same procedures and methods might actually constitute something akin to cognitive overtraining in which the creator "falls into a rut," "runs out of steam," "dries up," or in some other way succumbs to stylistic or intellectual mannerisms. To escape this creative cul-de-sac may require cross-training in which the person engages in some other creative activity that induces the individual to break away from the self-imposed stereotype or rigidity.

The disparate influences of overtraining and cross-training were suggested by an inquiry into the careers of fifty-nine opera composers (Simonton, 2000). Each of these composers produced at least one work that entered the operatic repertoire, and so all these creators could be said to have acquired world-class expertise in that domain at least once during the course of their career. All told, these same composers produced a total of 911 operas which varied immensely with respect to their contemporary and long-term success in the opera houses of the world (Simonton, 1998a). The question addressed by the study was whether the differential aesthetic impact of these 911 works could be explicated according to the expertise acquired at the time a given piece was composed. That expertise was measured multiple ways. One set of measures assessed the number of years accumulated since first lessons, since first compositions, and since first operas. Another set of measures gauged expertise in terms of cumulative products in four distinct categories: genre-specific operas, all operas, all vocal compositions, and all compositions.

The data analyses revealed several findings that severely compromised a straightforward expertise-acquisition explanation. In the first place, many of the effects were best described as nonmonotonic, single-peaked functions. Although the success of a work would increase with a certain amount of experience, after a certain point the influence would become negative, increasing experience causing a decline in the overall effectiveness of the operas produced. Moreover, these overtraining effects were especially prominent for more specialized forms of expertise acquisition. For instance, a composer who insisted on creating a long sequence of operas in the same genre, such as operetta, would display a conspicuous decline in creativity in comparison to a composer who switched from one genre to another, such as going from opera seria to opera buffa. Even more telling was the consequence of composing works outside the operatic form. Those composers who mixed it up by interspersing operatic output with symphonic and chamber music were more likely to see their operatic creativity maintain its vitality. Hence, those creators who specialized in a single operatic form ended up being less creative than those who displayed more versatility, contributing to multiple operatic genres and even to the repertoire beyond the opera house.

Using rather different methods, comparable effects have been found for scientific creativity (Root-Bernstein, Bernstein, and Garnier, 1993). Those scientists who displayed long, productive careers rich in high-impact contributions were those who were simultaneously involved in several research areas (see also Hargens, 1978). Their less influential colleagues, in contrast, tended to focus on just one topic at a time, pursuing it to exhaustion before switching to another research area. It is crucial to recognize that long-term, high-impact scientists are by no means dilettantes. The various topics that make up their research programs are interrelated so that they form a "network of enterprises" (Gruber, 1989; Simonton, 1992). The solution to one problem would often serendipitously provide an answer to a seemingly unrelated issue (see, for example, Poincaré, 1921). The cross-talk between separate projects has been identified as one of the key features separating genius-level creativity from that displayed by computer programs that attempt to simulate the creative process (Tweney, 1990).

Given the above empirical results, one conclusion becomes paramount: creativity cannot be reduced to mere expertise. Not only does it require more than mere expertise acquisition, but also a person may acquire too much expertise to maintain creative ability. To comprehend better the role of expertise in creative development, I now need to turn to the closely related concept of competency.

Does Creativity Presume Any Competencies?

The empirical research just reviewed does not exhaust all the findings that are difficult to reconcile with the simple notion that creativity is a form of acquired expertise. Another collection of findings concerns the distribution of successful and unsuccessful works across creative careers. Contrary to what one would predict from the standpoint of expertise acquisition, the career of the typical creator consists of a chaotic sequence of hits and misses, of successes and failures. A universally acclaimed masterpiece might be followed immediately by a widely criticized or ignored attempt (see, for example, Simonton, 1986, 1995a). The ratio of hits to total attempts does not increase over the course of the career, but rather tends to fluctuate randomly (for example, Quételet, 1835/1968; Simonton, 1977a, 1985, 1997a). Hence, creators do not seem able to acquire the expertise necessary to increase their odds of success. It is also telling that this same "equal-odds rule" applies not just to longitudinal changes, but to individual differences besides (Davis, 1987; Platz and Blakelock, 1960; Simonton, 1985, 1997a; White and White, 1978). Those creators who boast the most successes must also admit the most failures. The ratio of hits to total attempts is uncorrelated with the total number of hits. It is for this reason that W. H. Auden could write "the chances are that, in the course of his lifetime, the major poet will write more bad poems than the minor" (quoted in Bennet, 1980, p. 15). For instance, although some of Shakespeare's sonnets "bear the unmistakable stamp of his genius," others "are no better than many a contemporary could have written" (Smith, 1974, p. 1747). In general, hits and misses are randomly distributed both across and within creative careers, and even the most prolific creators never manage to acquire sufficient expertise to escape this fate (Huber, 1998a, 1998b, 2000).

This hit-or-miss feature of the creative career contrasts immensely with what is observed in those achievement domains where the importance of expertise is unquestionable. Who would buy tickets to hear a virtuoso cellist if there were no assurance that the interpretation would be reliably good, if not inspiring? What football coach would retain a kicker whose field-goal performance was too unpredictable to be relied on? This is not to say that instrumentalists or athletes cannot have off days. They do. Yet in general their performances are far more consistent than the uneven output of most creators. It is at this juncture that competency may provide a useful explanatory concept.

Here competency will be defined as any acquired skill or knowledge that constitutes an essential component for performance or achievement in a given domain. The concept recognizes that any given domain requires the acquisition of more than one component. For instance, achievement as an operatic composer presupposes competencies regarding melody, harmony, counterpoint, rhythm, form, orchestration, vocal writing, characterization, and dramatization. Accomplishments as a scientist presume competencies regarding literature search, hypothesis formation, research design, data collection and coding, statistical or mathematical analysis, and professional communication. The acquisition of any given competency may be enhanced by both general and specific abilities, and those supportive abilities may be to varying degrees innate. Nevertheless, the main contribution to the acquisition must come through training and practice. More important, a person who attains competency in all the components defining a creative domain is said to be competent in the corresponding domain. To be competent in a domain signifies a degree of skill and knowledge certainly higher than those of the novice, but not necessarily as high as a master. For instance, a doctoral degree in most academic disciplines designates this level of mastery. A Ph.D. identifies its recipient as rising above the novice level of the undergraduate without yet attaining the degree of proficiency expected of a world-class expert in the field. Now let us return to the problem of the random distribution of hits and misses across and within careers.

When it is said that a creator's output is uneven, that is not equivalent to asserting that incompetent products are randomly intermixed with competent products. On the contrary, the unsuccessful works usually remain highly proficient – well above what a novice could produce. The deficiency lies elsewhere. What the works fail to accomplish is to satisfy one or both requirements for a product to be deemed creative. Consider the following two outcomes:

1. The work exhibits the requisite competencies, but the product lacks sufficient originality. A product may be deficient in originality because it is too similar to what has already been offered before, whether by one's self (repetition) or others (imitation). This is one reason why movie sequels or remakes are seldom as successful as the original films. At best, the result is recognized as the old wine in a new bottle. As noted earlier, deficiency in originality is one of the adverse consequences of specializing excessively with respect to aesthetic genre or research topic.

2. The work displays all the necessary competencies, but the result is not adaptive. A product may be deficient in adaptiveness for many reasons besides being inept. The failed effort may constitute an experiment in which the creator boldly departed from procedures or principles well demonstrated in previous works. As chronic risk takers, creators will often try out new possibilities by breaking certain rules, by making different assumptions, by testing new techniques, by treating novel themes, or probing the limits of a given approach. But a payoff is far from guaranteed, making these experiments akin to "blind" trial-and-error

explorations (Campbell, 1960; Simonton, 1999a). Other times the product may fail because of circumstances beyond the creator's control. For instance, a theory might be rendered almost immediately untenable by the appearance of new data that refute it or by the publication of an alternative theory that handles the available data far better.

Whatever the specific cause, it is probably quite rare for an attempted contribution to fail because the creator's effort betrays complete ineptitude. Under the assumption that the individual has acquired all the relevant competencies, the product will always boast a minimal level of domain-relevant skill and knowledge. It is not a matter of the creator somehow lapsing back to the novice level in terms of acquired expertise. The worst film by Woody Allen probably remains better (at least in the sense of technical proficiency) than the best film to come out of any undergraduate film-production class. The attainment of the necessary competencies is a necessary but not sufficient basis for intellectual or aesthetic success. The offered product may prove competent, but uncreative.

IS CREATIVITY UNIQUE?

It should be apparent by now that creativity is far too complex a psychological phenomenon to be subsumed under a simple conceptual scheme. To some degree creativity can be considered an ability, but only by considering the capacity to encompass both cognitive and dispositional attributes. Each of these attributes may have non-trivial heritability coefficients, and yet the various genetic components may combine in a complex multiplicative fashion that makes inheritance quite capricious. Creativity presupposes a certain amount of domain-specific expertise, at least to the extent that the mandatory competencies are acquired. Creativity can be vitiated by excessive specialization ("overtraining") as well as vitalized by diversified interests and versatility ("cross-training"). In short, creativity is a complicated and dynamic mixture of various components, some innate and others experiential.

Although my focus throughout this chapter has been on creativity, I would argue that many other human capacities operate in an analogous fashion. That is, many capacities are an intricate and evolving combination of diverse components, each component developing through a distinctive proportion of genetic and environmental influences. To offer but one illustration, consider individual differences in leadership to be governed by similar multidimensional, multiplicative, nonlinear, and dynamic processes. Unlike many other abilities, but like creativity, for leadership ability there exists no widely accepted measure or "test," in part because leadership, like creativity, tends to be domain-specific (Bass, 1990). Ample evidence exists that leadership performance is an elaborate function of both cognitive and dispositional traits (Simonton, 1995b), at least some of which may partially originate via emergenic inheritance (Lykken, McGue, Tellegen, and Bouchard, 1992; see also Galton, 1869). In addition, empirical data show that developmental changes in leadership tend not to follow patterns expected by a straight-forward expertise-acquisition process (Lehman, 1953; Simonton, 1976, 1980, 1984c, 1998b). These contradictory patterns include (a) curvilinear, nonmonotonic age functions for measures of leadership performance and (b) apparent performance enhancements due to the acquisition of skills and knowledge outside the leadership domain. Like creativity, successful leadership may require the acquisition of certain minimal domain-relevant competencies without necessarily acquiring complete mastery (Bass, 1990; Simonton, 1987b).

Given these striking similarities, we certainly must wonder how many other human capacities have comparably complex etiologies. Given the real-world significance of creativity and leadership, we must contemplate the possibility that many capacities of genuine impor-tance also integrate cognitive abilities with dispositional traits, innate attributes with acquired skills, domain-specific knowledge with broad interests and versatility – these factors all interacting in a complicated and dynamic manner. When everything converges just right, the upshot is an Albert Einstein, or his analog in some other domain of achievement.

References

Amabile, T. M. (1982). Social psychology of creativity: A consensual assessment technique. *Journal of Personality and Social Psychology, 43*, 997–1013.
Amabile, T. M. (1996). *Creativity in context*. Boulder, CO: Westview.
Amelang, M., Herboth, G., & Oefner, I. (1991). A prototype strategy for the construction of a creativity scale. *European Journal of Personality, 5*, 261–285.
Baer, J. (1993). *Creativity and divergent thinking: A task-specific approach*. Hillsdale, NJ: Erlbaum.
Baer, J. (1994). Divergent thinking is not a general trait: A multidomain training experiment. *Creativity Research Journal, 7*, 35–46.
Barron, F. X. (1969). *Creative person and creative process*. New York: Holt, Rinehart & Winston.
Bass, B. M. (1990). *Bass & Stogdill's handbook of leadership: Theory, research, and managerial applications* (3rd Ed.). New York: Free Press.
Bennet, W. (1980, January–February). Providing for posterity. *Harvard Magazine*, pp. 13–16.

Bouchard, T. J., Jr. (1994). Genes, environment, and personality. *Science, 264,* 1700–1701.

Bramwell, B. S. (1948). Galton's "Hereditary " and the three following generations since 1869. *Eugenics Review, 39,* 146–153.

Burt, C. (1943). Ability and income. *British Journal of Educational Psychology, 12,* 83–98.

Burt, C. (1963). Is intelligence distributed normally? *British Journal of Statistical Psychology, 16,* 175–190.

Campbell, D. T. (1960). Blind variation and selective retention in creative thought as in other knowledge processes. *Psychological Review, 67,* 380–400.

Candolle, A. de (1873). *Histoire des sciences et des savants depuis deux siècles.* [History of sciences and scientists in the last two centuries.] Geneva, Switzerland: Georg.

Cattell, R. B., & Butcher, H. J. (1968). *The prediction of achievement and creativity.* Indianapolis, IN: Bobbs-Merrill.

Cox, C. (1926). *The early mental traits of three hundred geniuses.* Stanford, CA: Stanford University Press.

Davis, R. A. (1987). Creativity in neurological publications. *Neurosurgery, 20,* 652–663.

Dellas, M., & Gaier, E. L. (1970). Identification of creativity: The individual. *Psychological Bulletin, 73,* 55–73.

Dennis, W. (1954a, September). Bibliographies of eminent scientists. *Scientific Monthly, 79,* 180–183.

Dennis, W. (1954b). Productivity among American psychologists. *American Psychologist, 9,* 191–194.

Dennis, W. (1955, April). Variations in productivity among creative workers. *Scientific Monthly, 80,* 277–278.

Dennis, W. (1966). Creative productivity between the ages of 20 and 80 years. *Journal of Gerontology, 21,* 1–8.

Diamond, A. M., Jr. (1986). The life-cycle research productivity of mathematicians and scientists. *Journal of Gerontology, 41,* 520–525.

Dryden, J. (1885). Epistle to Congreve. In W. Scott & G. Saintsbury (Eds.), *The works of John Dryden,* Vol. 11 (pp. 57–60). Edinburgh, Scotland: Paterson (original work published 1693).

Elo, A. E. (1965). Age changes in master chess performance. *Journal of Gerontology, 20,* 289–299.

Ericsson, K. A. (1996a). The acquisition of expert performance: An introduction to some of the issues. In K. A. Ericsson (Ed.), *The road to expert performance: Empirical evidence from the arts and sciences, sports, and games* (pp. 1–50). Mahwah, NJ: Erlbaum.

Ericsson, K. A. (Ed.). (1996b). *The road to expert performance: Empirical evidence from the arts and sciences, sports, and games.* Mahwah, NJ: Erlbaum.

Ericsson, K. A., & Charness, N. (1994). Expert performance: Its structure and acquisition. *American Psychologist, 49,* 725–747.

Ericsson, K. A., Krampe, R. T., & Tesch-Römer, C. (1993). The role of deliberate practice in the acquisition of expert performance. *Psychological Review, 100,* 363–406.

Eysenck, H. J. (1995). *Genius: The natural history of creativity.* Cambridge, UK: Cambridge University Press.

Feist, G. J. (1998). A meta-analysis of personality in scientific and artistic creativity. *Personality and Social Psychology Review, 2,* 290–309.

Frensch, P. A., & Sternberg, R. J. (1989). Expertise and intelligent thinking: When is it worse to know better? In R. J. Sternberg (Ed.), *Advances in the psychology of human intelligence,* Vol. 5 (pp. 157–188). Hillsdale, NJ: Erlbaum.

Galton, F. (1869). *Hereditary genius: An inquiry into its laws and consequences.* London: Macmillan.

Galton, F. (1874). *English men of science: Their nature and nurture.* London: Macmillan.

Gardner, H. (1993). *Creating minds: An anatomy of creativity seen through the lives of Freud, Einstein, Picasso, Stravinsky, Eliot, Graham, and Gandhi.* New York: Basic Books.

Getzels, J., & Csikszentmihalyi, M. (1976). *The creative vision: A longitudinal study of problem finding in art.* New York: Wiley.

Getzels, J., & Jackson, P. W. (1962). *Creativity and intelligence: Explorations with gifted students.* New York: Wiley.

Goertzel, M. G., Goertzel, V., & Goertzel, T. G. (1978). *300 eminent personalities: A psychosocial analysis of the famous.* San Francisco, CA: Jossey-Bass.

Gough, H. G. (1979). A creative personality scale for the adjective check list. *Journal of Personality and Social Psychology, 37,* 1398–1405.

Gruber, H. E. (1989). The evolving systems approach to creative work. In D. B. Wallace & H. E. Gruber (Eds.), *Creative people at work: Twelve cognitive case studies* (pp. 3–24). New York: Oxford University Press.

Guilford, J. P. (1967). *The nature of human intelligence.* New York: McGraw-Hill.

Hargens, L. L. (1978). Relations between work habits, research technologies, and eminence in science. *Sociology of Work and Occupations, 5,* 97–112.

Hayes, J. R. (1989). *The complete problem solver* (2nd Ed.). Hillsdale, NJ: Erlbaum.

Helson, R., & Crutchfield, R. S. (1970). Mathematicians: The creative researcher and the average Ph.D. *Journal of Consulting and Clinical Psychology, 34,* 250–257.

Hocevar, D., & Bachelor, P. (1989). A taxonomy and critique of measurements used in the study of creativity. In J. A. Glover, R. R. Ronning, & C. R. Reynolds (Eds.), *Handbook of creativity* (pp. 53–75). New York: Plenum Press.

Howe, M. J. A. (1999). *The psychology of high abilities.* New York: New York University Press.

Howe, M. J. A., Davidson, J. W., & Sloboda, J. A. (1998). Innate talents: Reality or myth? *Behavioral and Brain Sciences, 21,* 399–442.

Huber, J. C. (1998a). Invention and inventivity as a special kind of creativity, with implications for general creativity. *Journal of Creative Behavior, 32,* 58–72.

Huber, J. C. (1998b). Invention and inventivity is a random, Poisson process: A potential guide to analysis of general creativity. *Creativity Research Journal, 11,* 231–241.

Huber, J. C. (2000). A statistical analysis of special cases of creativity. *Journal of Creative Behavior, 34,* 203–225.

Hudson, L. (1958). Undergraduate academic record of Fellows of the Royal Society. *Nature, 182,* 1326.

Hudson, L., & Jacot, B. (1986). The outsider in science. In C. Bagley & G. K. Verma (Eds.), *Personality, cognition and values* (pp. 3–23). London: Macmillan.

Johnson, S. (1781). *The lives of the most eminent English poets,* Vol. 1. London: Bathurst et al.

Krampe, R. T., & Ericsson, K. A. (1996). Maintaining excellence: Deliberate practice and elite performance in young and older pianists. *Journal of Experimental Psychology: General, 125,* 331–359.

Kroeber, A. L. (1944). *Configurations of culture growth.* Berkeley, CA: University of California Press.

Kuhn, T. S. (1970). *The structure of scientific revolutions* (2nd Ed.). Chicago: University of Chicago Press.

Lehman, H. C. (1953). *Age and achievement.* Princeton, NJ: Princeton University Press.

Lehman, H. C. (1962). More about age and achievement. *Gerontologist, 2,* 141–148.

Lotka, A. J. (1926). The frequency distribution of scientific productivity. *Journal of the Washington Academy of Sciences, 16,* 317–323.

Ludwig, A. M. (1995). *The price of greatness: Resolving the creativity and madness controversy.* New York: Guilford Press.

Lykken, D. T. (1982). Research with twins: The concept of emergenesis. *Psychophysiology, 19,* 361–373.

Lykken, D. T., McGue, M., Tellegen, A., & Bouchard, T. J., Jr. (1992). Emergenesis: Genetic traits that may not run in families. *American Psychologist, 47,* 1565–1577.

MacKinnon, D. W. (1978). *In search of human effectiveness.* Buffalo, NY: Creative Education Foundation.

Manis, J. G. (1951). Some academic influences upon publication productivity. *Social Forces, 29,* 267–272.

Martindale, C. (1989). Personality, situation, and creativity. In J. A. Glover, R. R. Ronning, & C. R. Reynolds (Eds.), *Handbook of creativity* (pp. 211–232). New York: Plenum Press.

McClelland, D. C. (1963). The calculated risk: An aspect of scientific performance. In C. W. Taylor & F. X. Barron (Eds.), *Scientific creativity: Its recognition and development* (pp. 184–192). New York: Wiley.

McClelland, D. C. (1973). Testing for competence rather than for "intelligence." *American Psychologist, 28,* 1–14.

McDowell, J. M. (1982). Obsolescence of knowledge and career publication profiles: Some evidence of differences among fields in costs of interrupted careers. *American Economic Review, 72,* 752–768.

McNemar, Q. (1964). Lost: Our intelligence? Why? *American Psychologist, 19,* 871–882.

Mednick, S. A. (1962). The associative basis of the creative process. *Psychological Review, 69,* 220–232.

Moles, A. (1968). *Information theory and esthetic perception* (J. E. Cohen, Trans.). Urbana, IL: University of Illinois Press (original work published 1958).

Nicholls, J. G. (1972). Creativity in the person who will never produce anything original and useful: The concept of creativity as a normally distributed trait. *American Psychologist, 27,* 717–727.

Ohlsson, S. (1992). The learning curve for writing books: Evidence from Professor Asimov. *Psychological Science, 3,* 380–382.

Platz, A., & Blakelock, E. (1960). Productivity of American psychologists: Quantity versus quality. *American Psychologist, 15,* 310–312.

Plomin, R., & Petrill, S. A. (1997). Genetics and intelligence: What's new? *Intelligence, 24,* 53–77.

Poincaré, H. (1921). *The foundations of science: Science and hypothesis, the value of science, science and method* (G. B. Halstead, Trans.). New York: Science Press.

Quételet, A. (1968). *A treatise on man and the development of his faculties.* New York: Franklin. (Reprint of 1842 Edinburgh translation of 1835 French original.)

Raskin, E. A. (1936). Comparison of scientific and literary ability: A biographical study of eminent scientists and men of letters of the nineteenth century. *Journal of Abnormal and Social Psychology, 31,* 20–35.

Richards, R., Kinney, D. K., Lunde, I., Benet, M., & Merzel, A. P. C. (1988). Assessing everyday creativity: Characteristics of the Lifetime Creativity Scales and validation with three large samples. *Journal of Personality and Social Psychology, 54,* 476–485.

Roe, A. (1953). *The making of a scientist.* New York: Dodd, Mead.

Root-Bernstein, R. S., Bernstein, M., & Garnier, H. (1993). Identification of scientists making long-term, high-impact contributions, with notes on their methods of working. *Creativity Research Journal, 6,* 329–343.

Rostan, S. M. (1994). Problem finding, problem solving, and cognitive controls: An empirical investigation of critically acclaimed productivity. *Creativity Research Journal, 7,* 97–110.

Schulz, R., & Curnow, C. (1988). Peak performance and age among super athletes: Track and field, swimming, baseball, tennis, and golf. *Journal of Gerontology, 43,* 113–120.

Seelig, C. (1958). *Albert Einstein: A documentary biography* (M. Savill, Trans.). London: Staples Press.

Shockley, W. (1957). On the statistics of individual variations of productivity in research laboratories. *Proceedings of the Institute of Radio Engineers, 45,* 279–290.

Simon, R. J. (1974). The work habits of eminent scientists. *Sociology of Work and Occupations, 1,* 327–335.

Simonton, D. K. (1976). Biographical determinants of achieved eminence: A multivariate approach to the Cox data. *Journal of Personality and Social Psychology, 33,* 218–226.

Simonton, D. K. (1977). Creative productivity, age, and stress: A biographical time-series analysis of 10 classical composers. *Journal of Personality and Social Psychology, 35,* 791–804.

Simonton, D. K. (1980). Land battles, generals, and armies: Individual and situational determinants of victory and casualties. *Journal of Personality and Social Psychology, 38,* 110–119.

Simonton, D. K. (1983). Formal education, eminence, and dogmatism: The curvilinear relationship. *Journal of Creative Behavior, 17,* 149–162.

Simonton, D. K. (1984a). Creative productivity and age: A mathematical model based on a two-step cognitive process. *Developmental Review, 4,* 77–111.

Simonton, D. K. (1984b). Is the marginality effect all that marginal? *Social Studies of Science, 14*, 621–622.

Simonton, D. K. (1984c). Leader age and national condition: A longitudinal analysis of 25 European monarchs. *Social Behavior and Personality, 12*, 111–114.

Simonton, D. K. (1985). Quality, quantity, and age: The careers of 10 distinguished psychologists. *International Journal of Aging and Human Development, 21*, 241–254.

Simonton, D. K. (1986). Popularity, content, and context in 37 Shakespeare plays. *Poetics, 15*, 493–510.

Simonton, D. K. (1987a). Developmental antecedents of achieved eminence. *Annals of Child Development, 5*, 131–169.

Simonton, D. K. (1987b). *Why presidents succeed: A political psychology of leadership.* New Haven, CT: Yale University Press.

Simonton, D. K. (1988). Age and outstanding achievement: What do we know after a century of research? *Psychological Bulletin, 104*, 251–267.

Simonton, D. K. (1989). Age and creative productivity: Nonlinear estimation of an information-processing model. *International Journal of Aging and Human Development, 29*, 23–37.

Simonton, D. K. (1991a). Career landmarks in science: Individual differences and interdisciplinary contrasts. *Developmental Psychology, 27*, 119–130.

Simonton, D. K. (1991b). Emergence and realization of genius: The lives and works of 120 classical composers. *Journal of Personality and Social Psychology, 61*, 829–840.

Simonton, D. K. (1992). Leaders of American psychology, 1879–1967: Career development, creative output, and professional achievement. *Journal of Personality and Social Psychology, 62*, 5–17.

Simonton, D. K. (1994). *Greatness: Who makes history and why.* New York: Guilford Press.

Simonton, D. K. (1995a). Drawing inferences from symphonic programs: Musical attributes versus listener attributions. *Music Perception, 12*, 307–322.

Simonton, D. K. (1995b). Personality and intellectual predictors of leadership. In D. H. Saklofske & M. Zeidner (Eds.), *International handbook of personality and intelligence* (pp. 739–757). New York: Plenum.

Simonton, D. K. (1997a). Creative productivity: A predictive and explanatory model of career trajectories and landmarks. *Psychological Review, 104*, 66–89.

Simonton, D. K. (1997b). When giftedness becomes genius: How does talent achieve eminence? In N. Colangelo & G. A. Davis (Eds.), *Handbook of gifted education* (2nd Ed., pp. 335–349). Boston: Allyn & Bacon.

Simonton, D. K. (1998a). Fickle fashion versus immortal fame: Transhistorical assessments of creative products in the opera house. *Journal of Personality and Social Psychology, 75*, 198–210.

Simonton, D. K. (1998b). Political leadership across the life span: Chronological versus career age in the British monarchy. *Leadership Quarterly, 9*, 195–206.

Simonton, D. K. (1999a). *Origins of genius: Darwinian perspectives on creativity.* New York: Oxford University Press.

Simonton, D. K. (1999b). Talent and its development: An emergenic and epigenetic model. *Psychological Review, 106*, 435–457.

Simonton, D. K. (2000). Creative development as acquired expertise: Theoretical issues and an empirical test. *Developmental Review, 20*, 283–318.

Simonton, D. K. (in press). Creativity assessment. In R. Fernández-Ballesteros (Ed.), *Encyclopedia of psychological assessment*. London: Sage Publications.

Smith, H. (1974). Sonnets. In G. B. Evans (Ed.), *The Riverside Shakespeare* (pp. 1745–1748). Boston: Houghton Mifflin.

Spearman, C. (1927). *The abilities of man: Their nature and measurement*. New York: Macmillan.

Sternberg, R. J., & Lubart, T. I. (1995). *Defying the crowd: Cultivating creativity in a culture of conformity*. New York: Free Press.

Sulloway, F. J. (1996). *Born to rebel: Birth order, family dynamics, and creative lives*. New York: Pantheon.

Tweney, R. D. (1990). Five questions for computationalists. In J. Shrager & P. Langley (Eds.), *Computational models of scientific discovery and theory information* (pp. 471–484). San Mateo, CA: Kaufmann.

Walberg, H. J., Strykowski, B. F., Rovai, E., & Hung, S. S. (1984). Exceptional performance. *Review of Educational Research, 54*, 87–112.

Waller, N. G., Bouchard, T. J., Jr., Lykken, D. T., Tellegen, A., & Blacker, D. M. (1993). Creativity, heritability, familiality: Which word does not belong? *Psychological Inquiry, 4*, 235–237.

White, K. G., & White, M. J. (1978). On the relation between productivity and impact. *Australian Psychologist, 13*, 369–374.

White, R. K. (1931). The versatility of genius. *Journal of Social Psychology, 2*, 460–489.

Zuckerman, H. (1977). *Scientific elite*. New York: Free Press.

9

Biological Intelligence

Robert J. Sternberg

Over the course of the years, there have been many diverse definitions of intelligence. A common feature of these definitions, however, has been intelligence as *the ability to adapt to the environment* (see, for example, "Intelligence and its Measurement," 1921; Sternberg and Detterman, 1986). There is perhaps no other feature of definitions of intelligence that has this level of universality.

What has been left unclear in these definitions and in the theories based on them is exactly what adaptation to the environment means. I argue in this essay that there are two distinct senses of adaptation to the environment, and that their meanings are quite different. Both constitute kinds of intelligence, one biological, the other, cultural. The focus of this article is on the biological.

Before discussing the proposed view of biological intelligence, I briefly review some previous approaches on which any new view must build, or at least, with which any new view must come to terms.

BIOLOGICAL APPROACHES TO INTELLIGENCE

Biological approaches typically seek to understand intelligence by directly studying the brain and its functioning rather than by studying

Preparation of this chapter was supported by Grant REC-9979843 from the National Science Foundation and by a government grant under the Javits Act Program (Grant No. R206R000001) as administered by the Office of Educational Research and Improvement, U.S. Department of Education. Grantees undertaking such projects are encouraged to express freely their professional judgments. This chapter does not, therefore, necessarily represent the positions or the policies of the U.S. government, and no official endorsement should be inferred.

primarily products or processes of behavior (Jerison, 2000; Vernon, Wickett, Bazana, and Stelmack, 2000). Early studies, like those by Karl Lashley (1950) and others seeking to localize biological bases of intelligence and other aspects of mental processes, were a resounding failure, despite great efforts. But Lashley had only relatively primitive tools for studying the brain. As tools for studying the brain have become more sophisticated we are beginning to see the possibility of finding physiological indications of intelligence. Some researchers (for example, Matarazzo, 1992) believe that we will have clinically useful psychophysiological indices of intelligence very early in the twenty-first century, although widely applicable indices will be much longer in coming.

Historically Important Biological Approaches

Hebb (1949) distinguished between two basic types of intelligence, Intelligence A and Intelligence B. Intelligence A is innate potential. It is biologically determined and represents the capacity for development. Hebb described it as "the possession of a good brain and a good neural metabolism" (p. 294). Intelligence B is the functioning of a brain in which development has occurred. It represents an average level of performance by a person who has matured. Although some inference is necessary in determining either intelligence, Hebb suggested that inferences about Intelligence A are far less direct than inferences about Intelligence B. Hebb argued that most disagreements about intelligence are over Intelligence A, or innate potential, rather than over Intelligence B, which is the estimated mature level of functioning.

Psychologists also distinguish an Intelligence C, which is the score one obtains on an intelligence test. It is the basis for inferring either of the other intelligences. Intelligence C was the basis for Boring's (1923) definition of intelligence in terms of whatever it is that intelligence tests measure.

Hebb's main interest was in Intelligence A, and his theory, the neuropsychological theory of the organization of behavior, can be seen in large part as an attempt to understand what Intelligence A is. The core of Hebb's theory is the concept of cell assembly. Hebb proposed that repeated stimulation of specific receptors slowly leads to the formation of an assembly of cells in the brain. More intelligent people have more elaborate sequences of cell assemblies.

Another biologically based theory that has had an influence on intelligence research and testing is that of Luria (1966, 1973, 1980). Luria suggested that the brain is a highly differentiated system whose parts are responsible for different aspects of a unified whole. In other words, separate cortical regions act together to produce thought and action of various kinds. Luria suggested that the brain comprises three main units. The first unit consists of the brain stem and midbrain structures, and is responsible for arousal. The second unit of the brain is responsible for sensory-input functions. The third unit includes the frontal cortex, and is involved in organization and planning.

The four main elements of information processing in Luria's theory are planning, attention, simultaneous information processing, and successive information processing. Simultaneous information processing is used in solving complex reasoning items, such as figural matrix problems or embedded-figures tasks in which one has to find a visual form embedded in more complex visual forms. Successive processing is used in tasks such as serial recall, in which one must learn and then repeat back a string of numbers, letters, hand movements, or other stimuli.

Some biological theories focus on the relation between hemispheric specialization and intelligence. Theories of hemispheric specialization can be traced back to a country doctor in France, Marc Dax, who in 1836 noted a connection between loss of speech, now known as aphasia, and damage to the left hemisphere of the brain. His claim was expanded upon by Broca (1861).

Hemispheric Specialization

This finding by Dax has been followed up by many researchers, most notably Sperry (1961). Sperry argued that each hemisphere of the brain behaves in many respects like a separate brain. He concluded from his research that visual and spatial functions are primarily localized in the right hemisphere, whereas linguistic functions are primarily localized in the left hemisphere. There is some debate, however, as to whether language is completely localized in the left hemisphere or spatial functions in the right hemisphere (for example, Farah, 1988, 1994, 1996; Gazzaniga, 1985). Levy (1974) further applied Sperry's theory to information processing, suggesting that the left hemisphere tends to process stimuli analytically, whereas the right tends to process it holistically. Continuing with this line of reasoning, Bogen (1975) suggested that the difference in processing of stimuli in the two hemispheres can be characterized in terms of what he refers to as propositional versus appositional information processing. "Propositional" applies to speaking, writing, and other verbal activities that are dominated by the left hemisphere, whereas "appositional" emphasizes the figural, spatial, non-verbal processing of the right hemisphere. The right hemisphere, in his view, understands patterns and relationships that are not susceptible to propositional analysis and that may not even be logical.

Gazzaniga (1985) took a different position and argued that the right hemisphere of the brain is organized modularly into relatively independent functioning units that work in parallel. Many of these modules operate at a level that is not even conscious, but that parallels our conscious thought and contributes to conscious processing. The left hemisphere tries to assign interpretations to the processing of these modules. Thus, the left hemisphere may perceive the individual operating in a way that does not make any particular sense or that is not particularly understandable. In other words, our thoughts precede our understanding of them.

Rate of Neural Transmission

Some biological theorists have pursued the notion that intelligent people act and think faster than less intelligent people. They attribute this difference to the speed of neural functioning, or peripheral nerve-conduction velocity (Reed, 1984).

This perspective on intelligence was originally seemingly supported by reaction-time studies (for example, Jensen, 1982). These studies showed that greater variability in response rate to a stimulus (for example, a light) was associated with lower scores on ability tests. More recent studies have attempted to measure conduction velocities more directly. Several studies suggest that the speed of conduction of neural impulses may correlate with intelligence as measured by IQ tests (for example, McGarry-Roberts, Stelmack, and Campbell, 1992; Reed and Jensen, 1992; Vernon and Mori, 1992), although the evidence is mixed. Some investigators (for example, Jensen, 1997; Vernon and Mori, 1992) have suggested that this research supports a view that intelligence is based on neural efficiency.

Vernon and Mori (1992) measured nerve-conduction velocity in the median nerve of the arm using electrodes. They found significant correlations between conduction velocity and IQ (around .4). However, they were unable to replicate these findings in later studies (Wickett and Vernon, 1994).

A meta-analysis of nine studies that have investigated the relation between peripheral nerve-conduction velocity and psychometrically measured intelligence yields mixed results (Vernon, Wickett, Bazana, and Stelmack, 2000). Some of the studies have yielded positive correlations (for example, Barrett, Daum, and Eysenck, 1990; Rijsdijk and Boomsma, 1997; Vernon and Mori, 1989, 1992; Vernon, Wickett, Bazana, and Stelmark, 2000); others have yielded trivial correlations (for example, Reed and Jensen, 1991; Rijsdijk, Boomsma, and Vernon, 1995); and yet another study showed mixed significant positive and negative correlations (Tan, 1996). Clearly, the jury is still out on the relation of peripheral nerve conduction velocity to IQ.

Electrophysiological Approaches

Electrophysiological research has suggested that complex patterns of electrical activity in the brain, which are prompted by specific stimuli, sometimes correlate with scores on IQ tests. Many of the early studies used simple sensory processing as the basis for eliciting the waveforms (Barry and Ertl, 1966; Caryl, 1994; Barrett and Eysenck, 1992; Ertl and Schafer, 1969; Shucard and Horn, 1972; Perry, McCow, Cunningham, Falgout, and Street, 1976). Typical correlations in these early studies were at about the .3 level between the latency of ERP waves elicited by visual stimuli and scores on tests of intelligence. But much, although certainly not all, of the work later failed to replicate (Barrett and Eysenck, 1994; Davis, 1971; Dustman and Beck, 1972; Shucard and Callaway, 1973; Widaman, Carlson, Saetermoe, and Galbraith, 1993), leaving the status of the work unclear.

In a typical study, Reed and Jensen (1992) used performance during a pattern-reversal task (for example, using a checkerboard where the black squares changed to white and the white squares to black) to measure two medium-latency event-related potentials, N70 and P100. The correlations between the latency measures and IQ were small (in the range of −.1 to −.2) but significant in some cases. (Correlations were negative because longer latencies corresponded to lower IQs.)

Studies looking at cognitive components of the event-related potential waveforms have yielded more consistently successful results. McCarthy and Donchin (1981) found that one event-related potential (P300) seems to reflect the allocation of cognitive resources to a given task. P300 is so named because it is a positively charged response occurring roughly 300 milliseconds after the stimulus is presented. Deary and

Caryl (1994) found, in a review of the literature, that the P300 amplitude most consistently showed correlations with measured intelligence. P300 has also been found to be a reliable measure of skills in responding to novelty and detection of unexpected target stimuli as well as stimulus classification (Kutas, McCarthy, and Donchin, 1977; Magliero, Bashore, Coles, and Donchin, 1984; Polich and Kok, 1995; Segalowitz, Unsal, and Dywan, 1992), so it would make some sense that the measure would correlate with intelligence.

Schafer (1982) has suggested that the tendency to show a large P300 response to surprising stimuli may reflect individual differences. More intelligent individuals should show greater P300 responses to unfamiliar stimuli, as well as smaller P300 responses to expected stimuli, than would less intelligent ones because they do not need to devote so much attention to familiar stimuli. Schafer reported a correlation of .82 between individual differences in event-related potentials and IQ. This level of correlation appears not to be generally replicable.

Although most investigators have used event-related potentials as proxy measures of speed of neural transmission, others have suggested that accuracy in transmission may be more important. Hendrickson and Hendrickson (1982) suggested that errors might occur in the passage of information through the cerebral cortex (see also Hendrickson & Hendrickson, 1980). These errors, which probably occur at synapses, are alleged to be responsible for variability in event-related potentials. Thus, it would follow that those individuals with normal neural circuitry that conveys information accurately will form correct and accessible memories more quickly than individuals whose circuitry is "noisy" and hence makes errors in transmission. They have shown a strong level of correlation between complexity of an event-related potential measure and IQ. The meaning of this correlation is unclear, however, and it has not replicated. Thus the Hendrickson and Hendrickson position must be viewed, at the present time, as speculative.

Metabolic Approaches

Support for neural efficiency as a measure of intelligence can be found by using a different approach to studies of the brain: studies of how the brain metabolizes glucose, a simple sugar required for brain activity, during mental activities. Haier and his colleagues (Haier, 1990; Haier et al., 1988; Haier et al., 1992) have found that higher psychometrically measured intelligence correlates with reduced levels of glucose metabolism during problem-solving tasks – that is, smarter brains consume less sugar (meaning that they expend less effort) than do less smart brains doing the same task. Further, Haier and colleagues found that cerebral efficiency increases as a result of learning in a relatively complex task involving visuospatial manipulations (such as in the computer game Tetris). As a result of practice, more intelligent individuals show not only lower cerebral glucose metabolism overall but also more specifically localized metabolism of glucose. In most areas of their brains, smarter persons show less glucose metabolism, but in selected areas of their brains (thought to be important to the task at hand), they show higher levels of glucose metabolism. It is interesting that, when at rest, more intelligent people seem to use *more* glucose than do less intelligent people, possibly suggesting that they are making use of the time at rest to do more thinking. A possible overall conclusion is that more intelligent people may have learned how to use their brains more efficiently.

A potential limitation of metabolic approaches is that causal inferences are attractive but not necessarily conclusive. For example, one cannot say for sure whether smarter or more expert people need to use less glucose, or whether people who need to use less glucose are smarter or more expert, or whether both are dependent on some third higher-order variable. Moreover, in a sense, Haier's results simply seem to remind us that experts need to expend less effort than novices to do a task. Why would we expect otherwise?

Brain Size Approaches

Perhaps it is not just how efficiently the brain processes information that matters for intelligence, but also, the sheer amount of brain capacity available to process information. The idea that the size of the brain may relate to intelligence was proposed by Broca (1861) and then later reintroduced by Galton (1883). Brain size is a proxy for processing capacity, but a proxy for brain size is head size. The correlation between head size and brain size in adults has been estimated variously, with .60 a typical estimate (Hoadley, 1929; Wickett, Vernon, and Lee, 2000). In infants and young children, the correlation is higher (Vernon et al., 2000).

Generally positive correlations have been found between various measures of head size and IQ. A meta-analysis of 35 studies with

54 independent samples and 56,793 participants revealed correlations ranging from .02 to .54, with a mean of .19 (Vernon et al., 2000). Thirty-six of the 54 correlations were statistically significant.

A more accurate estimate of the relationship of brain size to IQ can be obtained by using brain-imaging techniques that directly study the size of the brain. A meta-analysis of 15 samples with a total N of 657 revealed an unweighted mean correlation of .40. These data suggest, again, that there is some correlation.

Why do people have different head or brain sizes? Experience plays some role. Work by Greenough (for example, Comery, Shah, and Greenough, 1995; Fuchs, Montemayor, and Greenough, 1990; Jones and Greenough, 1996) and by Diamond (for example, Bennett, Diamond, Krech, and Rosenzweig, 1964; Diamond, Ingham, Johnson, Bennett, and Rosenzweig, 1976) shows that experience can alter the structure and therefore the function of the brain. In particular, these investigators have shown that experience can result in increases in brain weight, cortical thickness, and number of synapses. But genetics no doubt plays a role in brain size, as well.

Genetic and Behavior-Genetic Approaches

Researchers have explored the role of genetics in determining intelligence (see Sternberg and Grigorenko, 1997, for an in-depth review). Based on the existing research, it appears that approximately half the total variance in IQ scores is accounted for by genetic factors (Loehlin, 1989; Plomin, 1997). The percentages vary with age, however, with heritability of IQ generally increasing with age. It is also important to note that many researchers argue that the effects of heredity and the environment cannot be separated clearly (Bronfenbrenner and Ceci 1994; Wahlsten and Gottlieb, 1997), and that research attention should be devoted to understanding how heredity and environment work together to determine or influence intelligence (Jensen, 1997; Scarr, 1997). In any case, heritability can vary with population and environmental circumstances, so that any values of the heritability coefficient have to be considered in the context of the circumstances under which they are obtained.

Separated Identical Twins
Identical twins have identical genes. No one knows exactly why identical twinning occurs, but we do know that identical twins result when

a sperm fertilizes an egg, and then the newly formed embryo splits in two, resulting in two embryos with identical genes. Suppose that a set of identical twins is born, and then one of the twins is immediately whisked away to a new environment, chosen at random, so that no relationship exists between the environments in which the two twins are raised. The twins would have identical genes, but any similarity between their environments would be due only to chance. If we then created a number of such twin pairs, we would be able to estimate the contribution of heredity to individual differences in intelligence by correlating the measured intelligence of each individual with that of his or her identical twin. The twins would have in common all their heredity but none of their environment (except any aspects that might be similar due to chance).

Although purposely creating such a group of separated twins is unethical, sometimes real-life circumstances have created instances in which twins have been separated at birth and raised separately. In studies of twins reared apart, the various estimates tend to fall within roughly the same heritability-coefficient range of 0.6 to 0.8 (for example, Bouchard and McGue, 1981; Juel-Nielsen, 1965; Newman, Freeman, and Holzinger, 1937; Shields, 1962).

These relatively high figures must be interpreted with some caution, however. In many cases, the twins were not actually separated at birth, but at some point afterward, giving the twins a common environment for at least some time before separation. In other cases, it becomes clear that the supposedly random assortment of environments was not truly random. Placement authorities tend to place twins in environments relatively similar to those they left. These tendencies may inflate in some degree the apparent contribution of heredity to variation in measured intelligence, because variation that is actually environmental is included in the correlation supposed to represent only the effect of heredity.

Identical Versus Fraternal Twins

Another way to estimate heritability is to compare the correlation of IQs for identical versus fraternal twins. The idea is that, whereas identical twins share identical genes, fraternal twins share only the same genes as would any brother or sister. On average, fraternal twins share only 50 percent of their genes. To the extent that the identical and fraternal twin pairs share similar environments due to age, we should not get environmental differences due merely to variations in age among sibling pairs. If environments are nearly the same for both twins, differences in the correlation of intelligence scores between fraternal and identical twins should be attributable to heredity. According to a review by Thomas Bouchard and Matthew McGue (1981), these data lead to a heritability estimate of about 0.75, again suggesting a high level of heritability. More recent estimates are similar, although quite variable (Mackintosh, 1998).

These data may be affected by the fact that fraternal twins often do not share environments to the same extent that identical ones do, particularly if the fraternal twins are not same-sexed. Parents tend to treat identical twins more nearly alike than they do fraternal twins, even to the extent of having them dress the same way. Moreover, identical twins are likely to respond differently, perhaps seeking out more apparent identity with their twin. Thus, once again, the contribution of environment may be underestimated to some extent.

Adoption
Yet another way to examine hereditary versus environmental contributions to intelligence is by comparing the correlation between the IQs of adopted children with those of their biological parents, on the one hand, and their adoptive parents, on the other. Biological parents provide adopted children with their genes, and adoptive parents provide the children with their environments. To the extent that heredity matters, the higher correlation should be with the intelligence of the biological rather than the adoptive parents; to the extent that environment matters, the higher correlation should be that with the intelligence of the adoptive parents. In some families, it is also possible to compare the IQs of the adopted children to the IQs of either biological or adoptive siblings.

Many psychologists who have studied intelligence as measured by IQ believe the heritability of intelligence to be about 0.5 in children, and somewhat higher in adults (Mackintosh, 1998, Plomin, 1997), for whom the early effects of the child-rearing environment have receded. However, there probably is no one coefficient of heritability that applies to all populations under all circumstances. Changes in distributions of genes or in environments can change the estimates. Moreover, even if a trait shows a high heritability, we could not say that the trait cannot be developed. For example, the heritability of height is very high – about

0.9 – yet we know that over the past several generations, heights have been increasing.

Evolutionary Approaches

Evolutionary approaches to intelligence, which are perhaps most relevant to the goals of this essay, attempt to characterize how intelligence has evolved across various organisms (Jerison, 1982, 2000, 2001; Pinker, 1997). Jerison (2000), attempting to understand intelligence evolutionarily, defines intelligence as the "behavioral consequence of the total neural-information processing capacity in representative adults of a species, adjusted for the capacity to control routine bodily functions" (p. 216).

Most evolutionary based conceptions of intelligence are similar to Jerison's, which is in turn similar to conventional views of intelligence. Most view humans as the species at the top of the evolutionary scale of intelligence (Corballis, 2001). For example, Bradshaw (2001), Calvin (2001), and Cosmides and Tooby (2001) have viewed intelligence primarily in terms of problem-solving ability as applied to novel problems. Plotkin (2001) has emphasized acquisition of information from the environment. Byrne (2001) has viewed intelligence in all animal species largely in terms of mental or behavioral aptitudes, and suggested that the way intelligence is understood in animals is parasitic on everyday uses of the term *intelligence* as applied to humans.

Other approaches to evolutionary intelligence have been taken as well. For example, Bjorklund and Kipp (2001) as well as Stenhouse (1973) have suggested that cognitive inhibition is the key to intelligence from an evolutionary point of view – that more intelligent organisms are better able to inhibit instinctive reactions. From this point of view, it is not just what one does, but also what one does not do that is key to intelligence.

A Perspective on Biological Intelligence Based on Transmission of Genes

A common characteristic of most of the biological approaches described above is that they are *biological approaches* to intelligence rather than approaches to *biological intelligence*. The distinction may seem semantic, but I believe it is not. Intelligence is always based on adaptation to the environment, but the kind of adaptation dealt with by many theories seems to be cultural – the type of adaptation measured by proxy by conventional psychometric tests of intelligence. Biological adaptation, in contrast, takes a very different form.

THE NATURE OF ADAPTATION TO THE ENVIRONMENT

Humans and other organisms live within two kinds of environments that, although overlapping, are nevertheless conceptually distinct. The first kind of environment is biological/physical, and it is the environment in which adaptation means biological survival and transmission of one's genes to succeeding generations. If one succeeds in passing on one's genes in some degree, one is adaptive in some degree; if one does not survive to pass on one's genes, one is not adaptive. This sense of adaptation is the Darwinian sense (Darwin, 1859). Intelligence is in the adaptation to one's ecological niche (Flanagan, Hardcastle, and Nahmias, 2001).

The second kind of environment is cultural, and it is the environment in which adaptation means success in however it is culturally defined. Although humans may delight in viewing themselves as distinctive in having developed cultures, this claim to distinctiveness probably is largely a conceit. Other organisms have social groupings where certain behavior is acceptable and certain behavior not acceptable, and where certain kinds of behavior are preferred over others to varying degrees. Thus, at the very least, certain nonhuman primates (for example, chimpanzees, baboons, or gorillas) are more successful in their social groups than are others (Zentall, 2000). The same might be said for other animals as well.

Competencies and expertise that develop out of the two kinds of adaptations are potentially quite different. The first kinds of competencies are in attracting mates, producing viable children, and in making sure that they grow up so they can reproduce and propagate some of the same genes. The second kinds of competencies lie in surviving and thriving in one's cultural niche, and can apply even if one has no progeny at all.

The literature on intelligence has largely conflated the two kinds of adaptations. Even essays on the evolution of intelligence (for example, Jerison, 1982, 2000; Pinker, 1997; see essays in Sternberg and Kaufman, 2001) have at times conflated the two, with unfortunate consequences. Most evolutionary approaches place humans at the top of some kind of scale of intelligence. They view humans as supremely intelligent. From one point of view, humans may have more intelligence than cockroaches (as claimed by Godfrey-Smith, 2001); but from another, cockroaches may actually be better adapted to their ecological niche than humans, the point of view that we take below. So who is the expert – the human or the cockroach? It all depends on the environment to which one adapts. Cockroaches adapt better to different environments than do humans. So do bacteria. And sometimes, humans are the environment to which the bacteria adapt, with great success. Their adaptation does not always bode well for the human.

Intelligence as an Interaction

Intelligence is *never* simply a property of an individual. The differential and even many cognitive and biological approaches to intelligence have always been short-sighted in viewing intelligence as a property of an individual, whether measured by factors (see, for example, Brody, 2000), cognitive processes and strategies (see, for example, Deary, 2000; Lohman, 2000), or biological elements (see, for example, Vernon et al., 2000). Intelligence has meaning only in terms of interaction with an environment or set of environments, whether biological/physical or cultural. But the extent to which one develops competencies and from them, expertise (that is, very high levels of competencies, as recognized by some group that passes judgment – Sternberg, 1995; Sternberg and Horvath, 1998), depends on the kind of intelligence one talks about, and the kind of environment on which it acts.

Imagine someone who lives in a large locked box from early childhood. The child is weaned in infancy and then placed in the box. Meals are pushed in through a slot and the box has toilet facilities. Otherwise, there is nothing in the box. What does intelligence mean in this environment? The ability to read? There is nothing to read, any more than there is anything to read in a preliterate society. Knowledge of vocabulary? There is no one with whom to share one's knowledge of vocabulary, with whom to communicate via speaking, writing, listening, or reading. Skill in solving arithmetic problems? There are no arithmetic problems either. Skill in solving abstract analogy or matrix problems? There are no problems that require abstract thinking to solve in the environment.

Intelligence has meaning by virtue of the kinds of problems one needs to solve in some environment. If there are no meaningful problems to solve, there is no meaningful intelligence or intelligent problem solving.

Similarly, competencies and expertise exist only with respect to some kind of environmental niche.

Intelligence as a Systems Property

Intelligence is not merely the interaction of an individual organism with an environment. It is the interaction of one or more systems with the environment. One does not need a brain to be intelligent: Computers can act intelligently – can even beat world chess champions – but they have no brains, not, at least, in the biological sense. When one uses one's brain to act intelligently, one is always using a system. One uses one's hands to write or keyboard answers. One draws on interactions with parents and teachers to show knowledge transmitted by these parents and teachers. With poor socialization, one's intelligence is reduced. A child brought up in a closet will show low intelligence, without regard to any so-called inborn potential. One draws on writing systems created centuries before one was born, and on numeration systems that one often only vaguely understands. One writes answers in booklets or on computers created by others. Whole systems are always at work in the development and manifestation of intelligence. Intelligence is individual only in the sense that the individual embraces the contributions of countless others for his or her own purposes. Without these contributions, one truly could do relatively little.

What is Biological Intelligence?

Biological intelligence refers to an organism's ability to adapt to the biological/physical environment as measured by transmission of genes. Biological approaches to intelligence, curiously, have largely ignored this basic and, from an evolutionary point of view, singular fact. Such approaches have generally attempted to account for (a) how humans among other species have reached the top of the existing evolutionary scale in intelligence or (b) biological mechanisms that account for individual differences in human intelligence. In terms of cultural adaptation, humans have done extremely well, comparatively speaking. In terms of biological adaptation, however, they are middling at best, and probably worse (Gould, 1996). Humans occupy a dubious position in any scale of biological intelligence, for several reasons.

First, they are much less prolific than insects, bacteria, or any of a number of other life forms. Judged by spreading of genes, these other life forms do far better than humans. They are more expert in gene-diffusion. Viewing intelligence as a systems property, bacteria, viruses, and parasites regularly outwit humans, with hundreds of millions of deaths each year due to their ravages. Gould (1996) has noted that bacteria can be viewed as the most successful organisms in the world in terms of adaptation.

If one refers to the level of the individual virus or bacterium, the organism's biological intelligence might look pitiable, at best. For example, in killing a human, the organism brings on its own destruction. But its own survival is not, in any biological or other sense, its goal. Rather, its goal is transmission of its genes, which it does admirably, reproducing far faster and more prolifically than humans, and having devised elaborate mechanisms to ensure that its successors go on to infect other humans and thus continue the proliferation of the system. The organism is not, from its own point of view, fighting the human, any more than the human is fighting the fish it kills for consumption. Both organisms are merely doing their evolutionarily derived "thing," which is to ensure their own survival at least long enough to transmit genes to a future generation. Each develops competencies and then expertise in what suits it. In the cases of some organisms, especially parasites, very complex life cycles have evolved that enable the parasites to keep reproducing and invading successive hosts.

Second, on the whole, humans are among the most dubious life forms in terms of fostering the long-term survival of their genes. Humans have invented all kinds of weapons with the capability of destroying the entire species several times over. The world has more than enough atomic bombs to do the job. Several countries appear to have stockpiles of chemical and biological weapons that are also more than adequate to finish us off. Humans have created global warming that they do not know how to deal with, as well as threats to the ozone layer in the upper reaches of the atmosphere. Readers may take comfort in the fact that threats by terrorists or rogue countries have so far been limited to isolated times and places, and that threats of global warming and ozone depletion are so far under control. Dinosaurs, as a species, lasted millions of years, far more years than humans have lasted so far. Is it likely that nearly as much time will go by before any of these threats wipes out large swaths of the population or even the whole population of humans? Obviously, we do not know. But the signs are not, so far, encouraging. Is there really much doubt that terrorists will gain access to the weapons of destruction that can destroy massive amounts of humanity, or perhaps, that they already have?

Suppose, for the sake of argument, that humans do wipe themselves out in short order. Their genes do not continue to propagate because they have sown the seeds of their own destruction. A thousand, ten thousand, a hundred thousand, or a million years later some future civilization looks back at what humans have done to themselves. Will that civilization say humans were too smart for their own good, or that they lacked the intelligence even to maintain themselves a relatively short amount of time, on an evolutionary scale, as a species? We do not know what they will say. What we do know is that in terms of a strictly biological definition of intelligence, humans will have been rather unintelligent if they are responsible for their own mass destruction, as they have come near to being in two world wars and countless genocides. And who knows what future atrocities they will bring on themselves. High IQs do not particularly help dead people or the progeny they might have brought into the world had they lived long enough to do so.

These threats are not idle. A new global assessment of future threats to the United States, "Global Trends 2015: A Dialogue about the Future with Nongovernmental Experts" (as reported in Loeb, 2000) describes as perhaps the most dire threat the proliferation of weapons of mass destruction among terrorists and hostile governments. Over the short run, it may be possible to counter these threats with strong border control (which the United States most definitely does not have), antiterrorist weapons (notable by their conspicuous absence), or excellent intelligence (somewhat lacking due to the difficulties of infiltrating the organizations). But these threats will become increasingly serious and ultimately, perhaps overpowering.

Does any of this have anything to do with intelligence? Of course it does. Cultural intelligence – the kind measured by tests of intelligence and various kinds of cognitive abilities – presumes the success of biological intelligence. Dead organisms do not adapt to the cultural environment. If humans destroy themselves in a way that at this time appears to be unique across species, the concept of a high IQ will not be meaningful, except perhaps in the ironic sense that it is the high IQs of those who designed the weapons that served to create mass destruction.

Humans may be their own worst enemy, but they have no lack of other enemies. Psychologists and others may view intelligence in terms of the functioning of the brain or in terms of scores on IQ points. But biologically, survival and reproduction depend only a little on such things. Consider the following scenario.

Suppose the science-fiction thrillers prove to be correct. Alien life forms invade the Earth. The alien life forms are in the process of destroying humanity. As in many science-fiction novels and films, the aliens invade the body and hijack many of its systems. Humanity works at a desperate pace to fight back. There is some success, but the victories prove to be only in skirmishes. Battles are won but the war is being lost. The enemies seem to outclass all the efforts made to combat them. At best, humanity will be able to keep the aliens in check; at worst, humanity will soon go the way of the dinosaurs. Who knows who will win? And if the enemies are victorious, who knows which enemy will be the winner – the HIV virus, the tuberculosis bacillum, the malaria parasite, or some other alien life form?

When humans speak of the enemies of their bodies, they anthropomorphize them. It is customary to speak of the "war against cancer" or "outwitting the malaria parasite" or the "stealthy AIDS virus." It is easy to anthropomorphize because no matter how vigorously humans battle against these and other hostile life forms, at best these enemies are kept in temporary check. Humans may or may not want to refer to these organisms as "intelligent," but for those attacked by them, the wording does not much matter, especially if the alien life forms win the battle.

Viewed as a system, certain viruses, such as the HIV virus, have been enormously biologically intelligent, at least in comparison with humans. So far, the battle seems to be going to the aliens. What is even more bizarre is that the virus is, in effect, taking advantage of human patterns of behavior to ensure the human's destruction. AIDS is, in principle, an entirely preventable disease that has been on the increase despite our theoretical ability to control it. Tuberculosis and certain staphylococcus and salmonella infections have taken advantage of human behavior to become immune to all the drugs currently available to fight against them.

Humans can claim to have much bigger brains than viruses, bacteria, or parasites, none of which, in fact, have brains. But systemically, these organisms have already lasted longer than humans and are likely to outlast them. In the sense of adaptation to the environment, they seem to have certain systemic advantages over humans.

Cultural intelligence, of the kind measured by conventional intelligence tests, is important to humans. And important enough that they have redefined comparative intelligence across species largely in terms of the things that matter to humans.

Intelligence tests measure an aspect of adaptation to the environment in terms of the cultures that humans have created. The various theories of intelligence that have been proposed are far more applicable to cultural than to biological adaptation. They certainly have some relevance to biological adaptation: Smarter people may be less likely to engage in self-damaging behavior. On the other hand, smarter people also may create the instruments ultimately responsible for their own destruction.

Humans may well be at the top of some evolutionary scale in terms of cultural intelligence. In terms of biological intelligence, they are, at best, middling. They have been responsible, directly or indirectly, for the extinction of a number of species. At the rate they are going, they may soon be responsible for the extinction of their own. A species can excel in cultural intelligence, but not in biological intelligence. A species of this kind, such as the human one, may have its days numbered, in evolutionary time, in terms of small numbers of grains of sand. Humans have developed great competencies and wonderful levels of expertise. Unfortunately, they have devoted too much of these competencies and expertise to helping to bring about their own future destruction.

References

Barrett, P. T., Daum, I., & Eysenck, H. J. (1990). Sensory nerve conduction and intelligence: A methodological study. *Journal of Psychophysiology, 4*(1), 1–13.

Barrett, P. T., & Eysenck, H. J. (1992). Brain evoked potentials and intelligence: The Hendrickson Paradigm. *Intelligence, 16*, 361–381.

Barrett, P. T., & Eysenck, H. J. (1994). The relationship between evoked potential component amplitude, latency, contour length, zero-crossings, and psychometric intelligence. *Personality and Individual Differences, 16*, 3–32.

Barry, W., & Ertl, J. (1966). Brain waves and human intelligence. In F. B. Davis (Ed.), *Modern educational developments: Another look* (pp. 191–197). New York: Educational Records Bureau.

Bennett, E. L., Diamond, M. C., Krech, D., & Rosenzweig, M. R. (1964). Chemical and anatomical plasticity of the brain. *Science, 146*, 610–619.

Bjorklund, D. F., & Kipp, K. (2001). Social cognition, inhibition, and theory of mind: The evolution of human intelligence. In R. J. Sternberg & J. C. Kaufman (Eds.), *The evolution of intelligence.* Mahwah, NJ: Lawrence Erlbaum Associates.

Bogen, J. E. (1975). Some educational aspects of hemispheric specialization. *UCLA Educator, 17*, 24–32.

Boring, E. G. (1923, June 6). Intelligence as the tests test it. *New Republic,* 35–37.

Bouchard, T. J., Jr., & McGue, M. (1981). Familial studies of intelligence: A review. *Science, 212*, 1055–1059.

Bradshaw, J. L. (2001). The evolution of intellect: Cognitive, neurological and primatological aspects and hominid culture. In R. J. Sternberg & J. C. Kaufman (Eds.), *The evolution of intelligence.* Mahwah, NJ: Lawrence Erlbaum Associates.

Broca, P. P. (1861). Nouvelle observation d'aphemie produite par une lésion de la moitié postérieure des deuxième et troisième circonvolutions frontales gauches [New observations/recordings of aphemie produced by an injury of the rear half of the second and third frontal left convolutions]. *Bulletins de la Societé Anotomique de Paris, 36*, 398–407.

Brody, N. (2000). History of theories and measurements of intelligence. In R. J. Sternberg (Ed.), *Handbook of intelligence* (pp. 16–33). New York: Cambridge University Press.

Bronfenbrenner, U., & Ceci, S. J. (1994). Nature-nurture reconceptualized in developmental perspective: A bioecological model. *Psychological Review, 101*, 568–586.

Byrne, R. L. (2001). The primate origins of human intelligence. In R. J. Sternberg & J. C. Kaufman (Eds.), *The evolution of intelligence*. Mahwah, NJ: Lawrence Erlbaum Associates.

Calvin, W. H. (2001). Pumping up intelligence: Abrupt climate jumps and the evolution of higher intellectual functions during the ice ages. In R. J. Sternberg & J. C. Kaufman (Eds.), *The evolution of intelligence*. Mahwah, NJ: Lawrence Erlbaum Associates.

Caryl, P. G. (1994). Early event-related potentials correlate with inspection time and intelligence. *Intelligence, 18*(1), 15–46.

Comery, T. A., Shah, R., & Greenough, W. T. (1995). Differential rearing alters spine density on medium-sized spiny neurons in the rat corpus striatum: Evidence for association of morphological plasticity with early response gene expression. *Neurobiology of Learning and Memory, 63*, 217–219.

Corballis, M. C. (2001). Evolution of the generative mind. In R. J. Sternberg & J. C. Kaufman (Eds.), *The evolution of intelligence*. Mahwah, NJ: Lawrence Erlbaum Associates.

Cosmides, L., & Tooby, J. (2001). Unraveling the enigma of human intelligence: evolutionary psychology and the multimodular mind. In R. J. Sternberg & J. C. Kaufman (Eds.), *The evolution of intelligence*. Mahwah, NJ: Lawrence Erlbaum Associates.

Darwin, C. (1859). *The origin of species*. London: Murray.

Davis, F. B. (1971). *The measurement of mental capability through evoked-potential recordings*. Greenwich, CT: Educational Records Bureau.

Deary, I. J. (2000). Simple information processing. In R. J. Sternberg (Ed.), *Handbook of intelligence* (pp. 267–284). New York: Cambridge University Press.

Deary, I. J., & Caryl, P. G. (1994). Intelligence, inspection time, and cognitive strategies. In P. A. Vernon (Ed.), *Biological approaches to the study of human intelligence*. Norwood, NJ: Ablex.

Diamond, M. C., Ingham, C. A., Johnson, R. E., Bennett, E. L., & Rosenzweig, M. R. (1976). Effects of environment on morphology of rat cerebral cortex and hippocampus. *Journal of Neurobiology, 7*, 75–85.

Dustman, R. E., & Beck, E. C. (1972). Relationship of intelligence to visually evoked potentials. *Electroencephalography and Clinical Neurophysiology, 33*, 254.

Ertl, J., & Schafer, E. (1969). Brain response correlates of psychometric intelligence. *Nature, 233*, 421–2.

Farah, M. J. (1988). The neuropsychology of mental imagery: Converging evidence from brain-damaged and normal subjects. In J. Stiles-Davis,

M. Kritchevsky, & U. Bellugi (Eds.), *Spatial cognition: Brain bases and development* (pp. 33–56). Hillsdale, NJ: Lawrence Erlbaum Associates.

Farah, M. J. (1994). Beyond "pet" methodologies to converging evidence. *Trends in Neurosciences, 17*(12), 514–515.

Farah, M. J. (1996). Is face recognition "special"? Evidence from neuropsychology. *Behavioural Brain Research, 76,* 181–189.

Flanagan, O., Hardcastle, V., & Nahmias, E. (2001). Is human intelligence an adaptation? Cautionary observations from the philosophy of biology. In R. J. Sternberg & J. C. Kaufman (Eds.), *The evolution of intelligence.* Mahwah, NJ: Lawrence Erlbaum Associates.

Fuchs, J. L., Montemayor, M., & Greenough, W. T. (1990). Effect of environmental complexity on size of the superior colliculus. *Behavioral and Neural Biology, 54,* 198–203.

Galton, F. (1883). *Inquiry into human faculty and its development.* London: Macmillan.

Gazzaniga, M. S. (1985). *The social brain: Discovering the networks of the mind.* New York: Basic Books.

Godfrey-Smith, P. (2001). Environmental complexity and the evolution of cognition. In R. J. Sternberg & J. C. Kaufman (Eds.), *The evolution of intelligence.* Mahwah, NJ: Lawrence Erlbaum Associates.

Gould, S. J. (1996). *Full house.* New York: Harmony.

Haier, R. J. (1990). The end of intelligence research. *Intelligence, 14,* 371–374.

Haier, R. J., Nuechterlein, K. H., Hazlett, E., Wu, J. C., Pack, J., Browning, H. L., & Buchsbaum, M. S. (1988). Cortical glucose metabolic rate correlates of abstract reasoning and attention studied with positron emission tomography. *Intelligence, 12,* 199–217.

Haier, R. J., Siegel, B., Tang, C., Abel, L., & Buchsbaum, M. S. (1992). Intelligence and changes in regional cerebral glucose metabolic rate following learning. *Intelligence, 16,* 415–426.

Hebb, D. O. (1949). *The organization of behavior: A neuropsychological theory.* New York: Wiley.

Hendrickson, A. E. (1982). The biological basis of intelligence. Part I: Theory. In H. J. Eysenck (Ed.), *A model for intelligence* (pp. 151–196). Berlin: Springer-Verlag.

Hendrickson, A. E., & Hendrickson, D. E. (1980). The biological basis for individual differences in intelligence. *Personality and Individual Differences, 1,* 3–33.

Hendrickson, D. E. (1982). The biological basis of intelligence. Part II: Measurement. In H. J. Eysenck (Ed.), *A model for intelligence* (pp. 197–228). Berlin: Springer-Verlag.

Hoadley, M. F. (with Pearson, K.). (1929). On measurement of the internal diameters of the skull in relation: I. To the prediction of its capacity; II. To the "preeminence" of the left hemisphere. *Biometrika, 21,* 85–123.

"Intelligence and its measurement": A symposium (1921). *Journal of Educational Psychology, 12,* 123–147, 195–216, 271–275.

Jensen, A. R. (1982). Reaction time and psychometric *g.* In H. J. Eysenck (Ed.), *A model for intelligence.* Heidelberg, Germany: Springer-Verlag.

Jensen, A. R. (1997). The puzzle of nongenetic variance. In R. J. Sternberg & E. L. Grigorenko (Eds.), *Intelligence, heredity, and environment* (pp. 42–88). New York: Cambridge University Press.

Jerison, H. J. (1982): The evolution of biological intelligence. In R. J. Sternberg (Ed.), *Handbook of human intelligence*. New York: Cambridge University Press (pp.: 723–791).

Jerison, H. J. (2000). The evolution of intelligence. In R. J. Sternberg (Ed.), *Handbook of intelligence* (pp. 216–244). New York: Cambridge University Press.

Jerison, H. J. (2001). On theory in comparative psychology. In R. J. Sternberg & J. C. Kaufman (Eds.), *The evolution of intelligence*. Mahwah, NJ: Lawrence Erlbaum Associates.

Jones, T. A., & Greenough, W. T. (1996). Ultrastructural evidence for increased contact between astrocytes and synapses in rats reared in a complex environment. *Neurobiology of Learning and Memory, 65,* 48–56.

Juel-Nielsen, N. (1965). *Individual and environment; a psychiatric-psychological investigation of monozygotic twins reared apart.* New York: Humanities Press.

Kutas, M., McCarthy, G., & Donchin, E. (1977). Augmenting mental chronometry: The P300 as a measure of stimulus evaluation time. *Science, 197,* 792–795.

Lashley, K. S. (1950). In search of the engram. *Symposia of the Society for Experimental Biology, 4,* 454–482.

Levy, J. (1974). Cerebral asymmetries as manifested in split-brain man. In M. Kinsbourne & W. L. Smith (Eds.), *Hemispheric disconnection and cerebral function.* Springfield, IL: Charles C. Thomas.

Loeb, V. (2000, December 25). Future threats: A panel of experts outlines global conflicts and economic trends over the next 15 years. *The Washington Post Weekly Edition,* 16.

Loehlin, J. C. (1989). Partitioning environmental and genetic contributions to behavioral development. *American Psychologist, 44,* 1285–1292.

Lohman, D. F. (2000). Complex information processing and intelligence. In R. J. Sternberg (Ed.), *Handbook of intelligence* (pp. 285–340). New York: Cambridge University Press.

Luria, A. R. (1966). *The human brain and psychological processes.* New York: Harper & Row.

Luria, A. R. (1973). *The working brain.* New York: Basic Books.

Luria, A. R. (1980). *Higher cortical functions in man* (2d ed., rev. and expanded). New York: Basic Books.

Mackintosh, N. J. (1998). *IQ and human intelligence.* Oxford, UK: Oxford University Press.

Magliero, A., Bashore, T. R., Coles, M. G., & Donchin, E. (1984). On the dependence of P300 latency on stimulus evaluation processes. *Psychophysiology, 21*(2), 171–186.

Matarazzo, J. D. (1992). Biological and physiological correlates of intelligence. *Intelligence, 16*(3,4), 257–258.

McCarthy, G., & Donchin, E. (1981). A metric for thought: A comparison of P300 latency and reaction time. *Science, 211,* 77–9.

McGarry-Roberts, P. A., Stelmack, R. M., & Campbell, K. B. (1992). Intelligence, reaction time, and event-related potentials. *Intelligence, 16*(3,4), 289–313.

Newman, H. H., Freeman, F. N., & Holzinger, K. J. (1937). *Twins: A study of heredity and environment.* Chicago: University of Chicago Press.

Perry, N. W., McCow, J. G., Cunningham, W. R., Falgout, J. C., & Street, W. J. (1976). Multivariate visual evoked response correlates of intelligence. *Psychophysiology, 13,* 323–329.

Pinker, S. (1997). *How the mind works.* New York: W. W. Norton & Co.

Plomin, R. (1997). Identifying genes for cognitive abilities and disabilities. In R. J. Sternberg & E. L. Grigorenko (Eds.), *Intelligence, heredity, and environment* (pp. 89–104). New York: Cambridge University Press.

Plotkin, H. (2001). Intelligence as predisposed skeptical induction engines. In R. J. Sternberg & J. C. Kaufman (Eds.), *The evolution of intelligence.* Mahwah, NJ: Lawrence Erlbaum Associates.

Polich, J., & Kok, A. (1995). Cognitive and biological determinants of P300: An integrative review. *Biological Psychology, 41*(2), 103–146.

Reed, T. E. (1984). Residual latency (delay at the neuromuscular junction): Normative values and heritability in mice. *Behavior Genetics, 14*(3), 209–219.

Reed, T. E., & Jensen, A. R. (1991). Arm nerve conduction velocity (NCV), brain NCV, reaction time, and intelligence. *Intelligence, Vol 15,* 33–47.

Reed, T. E., & Jensen, A. R. (1992). Conduction velocity in a brain nerve pathway of normal adults correlates with intelligence level. *Intelligence, 16,* 259–272.

Rijsdijk, F. V., & Boomsma, D. I. (1997). Genetic mediation of the correlation between peripheral nerve conduction velocity and IQ. *Behavior Genetics, 27*(2), 87–98.

Rijsdijk, F. V., Boomsma, D. I., & Vernon, P. A. (1995). Genetic analysis of peripheral nerve conduction velocity in twins. *Behavior Genetics, 25*(1), 341–348.

Scarr, S. (1997). Behavior-genetic and socialization theories of intelligence: Truce and reconciliation. In R. J. Sternberg & E. L. Grigorenko (Eds.), *Intelligence, heredity and environment* (pp. 3–41). New York: Cambridge University Press.

Schafer, R. (1982). The relevance of the "here and now" transference interpretation to the reconstruction of early development. *International Journal of Psycho-Analysis, 63*(1), 77–82.

Segalowitz, S. J., Unsal, A., & Dywan, J. (1992). Cleverness and wisdom in 12-year-olds: Electrophysiological evidence for late maturation of the frontal lobe. *Developmental Neuropsychology, 8*(2–3), 179–298.

Shields, J. (1962). *Monozygotic twins brought up apart and brought up together.* London: Oxford University Press.

Shucard, D. W., & Callaway, E. (1973). Relationship between human intelligence and frequency analysis of cortical evoked response. *Perceptual & Motor Skills, 36,* 147–151.

Shucard, D. W., & Horn, J. L. (1972). Evoked cortical potentials and measurement of human abilities. *Journal of Comparative & Physiological Psychology, 78*(1), 59–68.

Sperry, R. W. (1961). Cerebral organization and behavior. *Science, 133,* 1749–1757.

Stenhouse, D. (1973). *The evolution of intelligence: A general theory and some of its implications.* New York: Harper & Row.

Sternberg, R. J. (1995). Expertise in complex problem solving: A comparison of alternative conceptions. In P. A. Frensch & J. Funke (Eds.), *Complex problem solving: European perspectives* (pp. 295–321). Hillsdale, NJ: Lawrence Erlbaum Associates.

Sternberg, R. J., & Detterman, D. K. (1986). *What is intelligence?* Norwood, N.J.: Ablex Publishing Corporation.

Sternberg, R. J., & Grigorenko, E. L. (Eds.). (1997). *Intelligence, heredity, and environment.* New York: Cambridge University Press.

Sternberg, R. J., & Horvath, J. A. (1998). Cognitive conceptions of expertise nad their relations to giftedness. In R. Friedman & K. Rogers (Eds.), *Talent in context* (pp. 177–191). Washington, DC: American Psychological Association.

Sternberg, R. J., & Kaufman, J. C. (Eds.). (2001). *The evolution of intelligence.* Mahwah, NJ: Lawrence Erlbaum Associates.

Tan, Ü. (1996). Correlations between nonverbal intelligence and peripheral nerve conduction velocity in right-handed subjects: Sex-related differences. *International Journal of Psychophysiology, 22,* 123–128.

Vernon, P. A., & Mori, M. (1989). Intelligence, reaction times, and nerve conduction velocity. *Behavior Genetics (abstracts), 19,* 779.

Vernon, P. A., & Mori, M. (1992). Intelligence, reaction times, and peripheral nerve conduction velocity. *Intelligence, 16*(3–4), 273–288.

Vernon, P. A., Wickett, J. C., Bazana, P. G., & Stelmack, R. M. (2000). The neuropsychology and psycholophysiology of human intelligence. In R. J. Sternberg (Ed.), *Handbook of intelligence* (pp. 245–264). New York: Cambridge University Press.

Wahlsten, D., & Gottlieb, G. (1997). The invalid separation of effects of nature and nurture: Lessons from animal experimentation. In R. J. Sternberg & E. L. Grigorenko (Eds.), *Intelligence, heredity, and environment* (pp. 163–192). New York: Cambridge University Press.

Wickett, J. C., & Vernon, P. A. (1994). Peripheral nerve conduction velocity, reaction time, and intelligence: An attempt to replicate Vernon and Mori. *Intelligence, 18,* 127–132.

Wickett, J. C., Vernon, P. A., & Lee, D. H. (2000). The relationships between factors of intelligence and brain volume. *Personality and Individual Differences, 29*(6), 1095–1122.

Widaman, K. F., Carlson, J. S., Saetermoe, C. L., & Galbraith, G. C. (1993). The relationship of auditory evoked potentials to fluid and crystallized intelligence. *Personality & Individual Differences, 15*(2), 205–217.

Zentall, T. R. (2000). Animal intelligence. In R. J. Sternberg (Ed.), *Handbook of intelligence* (pp. 197–215). New York: Cambridge University Press.

10

What Causes Individual Differences in Cognitive Performance?

Richard E. Mayer

INTRODUCTION

What are the determinants of individual differences in cognitive performance? Among the answers offered by the chapter authors are that cognitive performance depends on genes, ability, experiences, or knowledge. In this chapter, I provide a model of the determinants of individual differences in cognitive performance and show how it relates to some of the proposed answers provided by the contributors to this book. According to the model, ability and experience interact to produce specialized knowledge, which in turn enables cognitive performance. After describing the model, defining key terms, and examining key issues, I review eight major empirical findings cited by the chapter authors and show how these findings contribute to fleshing out the model. Overall, the book reflects psychology's multifaceted search for an understanding of individual differences in cognitive performance.

SEARCHING FOR THE DETERMINANTS OF INDIVIDUAL DIFFERENCES IN COGNITIVE PERFORMANCE

A student scores high on a standardized test of verbal ability. An expert memorizer listens to a list of fifty digits and recites them back without error. The head of a small company devises a successful plan to launch a new product. A young woman writes a moving poem about mental disabilities. These are examples of *cognitive performance* – that is, observable behavior on a cognitive task. What causes individual differences in

Preparation of this chapter was supported by a grant from the Office of Naval Research.

TABLE 10.1. *A Model of Individual Differences in Cognitive Performance*

Ability	+ Experience	= Knowledge →	Cognitive performance
Fluid intelligence Intelligence-as-process	Deliberate practice	Competency Expertise Crystallized intelligence Intelligence-as-knowledge	Intelligent behavior Successful test taking Expert performance
Is ability general or specific, cognitive or multidimensional, innate or modifiable?	Is the interplay mainly due to ability, experience or both?	Is knowledge general or specific, and declarative or procedural?	Is performance maximum or typical, and intelligent or creative?

cognitive performance – that is, why do people perform differently on cognitive tasks? This is the motivating question for the contributors to *The Psychology of Abilities, Competencies, and Expertise.*

The contributors offer a broad array of answers: Among the most prominent answers are that cognitive performance depends on your genes, on your general ability, on your life experiences, or on the specialized knowledge you have learned. Who is right? Across the chapters of this book, the authors offer reasoned arguments and empirical data to support each of these views. Twin studies show a strong correlation between the cognitive test scores of identical twins raised apart, suggesting evidence for the gene explanation. Scores on tests of general cognitive ability successfully predict how well students will do on school tests, suggesting evidence for the ability explanation. Music students whose parents encourage them to engage in large amounts of challenging practice are more likely to become accomplished pianists, suggesting evidence for the experience explanation. Finally, people who have learned specific strategies for how to remember a list of digits excel on digit span tasks, suggesting evidence for the knowledge explanation.

Model

How can the various answers be reconciled? In the top of Table 10.1, I offer a modest attempt to reconcile the various views about the sources of individual differences in cognitive performance. In particular, I provide a model of the sources of individual differences in cognitive performance. Starting on the right side (at "cognitive performance"), our first question is: Where does cognitive performance come from? I begin with the idea that cognitive performance depends on specialized knowledge (or domain-specific knowledge), as indicated by the entry labeled "knowledge." Consistent with strong themes in cognitive science, I propose that a person's knowledge enables a person's cognitive performance.

Although some scholars seem to focus solely on the knowledge-causes-performance explanation, I do not think this is the end of the story. We can go on to ask: Where do individual differences in knowledge come from? A reasonable answer is that knowledge comes from the interaction of one's ability and one's experiences, as indicated by the entries labeled "ability + experience." Whereas some scholars emphasize the role of ability or the role of experience, others offer an interactionist vision in which ability predisposes people to seek certain experiences that lead to the development of specialized knowledge.

Definitions

The middle of Table 10.1 lists some related terms for each of the entries: ability, experience, knowledge, and cognitive performance. Ability can be defined as one's potential for learning knowledge that supports cognitive performance. Related terms that fall under this heading include *fluid intelligence* and *intelligence-as-process*, which refer to general cognitive ability. Experience can be defined as one's interactions with the environment. A particularly important type of experience is *deliberate practice*, which refers to extensive, specialized forms of practice aimed at building expertise. Knowledge refers to learned cognitive representations that support cognitive performance. *Competency* can be defined as the specialized knowledge one has acquired that supports cognitive performance and *expertise* is a very high level of competency. Related terms falling under this heading are *crystallized intelligence* and *intelligence-as-knowledge*. Cognitive performance refers to observable behavior on cognitive tasks including *intelligent behavior*, *successful test taking*, and *expert performance*.

CENTRAL ISSUES

Nature of Ability

The bottom of Table 10.1 lists some fundamental questions raised by the model, which can be helpful in framing your reading of the book. There are three questions concerning the nature of ability. First, is ability general or specific? Dating from the earliest conceptions of intelligence by Galton and Binet, both views of ability were proposed (Sternberg, 1990). Galton conceived of intellectual ability as general – involving general facility in mental speed and perceptual discrimination. In contrast, Binet conceived of intellectual ability as specific – involving a collection of domain-specific skills and facts. These two conceptions of ability are also consistent with Cattell's (1971) classic distinction between fluid intelligence (which reflects general ability) and crystallized intelligence (which reflects specific knowledge).

How do the authors resolve this issue? Some simply reject the notion of ability as a useful concept. For example, Howe and Davidson opt for a non-theoretical approach because "we are dubious about the possibility of there being an ability construct that is genuinely explanatory." Other authors (such as Ackerman and Beier, or Krampe and Baltes) appear to accept both views: General cognitive ability (such as general intelligence) or even domain cognitive ability (such as verbal ability or spatial ability) fit under the label of *ability* in the model in Table 10.1, whereas highly specialized skills and facts go under the label of *knowledge* in the table. Thus, the distinction between general ability and specialized knowledge is reflected in Table 10.1 as a distinction between ability and knowledge. Many of the chapter authors make a similar distinction, such as Ackerman and Beier's distinction between ability and achievement or between intelligence-as-process and intelligence-as-knowledge, and Krampe and Baltes's distinction between cognitive mechanics and cognitive pragmatics.

A somewhat different distinction was proposed in Spearman's (1927) two-factor theory, which included the g-factor (general cognitive ability) and s-factors (specific cognitive abilities). The s-factors – such as verbal ability, mathematical ability, or spatial ability – are more general than specialized knowledge but more specific than general cognitive ability. The specification of specific abilities was advanced by Thurstone's (1938) theory of primary mental abilities, and reached its apex in Carroll's (1993) painstaking analysis of human cognitive factors.

With respect to Table 10.1, should ability be considered as a single monolithic factor or as a collection of more specific abilities? Several of the authors appear to favor the conception of ability as differentiated into specific abilities or talents. For example, Connell, Sheridan, and Gardner's chapter showcases Gardner's theory of multiple intelligences, which offers an influential alternative to the concept of general intelligence. Taking an entirely different approach, Grigorenko seems to come to the same conclusion about the modularity of ability. Research on savants demonstrates that it is possible to excel in one cognitive domain while showing low levels of cognitive functioning in general.

Is ability cognitive or multidimensional? Overall, several authors present convincing arguments that ability involves more than raw cognitive power. Ackerman and Beier describe intelligence as a complex of cognitive and personality factors, which they call *trait complexes*. Krampe and Baltes argue that intelligence "as measured by extant psychometric tests are but a weak reflection of the overall resources available to an individual." Howe and Davidson note that to become a successful musician requires non-cognitive traits such as drive and tenacity as well as cognitive skill. These authors show us that a full understanding of the nature of ability requires a better understanding of the relation between cognitive and personality factors.

Finally, is ability innate or modifiable? On the one hand, some of the authors point to twin studies and other evidence demonstrating a strong genetic influence on ability. For example, Sternberg notes that "half the total variance in IQ scores is accounted for by genetic factors." Simonton concludes that the talent underlying creative genius is "in a certain sense innate." Such views are consistent with Cattell's (1971) classic view that fluid intelligence is largely innate. On the other hand, some of the authors point to the strong role that experience plays in developing expert performance. For example, based on their case studies of successful musicians, Howe and Davidson state that "the proposal that someone is a good musician because he or she possesses abundant musical ability or a high degree of aptitude ... is not very convincing." A reasonable reconciliation is that ability is partly innate and partly modifiable, but the issue of innate ability is also involved in the next section on the interplay between ability and experience.

Nature of Experience

What is the nature of the interplay of ability and experience? Is it dominated by ability, dominated by experience, or based on an interaction of the two? The chapters by Sternberg and by Simonton tend to emphasize innate ability whereas the chapters by Ericsson and by Howe and Davidson tend to emphasize experience. A possible reconciliation is that genes and experience interact (as suggested by the plus sign in Table 10.1). For example, Ceci, Barnett, and Kanaya propose that a person's innate talents predispose the person to seek certain kinds of experiences in the environment. Thus, the *ability + experience* portion of Table 10.1 is consistent with the idea that innate ability and experience are inextricably intertwined. The interactionist view is somewhat consistent with those of most of the authors, except Ericsson, who sees no role for innate ability. Grigorenko notes, however, that "Ericsson and his colleagues are the only group of researchers in the field to take such an extreme position."

Nature of Knowledge

The third set of issues concerns the nature of the knowledge that supports cognitive performance. Is it general or specific? Is it declarative or procedural? The consensus among the authors is that the knowledge underlying cognitive performance is specific and includes both declarative knowledge (for example, facts and concepts) and procedural knowledge (for example, algorithms and strategies). Thus, the *knowledge* entry in Table 10.1 corresponds to specialized knowledge of facts, concepts, algorithms, and strategies.

Nature of Cognitive Performance

A fourth set of issues concerns the nature of cognitive performance. First, should we view cognitive performance as one's maximum performance (that is, one's very best performance under ideal conditions) or one's typical performance (that is, one's usual performance that can be replicated over time)? For example, Ackerman and Beier argue that most tests of cognitive ability seek to predict typical performance (such as academic grades). Thus, in Table 10.1, I use the term *cognitive performance* to refer to typical rather than maximum performance.

Second, is cognitive performance best thought of as intelligent performance or creative performance? In his chapter, Simonton provides a convincing argument that creative performance (that is, creating a product that is novel and useful) is qualitatively different from intelligent performance (that is, performing as an expert on some cognitive task). Creative performance is somewhat erratic whereas intelligent performance is more consistent. In Table 10.1, I use the term *cognitive performance* to reflect intelligent (or expert) performance rather than creative performance.

INTERESTING FACTS ABOUT COGNITIVE PERFORMANCE

The authors provide many interesting facts about cognitive performance, based mainly on research studies. In this section, I examine some of these facts and see how they relate to the model presented in Table 10.1.

Fact 1: Developmental Trends

The chapters by Ackerman and Beier and by Krampe and Baltes both report on age-related changes in specialized knowledge and general ability (which are respectively called intelligence-as-knowledge and intelligence-as-process by Ackerman and Beier, and cognitive mechanics and cognitive pragmatics by Krampe and Baltes). Performance on tests of specialized knowledge (or crystallized intelligence) tends to improve with age, whereas performance on tests of general cognitive ability (or fluid intelligence) tends to decline with age. As people progress from novice to expert in a domain, specialized knowledge gains power for predicting cognitive performance and general ability loses power for predicting cognitive performance.

In terms of the model in Table 10.1, cognitive performance appears to be related to both ability and knowledge, with knowledge taking on increasing importance as people become more experienced. Krampe and Baltes offer the following explanation: "In older adults, expertise-specific mechanisms can free performance from abilities and resources that are subject to age-related decrements in the normal population." It may be somewhat misleading to conclude that specialized knowledge can compensate for general ability, because general ability may have enabled the creation of specialized knowledge in the first place.

Fact 2: Flynn Effect

The Flynn effect refers to the finding that IQ has been increasing over the past one hundred years at the rate of five to nine points per decade (as summarized in the chapter by Ceci, Barnett, and Kanaya). These results seem to implicate experience rather than innate ability because genes cannot change so dramatically in such a short time. Ceci, Barnett, and Kanaya argue, however, that the Flynn effect can best be seen as an interaction between innate ability and experience; innate ability predisposes one to seek certain environmental experiences that in turn result in knowledge that supports cognitive performance. Thus, Ceci et al. propose that "differences among people arise mainly from genetically based differences in the experiences to which they are attracted." This is an example of a multiplier model because "initial genetic proclivities ... can be multiplied by the environment."

For example, reading performance may develop through successive multipliers. Children who seek reading activities acquire better vocabularies, which prime them to read more, learn more word meanings, and hence read even better. In short, Ceci et al. propose that "children who become better readers have selected an environment that will be conducive to further growth." According to Ceci et al., the same multiplier model explains the development of cognitive expertise: "practice can have a similar effect on the development of competencies by causing a slight improvement in performance that in turn leads to a choice to participate in more demanding activities and surround oneself with more stimulating company." In terms of the model in Table 10.1, this view is consistent with viewing "ability + experience" as an interactive process, rather than one in which ability or experience dominates.

Fact 3: Twin Heritability Effects

Several of the chapters (including those by Ceci et al. and by Sternberg) point to the results of twin heritability research, in which identical twins raised apart show a greater similarity in cognitive performance than do matched pairs who do not share as many genes. It is interesting that identical twin studies show that heritability increases with age and the potency of environmental factors seems to decrease. According to Ceci et al. (as noted in the previous section), genetic-based ability can predispose people to seek certain environmental experiences, which in turn lead to changes in specialized knowledge. Again, this view is consistent with saying that the "ability + experience" component in Table 10.1 represents an interaction of native ability and specific experience.

Fact 4: Deliberate Practice can Greatly Enhance Performance

The standard digit span in adults is about seven digits – that is, people can correctly listen to and recall a list about seven digits in length. Ericsson's chapter describes case studies in which fifty hours of concentrated training on how to remember digit lists resulted in a digit span of twenty, and two hundred to four hundred hours of training resulted in a digit span of eighty. Ericsson provides numerous other examples of how extended, specialized practice (which he calls *deliberate practice*) can have powerful effects on cognitive performance.

Based on these findings, Ericsson concludes that "expert performance is acquired." Experts are distinguished not by their innate talent but rather by their specialized knowledge: "mechanisms that mediate the superior performance are not nonmodifiable basic capacities, but surprisingly complex mechanisms that are highly specific to the task domain." According to Ericsson, the effectiveness of deliberate practice in creating expertise raises "doubts about the validity of the long-standing belief in stable innate capacities and any limiting such supposed innate capacities has on the individuals' ultimate performance potential." In terms of Table 10.1, this interpretation focuses mainly on the chain from experience to knowledge to cognitive performance. Although the role of ability appears to be minimized in Ericsson's account, multiplier models such as described by Ceci et al. provide a means for incorporating ability to complete Table 10.1.

Fact 5: Savants Show Outstanding Cognitive Performance on Highly Specialized Tasks

Grigorenko's chapter highlights the cognitive performance of savants who display outstanding performance in a specific domain such as mental arithmetic while displaying low cognitive functioning overall. Such findings suggest that the knowledge underlying cognitive performance may be domain-specific and modularized. In terms of Table 10.1, it appears that the knowledge component can best be thought of as specialized knowledge.

Fact 6: The Progress of Young Musicians Depends on Parental Support and Commitment to Practice

Howe and Davidson's chapter compares case studies of young musicians who do and do not attain later acclaim. Early signs of musical talent do not distinguish the successful from the unsuccessful musicians, suggesting that ability alone is not crucial in cognitive performance. However, successful musicians were more likely than unsuccessful musicians to be in the habit of practicing regularly and to have parents who encouraged them to practice. Such findings are consistent with Ericsson's claims for the role of deliberate practice in the development of expertise. In terms of Table 10.1, such results emphasize the chain from experience to knowledge to cognitive performance.

Fact 7: The Learning Curve for Creativity is not the Same for Expertise

The chapter by Simonton examines the creative output of great composers and other creative geniuses. Unlike experts who show ever-increasing performance with training over time, the output of creative people is best characterized as an inverted-U function, with performance peaking midway through training. In contrast to experts who consistently get better and better over time, case studies of creative people show a much more erratic pattern in which a major accomplishment can be followed by a major failure. Simonton also presents evidence that expertise is helped by overtraining and hurt by cross-training, whereas creativity is hurt by overtraining and helped by cross-training. Such results lead Simonton to conclude that "creativity cannot be reduced to mere expertise." Thus, the definition of cognitive performance in Table 10.1 focuses on expert performance rather than creative performance.

Fact 8: The Brains of Higher and Lower Ability People Behave Differently

Sternberg's chapter reviews research on the brain behavior of people who score low and high on tests of cognitive performance. Higher ability people show less brain activity (that is, lower levels of glucose metabolism) during cognitive testing than do lower ability people, suggesting less cognitive effort. In contrast, higher ability people show more brain activity (that is, higher levels of glucose metabolism) during rest than do lower ability people, suggesting that the higher ability people engage in more thinking. Such results are consistent with the idea that there is a biological basis for the individual differences in cognitive performance represented in Table 10.1.

CONCLUSION

The authors provide a thought-provoking search for the determinants of individual differences in cognitive performance. Although the authors sometimes use different terms and offer differing conceptual approaches, much of the discussion fits within the framework shown in

Table 10.1. Moving from right to left in the table, individual differences in cognitive performance depend on individual differences in specialized knowledge, which in turn depend on individual differences in the experiences of the learner fostered by individual differences in ability. Moving from left to right in the table, ability and experience interact to produce knowledge which in turn supports cognitive performance.

Thus, the model in Table 10.1 shows why it is possible to have so many answers to our question about the origins of individual differences in cognitive performance. Proponents of the knowledge explanation focus on the link from *knowledge* to *cognitive performance*. Proponents of the ability explanation can point to the link from *ability* to *cognitive performance*. Proponents of the experience explanation focus on the link from *experience* to *cognitive performance*. Proponents of the genes explanation focus on the genetic-based definition of *ability*. A fuller picture emerges, however, when all four of the components in Table 10.1 are given their rightful places.

The study of individual differences in human cognitive ability is a hot topic in cognitive science (Sternberg, 2000). This volume demonstrates that much progress has been made in understanding the determinants of individual differences in cognitive performance and the roles played by ability, experience, and knowledge. Additional research is needed to articulate more clearly the mechanism by which ability and experience interact to produce knowledge and the mechanism by which knowledge enables cognitive performance. A helpful step is a clearer specification of the nature of ability, experience, knowledge, and cognitive performance, including agreed-on definitions and means of measurement.

References

Carroll, J. B. (1993). *Human cognitive abilities*. New York: Cambridge University Press.
Cattell, R. B. (1971). *Abilities: Their structure, growth, and action*. Boston: Houghton Mifflin.
Spearman, C. (1927). *The abilities of man*. New York: Macmillan.
Sternberg, R. J. (1990). *Metaphors of mind*. New York: Cambridge University Press.
Sternberg, R. J. (Ed.). (2000). *Handbook of intelligence*. New York: Cambridge University Press.
Thurstone, L. L. (1938). *Primary mental abilities*. Chicago: University of Chicago Press.

Index